P9-BZF-080

ALSO BY ADAM GOPNIK

The King in the Window

Paris to the Moon

THROUGH THE CHILDREN'S GATE

THROUGH THE CHILDREN'S GATE

A Home in New York

ADAM GOPNIK

 ALFRED A. KNOPF • NEW YORK • TORONTO • 2006

THIS IS A BORZOI BOOK
PUBLISHED BY ALFRED A. KNOPF
AND ALFRED A. KNOPF CANADA

 Published in the United States by Alfred A. Knopf, a division of Random House, Inc., New York, and in Canada by Random House of Canada Limited, Toronto.
www.aaknopf.com
www.randomhouse.ca

Portions previously appeared in different form in *The New Yorker*.

Owing to limitations of space, permission to reprint previously published material can be found at the back of the book.

Library of Congress Cataloging-in-Publication Data
Gopnik, Adam.
Through the children's gate : a home in New York / Adam Gopnik.
p. cm.
ISBN 1-4000-4181-3
1. New York (N.Y.)—Description and travel. 2. Gopnik, Adam—Homes and haunts—New York (State)—New York. 3. Gopnik, Adam—Family. 4. New York (N.Y.)—Biography. 5. New York (N.Y.)—Social life and customs. 6. Home—Social aspects—New York (State)—New York. 7. Home—New York (State)—New York—Psychological aspects. I. Title.
F128.55.G67 2006
917.47'10444—dc22 2006045260

Library and Archives Canada Cataloging in Publication Data
Gopnik, Adam
Through the children's gate : a home in New York / Adam Gopnik.
ISBN-13: 978-0-676-97826-1
ISBN-10: 0-676-97826-6
1. Gopnik, Adam—Homes and haunts—New York (State)—New York. 2. Children—Homes and haunts—New York (State)—New York. 3. New York (N.Y.)—Description and travel. I. Title.
F128.55.G67 2006a 974.7'1044 C2006-902585-1

Manufactured in the United States of America
First Edition

Once again:

For Luke and Olivia

(obviously)

For Martha

(actually)

And for Henry Finder and Ann Goldstein

(miscellaneously)

The world is never ready
for the birth of a child

Our ships are not yet back from Winnland
We still have to get over the S. Gothard pass.
We've got to outwit the watchmen on the desert of Thor,
fight our way through the sewers to Warsaw's center,
gain access to King Harold the Butterpat
and wait until the downfall of Minister Fouche.
Only in Acapulco
Can we begin anew.

—from "A Tale Begun," Wislawa Szymborska

INTERVIEWER: *Sir, how do you survive in New York City? What do you eat?*
SID CAESAR (as The Wild Boy): *Pigeon.*
INTERVIEWER: *Don't the pigeons object?*
SID CAESAR: *Only for a minute.*

—from *Your Show of Shows* (attr. Mel Brooks)

CONTENTS

THROUGH THE CHILDREN'S GATE

Through the Children's Gate: Of a Home in New York

In the fall of 2000, just back from Paris, with the sounds of its streets still singing in my ears and the codes to its courtyards still lining my pockets, I went downtown and met a man who was making a perfect map of New York. He worked for the city, and from a set of aerial photographs and underground schematics he had turned every block, every highway, and every awning—every one in all five boroughs!—into neatly marked and brightly colored geometric spaces laid out on countless squares. Buildings red, streets blue, open spaces white, the underground tunnels sketched in dotted lines . . . everything in New York was on the map: every ramp to the Major Deegan Expressway and every abandoned brownstone in the Bronx.

The kicker was that the maniacally perfect map was unfinished and even unfinishable, because the city it described was too "dynamic," changing every day in ways that superceded each morning's finished drawing. Each time everything had been put in place—the subway tunnels aligned with the streets, the Con Ed crawl spaces with the subway tunnels, all else with the buildings above—someone or other would come back with the discouraging news that something had altered, invariably a lot. So every time he was nearly done, he had to start all over.

I keep a small section of that map in my office as a reminder of several New York truths. The first is that an actual map of New York recalls our inner map of the city. We can't make any kind of life in New York without composing a private map of it in our minds—and these inner maps, as Roger Angell once wrote, are always detailed, always divided into local squares, and always unfinished. The private map turns out to be as provisional as the public one—not one on which our walks and lessons trace grooves deepening over the years, but one on which no step, no thing seems to leave a trace. The map of the city we carried just five years ago hardly corresponds to the city we know today, while the New Yorks we knew before that are buried completely. The first New York I knew well, Soho's art world of twenty years ago, is no less vanished now than Carthage; the New York where my wife and I first set up housekeeping, the old Yorkville of German restaurants and sallow Eastern European families, is still more submerged, Atlantis; and the New York of our older friends—where the light came in from the river and people wore hats and on hot nights slept in Central Park—is not just lost but by now essentially fictional, like Narnia. New York is a city of accommodations and of many maps. We constantly redraw them, whether we realize it or not, and are grateful if a single island we knew on the last survey is still to be found above water.

I knew this, or sensed some bit of it, the first time I ever saw the city. This was in 1959, when my parents, art-loving Penn students, brought my sister and me all the way from Philadelphia to see the new Guggenheim Museum on its opening day. My family had passed through New York a half century earlier, on the way to Philadelphia. My grandfather, like every other immigrant, entered through Ellis Island, still bearing, as family legend has it, the Russian boy's name of "Lucie," which I suppose now was the Russianized form of the Yiddish Louis, actually, same as his father's. The immigration officer explained with, as I always imagined it, a firm but essentially charitable brusqueness that you couldn't call a boy Lucy in this country. "What shall we call the boy, then?" his baffled and exhausted parents asked. The immigration officer looked around the great hall and drew the quick conclusion. "Call him Ellis," he said, and indeed my grandfather lived and died in honor of the New York island as Ellis Gopnik—though Ellis was regarded as a touch too New York for Philadelphia, and Lucie-Ellis actually lived and died known to all as Al.

For the Guggenheim occasion, my mother had sewn a suit of mustard-colored velvet for me and a matching dress for my sister, and we stood in line outside the corkscrew building, trying to remember what we had been taught about Calder. Afterward, we marched down the ramp of the amazing museum and then walked along Fifth Avenue, where we saw a Rolls-Royce. We ate dinner at a restaurant that served a thrilling, exotic mix of blintzes and insults, and that night we slept in my great-aunt Hannah's apartment at Riverside Drive and 115th Street. A perfect day.

I remember looking out the window of the little maid's room where we had been installed, seeing the lights of the Palisades across the way, and thinking, *There! There it is! There's New York, this wonderful city. I'll go live there someday.* Even being in New York, the actual place, I found the idea of New York so wonderful that I could only imagine it as some other place, greater than any place that would let me sleep in it—a distant constellation of lights I had not yet been allowed to visit. I had arrived in Oz only to think, *Well, you don't* live *in Oz, do you?*

Ever since, New York has existed for me simultaneously as a map to be learned and a place to aspire to—a city of things and a city of signs, the place I actually am and the place I would like to be even when I am here. As a kid, I grasped that the skyline was a sign that could be, so to speak, relocated to New Jersey—a kind of abstract, receding Vision whose meaning would always be "out of reach," not a concrete thing signifying "here you are." Even when we are established here, New York somehow still seems a place we aspire to. Its life is one thing—streets and hot dogs and brusqueness—and its symbols, the lights across the way, the beckoning skyline, are another. We go on being inspired even when we're most exasperated.

If the energy of New York is the energy of aspiration—let me in there!—the spirit of New York is really the spirit of accommodation—I'll settle for this. And yet both shape the city's maps, for what aspirations and accommodations share is the quality of becoming, of not being fixed in place, of being in every way unfinished. An aspiration might someday be achieved; an accommodation will someday be replaced. The romantic vision—we'll get to the city across the river someday!—ends up harmonizing with the unromantic embrace of reality: We'll get that closet cleaned out yet.

In New York, even monuments can fade from your mental map under the stress of daily life. I can walk to the Guggenheim if I want to, these days, but in my mind it has become simply a place to go when the coffee shops are too full, a corkscrew Three Guys, an alternative place to get a cappuccino and a bowl of bean soup. Another day, suddenly turning a corner, I discover the old monument looking just as it did the first time I saw it, the amazing white ziggurat on a city block, worth going to see.

This doubleness has its romance, but it also has its frustrations. In New York, the space between what you want and what you've got creates a civic itchiness: I don't know a *content* New Yorker. Complacency and self-satisfaction, the Parisian vices, are not present here, except in the hollow form of competitive boasting about misfortune. (Even the very rich want another townhouse but move into an apartment, while an exclusive subset of the creative class devotes itself to dreaming up things for the super-rich to want, if only so they alone will not be left without desire.)

I went back to New York on many Saturdays as a child, to look at art and eat at delis, and it was, for me, not only the Great Romantic Place but the obvious engine of the working world. After a long time away, I returned, in 1978 with the girl I loved. We spent a miraculous day: Bloomingdale's, MoMA, dinner at Windows on the World, and then the Carnegie Tavern, to hear the matchless poet Ellis Larkins on the piano, just the two of us and Larkins in a cool, mostly empty room. (A quarter century later, I haven't had another day that good.) We were dazzled by the avenues and delighted by the spires of the Chrysler Building, and we decided that, come what might, we had to get there.

For all that the old pilgrimage of the young and writerly to Manhattan had become, in those years, slightly Quixotic, we determined nevertheless to make it—not drawn to the city romantically, as we were later to the idea of Paris, but compelled toward it almost feverishly—deliriously, if you like—as the place you needed to be in order to stake a claim to being at all. This feeling has never left me. I've lived elsewhere, but nowhere else feels so entirely, so delusionally—owing more to the full range of emotional energies it possesses than to the comforts it provides—like home.

A home in New York! However will we have one? The exclamation of hope is followed at once by the desperate, the impossible, question. The idea of a home in Manhattan seems at once self-evident and still just a touch absurd, somehow close to a contradiction in its own shaky terms, so that to state it, even quietly, is to challenge some inner sense of decorum, literary if not entirely practical. In literature, after all, New York is where we make careers, deals, compromises, have breakdowns and break-ins and breaks, good and bad. But in reality what we all make in Manhattan are homes (excepting, of course, the unlucky, who don't, or can't, and act as a particularly strong reproach to those of us who do). The Life is the big, Trumpish unit of measure in New York, but the home, the apartment with its galley kitchen and the hallways with its cooking smells, is the real measure, the one we know, and all we know. We make as many homes in New York as in any other place. To make a home at all in New York is the tricky part, the hard part, and yet, at the same time, the self-evident part. Millions of other people are doing it, too. Look out your window. "Do New York!" Henry James implored Edith Wharton in a famous letter, meaning encompass it, if you can, but when we try to do New York, it does us and sends us reeling back home. (When the great James tried to come back home to do it, what he did was the house on Fourteenth Street where he was born, and the other homes, around the corner on Sixth.)

I still recall our first efforts at making a home, when my wife and I arrived on a bus from Canada and moved into a single nine-by-eleven basement room, on East Eighty-seventh Street. I remember it, exactly a quarter century after, with something approaching disbelief: How did we use so many toggle bolts on three walls? But doing it a second time doesn't seem easier, or more supple; I can't walk into a housewares store in Manhattan without feeling myself the victim of a complicated confidence trick, a kind of cynical come-on. We're really going to use a toaster and a coffee-maker every morning? And then, of course, we do, just like they do in Altoona, just like we did . . . back home.

To make a home in New York, we first have to find a place on the map of the city to make it in. The map alone teaches us lessons about the kind of home you can make. So the first New York home we made was in one of many small basement apartments strung along First Avenue. Then there was Soho in its Silver Age, when the cheese counter at Dean & DeLuca and the art at Mary Boone conspired to convince one that a Cultural Moment was under way. But that era has passed—a world gone right under, as they all do here—and coming home this time, we hoped to land in one of the more tender squares on the map, the one that kids live in.

We came back to New York in 2000, after years away, to go through the Children's Gate, and make a home here for good. The Children's Gate exists, and you really can go through it. It's the name for the entrance to Central Park at Seventy-sixth Street and Fifth Avenue. The names of the gates—hardly more than openings in the low stone wall describing the park—are among its more poetic, less familiar monuments. In a moment of oddly Ruskinian whimsy, Frederick Law Olmsted and Calvert Vaux gave names to all the entrances of Central Park, calling them gates, each accommodating a class of person to enter there: a park for all the people with entrances for every kind. There was, and is, the Miners' Gate, and the Scholars' Gate, and—for a long time this was my favorite—the Strangers' Gate, high on the West Side. The Children's Gate is one of the lesser known, though the most inviting of all. On most days you can't even read its name, since a hot-dog-and-pretzel vendor parks his cart and his melancholy there twelve hours a day, right in front of where the stone is engraved. It's a shame, actually. For though it's been a long time since a miner walked through his gate, children really *do* come in and out of theirs all day and, being children, would love to know about it. Now my family had, in a way, decided to pass through as children, too.

This was true literally—we liked the playground and went there our first jet-lagged morning home—and metaphorically: We had decided to leave Paris for New York for the romance of childhood, for the good of the children. We wanted them to go not to baffling Parisian schools—where they would have gotten a terrific education, been cowed until seventeen, and only then begun to riot—but to a New York progressive school, where they'd get a terrific education and, we hoped, have a good time doing it. Childhood seemed too short to waste on preparation. And we wanted them to grow up in New York, to be natives here, as we could never be, to come in through the Children's Gate, not the Strangers' Gate.

A crowd came through the gate with us. Twenty-five years ago, Calvin Trillin could write of his nuclear family of two parents and two kids as being so strange a sight in New York that it was an attraction on bus tours, but by the time we came home, the city had been repopulated—some would say overrun—with children. It was now the drug addicts and transvestites and artists who were left muttering about the undesirable, short element taking over the neighborhood. New York had become, almost comically, a children's city again, with kiddie-coiffure joints where sex shops had once stood and bare, ruined singles bars turned into play-and-party centers. There was an excess of strollers so intense that notices forbidding them had to be posted at the entrances of certain restaurants, as previous generations of New Yorkers had warned people not to hitch their horses too close to the curb. There were even special matinees for babies—real babies, not just kids—where the wails of the small could be heard in the dark, in counterpoint to the dialogue of the great Meryl Streep dueting with a wet six-month-old. Whether you thought it was "suburbanized," "gentrified," or simply improved, that the city had altered was plain, and the children flooding its streets and parks and schools were the obvious sign.

The transformation of the city, and particularly the end of the constant shaping presence of violent crime, has been amazing, past all prediction, despite the facts that the transformation is not entirely complete and the new city is not entirely pleasing to everyone. Twenty some years ago, it was taken for granted that New York was hell, as Stanley Kauffmann wrote flatly in a review of Ralph Bakshi's now oddly forgotten New York cartoon-dystopia *Heavy Traffic,* and every movie showed it that way, with the steam rising from the manholes to gratify the nostrils of the psychos, as if all the infernal circles, one through thirty, inclusive, were right below. E. B. White was asked to update his famous essay about the city, and that unweepy man, barely able to clear the bitter tears from his prose, declined to write about a city he no longer knew. In the seventies, Robert Caro's life of Robert Moses, blankly subtitled "And the Fall of New York," was the standard version of What Had Happened.

Everyone has a moment of personal marvel about how far things have gone or changed: Twenty-three years ago, I recall, they were toting bodies out of the Film Center on Ninth Avenue, and (nice lost word) the degenerates were brooding on it at the Film Center Café. Now the Film Center shines and the café across the street serves mussels and croissant sandwiches, having kept its Art Moderne front, so "period," if nothing else. The scale of this miracle—and for anyone who remembers the mood of the city in the early seventies, miracle it is—leads inevitably to a rebound of complaint. It Is Not So Miraculous At All. Or: You call *that* a miracle? The cross-dressers in the Village sniff at the influx of nuclear families as the fleeing nuclear families once sniffed at the cross-dressers. Some of the complaining is offered in a tone of intelligent, disinterested urban commentary: The service and financial and media industries, they say, are too unstable a base for a big city to live and grow on (though, historically speaking, no one seems able to explain why these industries are any more perilous than the paper-box or ladies' lingerie industries of forgotten days).

Most of the beefs are aesthetic and offered in a tone of querulous nostalgia: What happened to all that ugliness, all that interesting despair, all that violence and seediness, the cabdrivers in their undershirts and the charming hookers in their heels? This is standard-issue human perversity. After they gentrify hell, the damned will complain that life was much more fun when everyone was running in circles: *Say what you will about the devil, at least he wasn't antiseptic. We didn't come to hell for the croissants.* But the lament has a subtler and more poignant side, too. All of us, right and left, make the new Times Square a butt of jokes—how sickening it still is to be forced to gaze at so much sleaze and human waste, to watch the sheer degradation of people forced to strut their wares in lust-inducing costumes before lip-licking onlookers, until at last *The Lion King* is over and you can flee the theater. These jokes are compulsive and irresistible because they speak to our embarrassment about our own relief, and to a certain disappointment, too. Safety and civic order are not sublime; these are awfully high rents to be paying to live, so to speak, in Minneapolis.

Still, croissants and crime are not lifestyle choices, to be taken according to taste; the reduction of fear, as anyone who has spent time in Harlem can attest, is a grace as large as any imaginable. To revise Chesterton slightly: People who refuse to be sentimental about the normal things don't end up being sentimental about nothing; they end up being sentimental about *anything*, shedding tears over old muggings and the perfect, glittering shards of the little crack vials, sparkling like diamonds in the gutter. *Où sont les neiges d'antan?*: Who cares if the snows were all of cocaine? We saw them falling and our hearts were glad.

The more serious argument is that the transformation is Parisian in the wrong way: the old bits of the city are taken over by the rich (or by yuppies, which somehow has a worse ring) while the poor and the unwashed are crowded right off the island. By a "city," after all, we mean more than an urban amusement park; we mean a collection of classes, trades, purposes, and functions that become a whole, giving us something more than rich people in their co-ops and condos staring at other rich people in their co-ops and condos. Those who make this argument see not a transformation but an ethnic cleansing, an expulsion of the wrong sort. Still, it is hard to compare the *Mad Max* blackout of '77 with the *Romper Room* blackout of '03 and insist that something has gone so terribly wrong with the city. No one can credibly infer a decline, which leads us back to the Times Square Disneyfication jokes. And toward remaking the old romance.

It is a strange thing to be the serpent in one's own garden, the snake in one's own grass. The suburbanization of New York is a fact, and a worrying one, and everyone has moments of real disappointment and distraction. The Soho where we came of age, with its organic intertwinings of art and food, commerce and cutting edge, is unrecognizable to us now—but then that Soho we knew was unrecognizable to its first émigrés, who by then had moved on to Tribeca. This is only to say that in the larger, inevitable human accounting of New York, there are gains and losses, a zero sum of urbanism: The great gain of civility and peace is offset by a loss of creative kinds of vitality and variety. (There are new horizons of Bohemia in Brooklyn and beyond, of course, but Brooklyn has its bards already, to sing its streets and smoke, as they will and do. My heart lies with the old island of small homes and big buildings, the sounds coming from one resonating against the sounding board of the other.)

But those losses are inevitably specific. There is always a new New York coming into being as the old one disappears. And that city—or cities; there are a lot of different ones on the same map—has its peculiar pleasures and absurdities as keen as any other's. The one I awakened to, and into—partly by intellectual affinity, and much more by the ringing of an alarm clock every morning at seven—was the civilization of childhood in New York. The phrase is owed to Iona Opie, the great scholar of children's games and rhymes, whom I got to interview once. "Childhood is a civilization with its own rules and rituals," she told me, charmingly but flatly, long before I had children of my own. "Children never refer to each other as children. They call themselves, rightly, people, and tell you what it is that people like them—their people—believe and do." The Children's Gate exists; you really can go through it.

B*ut why such a fuss about children in New York, or anywhere?* I hear some level head (not you, reader) sigh. *Can't we simply accept childhood, really, as children do, as just a preface to personhood?* If love of one's children is a natural emotion—Dr. Johnson thought not, but Mrs. Thrale, quite rightly, I'd say, told him he was full of it—to love one's children nearly to the exclusion of, or at least above, all else, is a different thing, at least for a man. An obsessive love of our children is proof that we are unhappy about something else, Queen Marie of Rumania once said—and who am I, are we, to argue with Queen Marie of Rumania?

Struggling to reflect on a subject about which I cannot help but obsess—my heart lifts when they wake up and falls a little when they go to school, and I feel myself possessed by the kind of compulsive all-day mindfulness once the exclusive province of mothers—I see that this is a product, a "construction," of one particular period, a paternal archetype no less historical than the distant father who left nursing to the nursery even if the magnitude of the love he felt was no less or greater than we may feel. Kenneth Clark kept his children in an entirely separate house on his property; they were led in to say good evening just before the grown-ups sat down to dinner, and then they were dismissed again. Yet in his autobiography, Clark writes that nothing in his life had given him as much joy as his kids, and I don't doubt that, on his own terms, he was telling the truth.

The new paternal feeling is partly an effect of feminism, which required that mothers surrender exclusive child-love for freedom, and partly the consequence of many parents' advanced childbearing age. The father is no longer a kid on the make but a man who has, to some brief degree, been made, and who therefore has more time to cook dinner and wipe noses than his own father did. And the self-consciousness that now comes with child rearing comes from that, too. My own dad—father of six, grandfather of fourteen—said once that the greatest difference in life is between having children at (so to speak) twenty and having them at (so to speak) forty: When we're twenty, they are just there, smaller fellow climbers on the same mountain; at forty, we have been up the mountain once already, and we become their Sherpas, carrying their equipment, checking their oxygen supply, hoisting them up to the peak and telling them they did it all themselves, just as generations of Sherpas did for generations of Englishmen. The new love of childhood and parenting is also the consequence of a kind of boot-strapping into "adulthood." For those of us who lingered in boyishness, child rearing and child-love, far from being regressive, are part of the forced march to maturity: You have to do a thing, and here is a thing you have to do.

Whatever the origins—and I leave it to some meatier-minded cultural historian to trace them all—what child rearing is, when you live it, is a joy. It should be seen as we really do feel it—less as a responsibility imposed than as a great gift delivered up to us, just as the troubadour poets opened up romantic love for everyone, so that it can still serve Lorenz Hart or Paul McCartney.

Children reconnect us to romance. For children, as my sister Alison, the developmental psychologist who makes sapient, recurring appearances in these tales, has written, every morning is the first morning in Paris, every day is the first day of love: The passions that for us grown-ups rise and fall only in exceptional circumstances, unexpected storms on the dull normal beach where the tide breaks unchangingly, rise every day for them. Shock, hatred, infatuation: "I hate you," they cry, slamming the door, and they mean it; and then the door opens fifteen minutes later for dessert. They compel us to see the world as an unusual place again. Sharing a life with them is sharing a life with lovers, explorers, scientists, pirates, poets. It makes for interesting mornings.

And then they are not here to do better, or to be smarter, or to get ready: They are here to *be,* and they know it. We delight in children because they keep the seven notes of enlightenment, as the Buddha noted them. Keep them? They sing them, they *are* them: energy, joy, concentration, attentiveness, mindfulness, curiosity, equanimity. (Well, not the last, maybe, but they still keep it better than we do; they are often in pain but rarely in panic.) Detachment, too—they are detached from us in ways that we know only after; they study us exactly as monks contemplate the world, to free themselves from needing us. Their ultimate enlightenment lies in that emancipation. What we didn't grasp before is how badly the world feels about being abandoned by the monks. As parents we are, briefly, objects of intellectual desire; we are, for a moment, worlds. We should be proud to have been as large as worlds, but instead, we are merely sad to be abandoned. The risk of sentimentality lies only in failing to see that the most charmed thing they will do is leave us. They have to renounce their attachment to us as the adept abandons his attachment to the world. All we can hope for is the pleasure the world takes in once having been seductive enough to attach somebody to it. All we can expect from children is the memory the monk has of the time he was attached. We can hope for their pity, and their tolerance, and a spring visit after we have been banished to Florida and white shorts and socks.

There's no bad place to watch children grow, but Manhattan is a good one. The intersection of two very small points with one very big place, the constant daily back-and-forth between small emerging consciousness and huge indifferent stuff, is always instructive. Having them, you get a much clearer sense of the city's sharp edges and smooth spots, of the grace it gives to things—the literature of epiphanies received at the Museum of Natural History by now is larger than that of miracles found at Lourdes—and of the grace it denies, as well, of its *overwhelmingness.* When you get on the subway together at five o'clock, you have to hold them tight, as if you were white-water rafting and they might fall into the river; they could just get swept away by the crowd. They show you quiet places—my son, Luke, once gave me a back massage on Father's Day in a little glade in the park that time and man had forgotten—and they get you to take them to noisy ones you had sworn off for good. My daughter, Olivia, and I go every year at Christmas to Tiffany to window-shop and gape at the giant diamonds, and the sheer press of tourists seems for once like a benediction, not a curse.

Your children make their own maps, which enlarge and improve your own. They inscribe permanent illustrative features on your map, like the spouting beasts on medieval ones. There's a spot on University Place where Olivia, furious at being too small to go bowling at Bowlmor Lanes nearby, yelled at me, "I used to love you! And now I don't even like you!" When I pass it now, she is still there, still indignant and still yelling. And if their maps are mutable, well, you believe, every child's map is meant to be, only to emerge in adulthood as the Only Map There Is, the one they're stuck with. The image of me they settle on, I would shudder to see—but I hope their map of New York will be bright and plain: That's where we grew up, weirdly enough. My two, I hardly need add, though distinct enough for me, here in these pages stand in for, if not a million, than many others: They could be Jacob and Sasha, or Ben and Sophie, or Emma and Gabriel. The miraculous thing about children is that they really are all alike—boom, here comes three and an imaginary friend; whoosh, there goes eleven and the first stirrings of passion—and all utterly unique. They are radically themselves and entirely of their kind. Just like us, actually. The city doesn't change that, but it does italicize it: among eight million souls, these two.

For us, at least, these five years, the children's sober buoyancy bounced us through the gate and into the park even in the darkest times. It might have done so in any circumstances, but it *really* did so then. I ended the story of the five years we lived in Paris with the birth of a baby—on, as it happened, September 11, 1999, the happy end of a rich decade spent under a Pax Americana as vast and essentially benevolent as the British nineties had been a century before, with an optimistic material civilization at the height of a power so absolute as to be nearly absurd in its creation of a soft empire of signs.

Two years later, we were preparing to celebrate that baby's second birthday when a phone call came. The rest is history, as we say of an unforgettable event with a unsettled meaning, unsettled because the meanings assigned to catastrophic events fluctuate so entirely as the rest of what happens unfolds that to claim to understand an event's meaning even long after, much less right away, is absurd. Was this the first Gothic sack of Rome, or Sarajevo 1914, or simply the Manson family to the power of ten? Or the sinking of the *Lusitania* for our time? We don't know yet, and we might not know for a long time, or ever. Searching for a remotely adequate historical parallel for the destruction of a capital's two biggest buildings in a single morning, one finds it only in the catastrophes that signal the ends of civilizations: the sacking of the Temple, the overthrow of Rome.

Anyone with a minimal sense of history recognizes that it must have changed everything, and anyone with a minimal sense of reality knows that it has not. For the other truth, almost unsayable to this day, was that the disaster left, and leaves, the rituals and facts and even the comforts of the city practically unaltered. There was an assault, but no sack. We went home that night, even a mile from the site, to phones that worked and refrigerators that hummed in the background as we tried to make sense of a catastrophe that had not, as catastrophes had usually before, left a devastated epicenter emanating waves of other destruction. This catastrophe was as specific and exact in its place as it was nightmarish in its murderousness. As I wrote at the time, it was as though the *Titanic* had been sunk on the street before us, and we had watched it go down and then walked home.

The amazing thing was to witness the recovery and to learn from it. Those of us who had walked in through the Children's Gate had to choose to flee or stay; and choosing to stay, we chose to live, and so we chose to hope—to secure as much happiness for our kids as we could find, or make. Our own tiny family predicament echoed the larger one: We had, from then on, both to honor the memory of September 11 and to celebrate Olivia's birthday, and we had to do both, at once, as well as we could. (We were doing two things at once, the minimal number necessary for life.) There isn't any heroism in carrying on, because there isn't any choice. But not having any choice at least puts you in hailing distance of what real heroes do when they don't have any choice about what to do and do it anyway.

What was certainly true (and moving) was that New York was transformed and, for the first time in its history, became, in the world's eyes, vulnerable and fragile. New York, the Rome of the virtual age, suddenly became the Venice of the new millennium: the beautiful endangered place that could just shatter and be flooded and break. This was very different from what it had been back in the seventies, when it was ruined and doomed. Now the ruin was less but the fear, for a while anyway, larger. All the secular rituals of existence in New York went on, made newly poignant by a recognition that they could not be practiced complacently. A charge of fragility entered every family snapshot, every picnic on the Great Lawn, every New Age birthday party with a yoga mat given to each child. It even took the comic form of an awareness that filled the children's eyes, of how low low-flying planes ought to be.

Flight was a rational possibility and—who knows?—may yet turn out to have been the rational response. But not very many fled, perhaps as much out of stolidity and fatigue as anything, and as we all went on living and choosing to live, we had no choice but to go on hoping. The tenor of our lives and the shape of our manners, in that space between sporadic fear and real pleasure, did change, in subtle ways worth setting down. There is, I think, no sense in talking about a "post-9/11" New York: History and individual experience don't intersect that neatly except in cheap journalism and bad novels. History and experience run on different tracks, and when history knocks experience off its own, we know the force of the collision from the dents on the people's hats and hearts. Fear changes minds, and minds change the forms of manners—but it changes as smoke changes the air in a room, subtly and in ways that can be recorded only by sensing the atmosphere. (The best novel about World War I is *Mrs. Dalloway*, in which the consequences of that catastrophe lie not in some overt transformation of that city and its manners, which are proceeding more or less just as they have for so long, but in the small tugs of gravity that work on hearts, coming from a new but still-distant planet: the mad veteran in the park on the shining morning with the party at its end.)

Manners changed just enough to be traceable. Our time in New York, to use a homely metaphor, was spent waiting for the other shoe to drop; and when it didn't drop—or hasn't dropped, not quite yet—we learned to live on one foot, hopping along spiritually in more or less normal times. It turns out that we can live quite happily on one leg, enough that the memory of two legs seems odd. Every age and city are scared of *something*, anyway. The real question that pressed itself upon us as parents was how to let our children live in joy in a time of fear, how to give light enough to live in when what we saw were so many shadows.

. . .

New York, in times likes these, could seem an unfair place to have and to raise children. But then, there is no right time, never a serene and happy plateau in which to have them. As the great Szymborska reminds us in the little epigraph to this book, there has never been, throughout human history, a good moment to have a child: There is always something enormous and threatening happening, or about to happen, that makes it unwise. The Vandals are coming, the Gothard Pass is closed . . . we will have to get safely to sunny Acapulco for it to be possible, and we will never get to Acapulco.

And yet, we have them still and have to bring them up in the moment and the city that the time being gives us. That having them is more volitional than it used to be—no one caught in the snow in the Gothard Pass could imagine *debating* having kids; they just had them, as one had sex and its consequences—doesn't alter that. Having them in New York is just like having them anywhere else, only more so. The difference is that the speed of the city, its rhythm, accelerates the play between what happens outside in the world and what happens inside in their minds. It all happens, perhaps, one beat faster, sooner, weirder, with more nervous energy and too little breathing room. Their imaginary playmates are as busy as their parents. As Sid Caesar pointed out, playing the part of a feral child in the city, the pigeon *does* object to being eaten here, but only for a minute. Then it's gone, and another bird is in its place, eating and being eaten. No one mourns the vanished pigeon.

The odd thing is that a compensatory instinct—or is it merely guilt? In any case, whatever makes us all, in every circumstance, beat back against the current of our time—makes New York parents more concerned to live a life defined, however quaintly, as normal than people elsewhere. In my experience, at least, it is liberal parents who tend to be the most socially conservative—the most queasy at the endless ribbon of violence and squalor that passes for American entertainment, more concerned to protect their children from it. One might have the impression that it is the Upper West Side atheist and the Lancaster County Amish who dispute the prize for who can be most obsessive about having the children around the table at six p.m. for a homemade dinner from farm-raised food. Morals and manners proceed in twisting spirals of contradiction more often than in neat sandwiches of sameness, and the attitudes of the prohibitive and the secular end up resembling each other. We try to find a way to say grace every night, too, although in our own way. We hold hands, and clink glasses.

In these circumstances, simple elemental things—Christmas shopping, or skating, the whole middle-class carousel of grocery shopping and piano lessons and baseball practice, which until then one had practiced (or at least chronicled) ironically—took on a new edge, not of heroism, certainly, but of poignant significance, at least for the parents.

In the end, ordinary life, sheltered from the abysmal winds of History, is what we all hope to preserve as long as the universe will allow. In my work for *The New Yorker,* I am made to be busily conscientious as a reporter can be, spending days on Rikers Island and nights in telecom hotels. In one atypical burst of civic virtue, I helped the High Line happen. But once again I have left most of that writing out of this book. We can write about *the* world only by writing about *a* world, and that world the one we think, at least, we really know. Journalism is made from the outside in; but writing is made from the inside out. Applicable metaphors, not all-over views, are what writers and readers trade in. The metaphors of experience each writer finds in his own backyard, or air shaft, or palace gardens, have, of necessity, different colors—some are gold and some are green and some merely gray—but in the end, the shapes we know are all the same: the arc of desire and disappointment, the rising half circle of hope, the descending crescent of aging, the scribble of the city or the oval of the park, or just the long, falling tunnel of life. Each of these shapes is to be found in any life lucky enough to have any shape at all. (The comic-sentimental essay is, in any case, a kind of antimemoir, a nonconfession confession, whose point is not to strip experience bare but to use experience for some other purpose: to draw a moral or construct an argument, make a case or just tell a joke.)

And so some tiles on the map of the real city of New York, some of its streets and secrets and the games children and adults play within it, are my subject. Manners matter; children count out of all proportion to their size; and the poetic impulse, however small its objects, is usually saner than the polemical imperative, however passionate its certitudes. Comic writers should not have credos, perhaps, but if I had one, that would be the one I would have. These are stories about the manners, the children, and the objects of the professional classes in what was and remains the world's real capital, in a time of generalized panic and particularized pleasures, about the secular rituals of material but not unmindful people, a handful of manners pressed between the pages of a book. They are stories and images of a class in many ways privileged, but one whose privileges are always provisional, as rooted in this year's harvest of symbolic transactions as any farmer's are in this year's harvest of soybeans, and touched always by a certain precariousness, the permanent precariouness of the professional classes in a plutocratic society.

As for living within ambiguities and seeing two things at once while you do, well, children do it all the time. Olivia, at three, always cried when she entered a New York cab, "I want to see New York! I want to see New York!," meaning that she wanted to look at the schematic map of Manhattan posted on the back of the front seat, and she'd stare at it while the city sped along beside her. The picture and the city were, to her, about equally interesting. This book is like that map, like that moment: a picture of a place that remains intrinsically elsewhere, out the window. New York is always somewhere else, across the river or on the back of the front seat, someplace else, while the wind of the city just beyond our reach rushes in the windows. We keep coming home to New York to try and look for it again.

Through it all that first feeling, on a night more than forty years ago, remains my major feeling: I am so pleased to be here that I can hardly believe I am. What New York represents, perfectly and consistently, in literature and life alike, is the idea of Hope. Hope for a new life, for something big to happen, hope for a better life or a bigger apartment. When I leave Paris, I think, *I was there*. When I leave New York, I still think: *Where was I?* I was there, of course, and I still couldn't grasp it all. I love Paris, but I *believe* in New York and in its trinity of values: plurality, verticality, possibility. These are stories of happiness in shadow: the shadow of a darkening time and the shadow of human mortality both. I feel the shadows, as we all do, and cringe maybe even more than most. But I try to remember that darkness is a subject, too, and need not always be too sad a one. Shadows are all we have to show us the shapes that light can make.

A Hazard of No Fortune

Home again, to begin once again at the beginning. Apartment-hunting is the permanent New York romance, and the broker and his couple the eternal triangle. A man and woman are looking for a place to live, and they call up a broker, and he shows them apartments that are for sale or rent, but the relationship between those three people is much more complicated than the relationship between someone who knows where homes can be found and two people who would like to find one. For one thing, the places are not really his to sell, not really theirs to buy. A tangle of clients and banks, bids and mortgages, co-op boards and co-op skeptics surrounds their relationship. *Hypothèque* is the French word for mortgage, and a hypothetical air attends every step you take: if you could . . . if they would . . . if the bank said . . . if the board allows. . . .

Yet the broker, at the top of the triangle, is a happy man. First he forms a liaison with the wife, which unites them against all the things that husbands have—doubt, penury, a stunted imagination. Together, the broker winks at the wife; they will scale the heights, find a poetic space, a wking brk frplce, something. But by late morning he has formed a second, darker, homoerotic alliance with the husband. The two guys share musky common sense, and their eyes exchange glances—she's so demanding, pretty much impossible. Now, a couple of guys like us, we could be happy together, take what we can get, fix a place up. The skilled broker keeps the husband and wife in a perpetual state of uncertainty about whose desires will be satisfied.

Over lunch, it becomes plain that the broker has a past, as lovers will. He did something else before—he was a journalist, or a banker, or in advertising. He chose to be a broker because it gave him freedom, and then (he admits) in the nineties it began to give him money, more money than he ever thought possible. He looks sleek in his Italian suit, while his couple feel for the moment like out-of-towners, hicks in cloth coats and rubber boots. As coffee arrives, the couple hear his cell phone buzzing, muffled somewhere near his heart. He finds the phone, mutters into it, then speaks up: "Hey, I'm in the middle of lunch." But the husband and wife are temporarily bound together: There is another—one he may love more than us.

The only time the broker loses his poise is when the Rival Broker is waiting for him in the lobby of the building where she has the "exclusive." Ethics and tradition insist that the two brokers show the apartment together, and suddenly the broker, so suave, so sexy, becomes an ex-husband, the two brokers like a couple after a bad divorce, polite only for the sake of the child—the apartment.

The billets-doux of the couple's relationship with the broker are the layouts, the small black-and-white schematic maps of apartments, with key descriptive points set off in bullets: "Triple mint" (meaning not actually falling down); "Room to roam" (a large, dark back room); "Paris rooftops" (a water tower looms in the window of the bedroom). A New York apartment layout is the only known instance of a blueprint that is more humanly appealing than the thing it represents.

One apartment succeeds another. There are the absurd apartments, nestled in towers among towering buildings four feet away, so that every sunless window shows another sunless window, and you could wake every morning to reach out and touch your pallid neighbor with your pallid hand. There are the half-shrunk apartments, with a reasonable living room and two more rooms carved out behind that you have to enter sideways. Then there are the apartments that are genuinely unique to New York. A hugely expensive "duplex" in the West Seventies, for instance, turns out to be a basement and a sub-basement—the basement where you used to put up your sloppy cousin from Schenectady, the one who never took off his Rangers sweater, and the windowless sub-basement where the janitor was once found molesting children. The apartment's chief attraction is wistfully announced on its blueprint. It is "Near Restaurants."

When you're in a tiny hotel room, apartments begin to crowd your imagination and haunt your nights. They turn into bright-eyed monsters, snaking through your dreams like subway cars. Last Christmas, having decided to try to bring my family home after five years abroad, I found myself walking in fact, and then in spirit, through all these apartments, again and again. As a distraction, I picked up a book I had packed for the journey, William Dean Howells's *A Hazard of New Fortunes.* A little over a hundred years old, it's still the best book about middle-class life—or is it upper-middle? anyway, the lives of salaried professionals—in New York, a great American novel. Instead of fussing about hunting whales or riding rafts or fighting wars, or any of those other small-time subjects, it concerns something really epic: a guy in the magazine business looking for an apartment in Manhattan.

Howells is out of favor now. All literary reputation-making is unjust, but Howells is the victim of perhaps the single greatest injustice in American literary history. The period from 1880 to 1900, Henry Adams once said, was "our Howells-and-James epoch," and the two bearded grandees stood on terms as equal as the Smith Brothers on a cough-drop box. But then Howells got identified, unfairly, with a Bostonian "genteel" tradition, nice and dull. Now James gets Nicole Kidman and Helena Bonham Carter, even for his late, fuzzy-sweater novels, along with biography after biography and collection after collection, and Howells gets one brave, doomed defense every thirty years. Yet Howells, though an immeasurably less original sensibility than James, may be the better novelist, meaning that Howells on almost any subject strikes you as right, while James on almost any subject strikes you as James. Howells's description in *A Hazard* of New York, and of New York apartment-hunting, at the turn of the century comes from so deep a knowledge of what capitalism does to the middle classes, and how it does it to them, that it remains uncannily contemporary. We've spent billions of dollars to prevent our computers' mistaking 2000 for 1900; *A Hazard of New Fortunes* suggests that the error may have been a kind of truth.

In the novel, a diffident and ironic literary man, Basil March, sublets his house in Boston and comes to New York to edit a new magazine, a fortnightly to be called *Every Other Week*. It is to be the first "syndicate" magazine, with the contributors sharing in the profits. (These days it would be an Internet launch.) Gradually, we learn that the money behind the magazine comes from a backwoods Pennsylvania Dutch natural-gas millionaire named Dryfoos, who, newly arrived in New York, has invested in the magazine as a worldly diversion for his unworldly son, Conrad, who dreams of becoming a priest. (Howells began writing *A Hazard* in the late eighties, when he moved to New York from Cambridge, after editing *The Atlantic Monthly* for ten years.)

Although the action of *A Hazard* eventually takes in the more "panoramic" material of strikes and riots, Howells's genius was to devote the first hundred or so pages of his book to the Marches' apartment-hunting. Isabel March, Basil's wife, who is an old Bostonian, joins him for the search, leaving the children behind in Beantown. They begin with the blithe certainty that it will take a couple of days. "I cut a lot of things out of the *Herald* as we came on," she tells her husband at their hotel on the first morning, taking "a long strip of paper out of her handbag with minute advertisements pinned transversely upon it, and forming the effect of some glittering nondescript vertebrate." She goes on, "We must not forget just what kind of flat we are going to look for":

> "The sine qua nons are an elevator and steam heat, not above the third floor, to begin with. Then we must each have a room, and you must have your study and I must have my parlor; and the two girls must each have a room. With the kitchen and dining room, how many does that make?"
>
> "Ten."
>
> "I thought eight. Well, no matter. . . . And the rooms must all have outside light. And the rent must not be over eight hundred for the winter. We only get a

> thousand for our whole house, and we must save something out of that, so as to cover the expenses of moving. Now, do you think you can remember all of that?"

The modern reader waits for the shock to strike, and it does. They wander from one apartment building to another—all named, with unchanged real estate developers' pretension, after classical writers. ("There is a vacant flat in the Herodotus for eighteen hundred a year, and one in the Thucydides for fifteen," she sees, lamenting, "What prices!") They visit six apartments in the afternoon, then four more that night. They are all too small, too expensive, too strange—too, well, New York.

> One or two rooms might be at the front, the rest crooked and cornered backward through increasing and then decreasing darkness till they reached a light bedroom or kitchen at the rear. . . . If the flats were advertised as having "all light rooms" [the janitor] explained that any room with a window giving into the open air of a court or shaft was counted a light room.

Basil blames the brokers: "There seems to be something in the human habitation that corrupts the natures of those who deal in it, to buy or sell it, to hire or let it. You go to an agent and tell him what kind of a house you want. He has no such house, and he sends you to look at something altogether different upon the well-ascertained principle that if you can't get what you want, you will take what you can get." And yet the Marches become not repelled by apartment-seeking but addicted to it:

> It went on all day and continued far into the night, until it was too late to go to the theater, too late to do anything but tumble into bed and simultaneously fall on sleep. They groaned over their reiterated disappointments, but they could not deny that the interest was unfailing.

The Marches become mesmerized by the ads, the layouts, the language. "Elegant large single and outside flats" were offered with "all improvements—bath, icebox, etc." Soon the search for an apartment becomes a consuming activity in itself, self-propelling, self-defining—a quest. "Now we are imprisoned in the present," Basil says of New York, "and we have to make the worst of it."

Imprisoned in the present. It seems not to matter when or with how much money you look for an apartment in New York. I've done it officially three times: once as a grad student looking for one room for two, with thirty-five hundred dollars in my pocket to last the year; once as a "yuppie" (we were called that, derisively, before the world was ours), looking for a loft or a one-bedroom; and now as a family guy with a couple of kids. The numbers and the figures change, but the experience remains the same and feels different from the way it feels anywhere else, with a jag of raised hopes and dashed expectations.

The city is, it's true, shinier than it has ever been. It gleams. It is as if the "broadband pipe," the philosophers' stone of our era, had already come into existence as a blast hose and washed off the grime. The newsstands that once seemed to stock mainly *SCREW* now stock *InStyle* and *Business 2.0.* Even the smells have changed. The essential New York smell twenty years ago was still Italian and Wasp: tomato and olive oil and oregano, acid and pungent, mingled with the indoor, Bloomingdale's smell of sweet, sprayed perfumes. Now, inside the giant boxes that have arrived from America, from the malls (the Gap and Banana Republic and Staples), there is a new, clean pharmacy smell, a disconcerting absence of smells, the American non-smell.

The New Yorkers who arrived in the seventies, the post–*Annie Hall* wave of immigrants, are dismayed by the new shine. They liked the fear and dilapidation that they saw when they came, since it meant that living here required courage. Life in New York was a broken-field run, demanding, even in the "nice" neighborhoods, a continual knowing, sideways-glancing evaluation of everyone else on the street and what kind of threat each person might represent—white faces in dark shoes searching fearfully for dark faces in white shoes. Today the rich stroll down the street as though the place belongs to them. (It always did, but now they show it.) A lot of New York existence is like a fantasy mordantly imagined in the 1970s: Picture a city with polite taxi drivers and children in strollers crowding the avenues, where everyone is addicted to strong, milky coffee.

The horizon seems so secure that places to live these days seem to be conjugated in the future indefinite—some of the apartments one looks at are purely notional, like Priceline.com profits. Not only do the neighborhoods not quite exist yet—whole blocks are now annexed to Tribeca that five years ago were shabby streets fringing City Hall—but the apartments themselves don't exist. Amid the noise and dust of construction work, you enter a "welcome" shed, where you are shown eight-by-eight-inch samples of "finishes": brushed aluminum for the kitchen appliances, maple for the floors, white pine for the kitchen cabinets, one blue tile that is meant to stand for the finished bathroom. The eight-by-eight samples are stapled to a sheet of Masonite, like a science project done the night before the science fair.

You sign a paper promising not to sue if you are killed while examining the nonexistent apartments. This is fair; you are simply acknowledging that searching for an apartment in New York is potentially fatal, like scaling Everest. ("They got up to 3-C in plenty of time, but they dawdled in the kitchen and didn't begin the descent back until it was already growing dark and the squalls were threatening in the service elevator.") You walk into a vast space, into the dust and crashing sounds of an entire world being emptied out, century-old plaster spilling down chutes. The broker leads you up a steep plank to a two-by-four square hole. You duck down and squeeze through—it is like the entrance that leads the Artful Dodger and Oliver into Fagin's den. Then you are in the remains of the wrecked warehouse, with a row of three windows down at one end and perhaps silver tape laid out on the floor: your home. The second broker leads you to the corner window. "I love this line," she sighs with pleasure. "Extrapolate from the finishes," someone orders.

. . .

But the Marches have been here, too; you see their Gilded Age forms, like ghosts on North Moore Street, and they are in the same bewildered state: "Mrs. March had out the vertebrate, and was consulting one of its glittering ribs and glancing up from it at a house before which they stood. 'Yes, it's the number—but do they call this being ready October 1st?' "

Isabel boldly goes into the empty place and, "with the female instinct for domiciliation which never failed her," she begins to settle the family in the still unfinished house as the landlord "lent a hopeful fancy to the solution of all her questions." Isabel explains to her skeptical husband, "It's the only way I can realize whether it will do for us. I have to dramatize the whole thing."

Dramatize the whole thing. You can take the Marches with you everywhere in New York. In their day, too, people were haunted by the sixties—the strife at home—which they had agreed to identify in retrospect as a time of true idealism, since mislaid. And then, one also begins to sense, their boom was like ours in its subtle articulation into two phases. In the first phase, having money became a way of entering an older, existing society; in the second, money created its own society. Howells's early novel *The Rise of Silas Lapham* described the plight of the typical millionaire-adventurer trying and failing to make his way in Boston society of the 1870s, "hemmed in and left out at every turn by ramifications that forbid him all hope of safe personality in his comments." By the time of *A Hazard*, money is the only ramification left.

Although our boom sometimes seems one continuous curve of money and manners that began around 1984, it, too, has had two phases. In the eighties, the familiar mechanisms that gave new money the appearance of old—turning money into charity or culture—still operated, at times feverishly. Newly rich men in the eighties were driven by the same amalgam of guilt and gilt that drove the robber barons of the Gilded Age to have their portraits made by Sargent and buy Renaissance or even Impressionist pictures. To buy a risky picture in the 1980s—a Fischl, a Salle, a Koons—was to give commercial risk the patina of aesthetic risk. The circles of social life turned more or less the same elaborate machinery that they had turned a century earlier: The cogs in the greed wheel turn the money wheel, which turns the culture wheel, which turns the social wheel, until at last the aspirant gains a seat at the central wheel table, where the hostess is called "Mrs." (Mrs. Wrightsman, Mrs. Astor), and he has at last arrived.

By the nineties, new rules had begun to fall into place, just as they did in Howells's nineties. Everyone in *A Hazard,* rich or poor, is an immigrant: There are no native New Yorkers, no indigenous established society. There are just people with new money, or people dependent on it, having dinners for one another. The unwashed Dryfooses, Isabel discovers to her shock, do not know that they are out of society, because they do not know there is a society to be in. (The Dryfoos daughters don't even take piano lessons; they play the banjo.) Dryfoos buys the magazine to occupy his son, not to achieve a social position; when he wants to have a dinner party to celebrate the new magazine, it turns into a glorified office party, the same old faces. In today's New York, too, the parties that people talk about seem to be glorified office parties, propelled not by hostesses but by verbs and gerunds: launches and start-ups and initial public offerings.

In a society in which money has gained its sovereign virtue, art—and the ascension it symbolizes—no longer matters in quite the same way. When George Bellows's 1910 painting *Polo Crowd* was bought by an unnamed millionaire a few months ago, it violated essential Veblenian status-creating principles. The picture was being sold by the Museum of Modern Art because "it did not fit into its collection"; i.e., wasn't good enough. It went for three times the estimate. The guy who paid $27.5 million for the painting didn't buy it because he wished to acquire status from it; its status had been officially denied by the status-granting institution. *He bought it because he liked it.* Society totters.

Isabel has the apartment dream, too! "It was something about the children at first," she tells Basil, and then it was "of a hideous thing with two square eyes and a series of sections growing darker and then lighter, till the tail of the monstrous articulate was quite luminous again." March says, laughing, "Why, my dear, it was nothing but a harmless New York flat—seven rooms and a bath."

Haunted by that dream, Isabel returns to Boston, and Basil, in a fit of resignation, rents a horrible furnished apartment that she has seen and rejected. "He was aware more than ever of its absurdities, he knew that his wife would never cease to hate it," but he also "felt a comfort in committing himself and exchanging the burden of indecision for the burden of responsibility."

The magazine begins to prosper, and March tries to do good with Dryfoos's money by going downtown to offer work to a German-American socialist translator named Lindau, who taught him Heine back in the Midwest when he was a boy. He finds Lindau living in Chinatown, on Mott Street. "But what are you living here for, Lindau?" he asks. Lindau explains that he has come here to see poverty. "How much money can a man honestly earn without wronging or oppressing some other man?" Lindau asks, and then answers his question: "It is the landlords and the merchant princes, the railroad kings and the coal barons . . . it is these that make the millions, but no man earns them. What artist, what physician, what scientist, what poet, was ever a millionaire?"

"That's Tom and Nicole's, that's Barbra's, that's Bruce's, that's the one Bruce gave to Demi after the divorce, that's Madonna's," the broker goes, pointing upward at all the great turrets, the high crowning spires, of the classic apartment buildings of Central Park West. Apparently, they all belong, like feudal keeps, to the stars who have immigrated to New York, as Howells did, as the Marches did. Perhaps they wave at one another, tower to tower, in the morning, as neighbors should.

Isabel and Basil, you realize, were the first victims of a persistent American illusion: Even the upper-middle classes in a plutocratic society, Howells believed, are always in precarious shape and usually don't know it. In New York, they do. Outside New York, the bourgeoisie does tend to live in ways not entirely unlike the rich. The Marches' little house in Boston, though hardly grand, is a house, with a house's accoutrements and pleasures, as would be the case in Cambridge (or Philadelphia) today. New York tends to invite the middle classes to live alongside the rich, and then makes visible the true space between them, draws a line in outside light. Unlike London and Paris, the two other great capitals of bourgeois civilization, Manhattan has never really been symbolized by middle-class housing. The sweep of semi-detached houses in Knightsbridge or Kensington, the long boulevards filled with bourgeoisie in the sixteenth and eighth arrondissements of Paris, sum up the image of those places. New York, on the other hand, is famous for William Randolph Hearst's penthouse and Sister Eileen's basement apartment, or, more recently, for the Trump Tower aerie and the Tribeca loft. A nuclear family living in a little house in Manhattan is a sight. The old enclaves of the true bourgeoisie, Riverside Drive and York Avenue, were on the margins of the island, and their high period was a short one. (My great-aunt, like everybody else's, moved into a fifteen-room apartment on Riverside Drive in the forties, and it had been broken up by the sixties, barely a generation's worth of extra closets. Each of its divided parts now costs more money than my great-uncle made in a lifetime.)

At one moment in *A Hazard*, Isabel and Basil pretend to be millionaires simply to see what lies beyond their means. "They looked at three-thousand- and four-thousand-dollar apartments and rejected them for one reason or another which had nothing to do with the rent; the higher the rent, the more critical they were." Inspired by them, we decided to do it, too.

What you find, though, when you search—well, not the spires (what, are you kidding?) but the spaces that hold up the spires—isn't luxury, twisting staircases and panoramic windows, but the old American representations of normalcy and domestic comfort. What you find isn't Fred Astaire's apartment in *Daddy Long Legs* but Meg Ryan's apartment in a Nora Ephron movie, the apartment where Hannah lived in the Woody Allen film, the flat that Mr. Blandings is desperate to escape in order to build his dream house. There are kitchens that look like kitchens, living rooms like living rooms, bedrooms like bedrooms. A millionaire's life in New York is still what normal life looks like on a cereal box. And this is exactly what draws the people in the spires to live in the spires: The movie star who moves here announces that he likes New York because he can live like a normal person, because his kids can have normal lives, and, in a weird way, he means it.

For Howells, the inevitable result of plutocracy, exemplified by the apartment madness and Lindau's despair, is popular revolt and its repression. A trainmen's strike threatens to paralyze the city, and Basil, in a fit of reportorial responsibility, goes to "cover" the strike and sees Lindau struck down by a policeman—and then sees Dryfoos's saintly young son lose his life in an attempt to rescue the old socialist.

Howells himself became a Tolstoyan (i.e., mushy) socialist, and he wrote for Basil March a long concluding speech in which March realizes that the hazard of new fortunes is his, too. "What I object to is this economic chance world in which we live and which we men seem to have created," he tells Isabel. A workingman should be guaranteed his livelihood and his repose, and it is insupportable that he is not:

> At my time of life—at every time of life—a man ought to feel that if he will keep on doing his duty he shall not suffer in himself or in those who are dear to him, except through natural causes. But no man can feel this as things are now, and so we go on. Pushing and pulling, climbing and crawling, thrusting aside and trampling underfoot, lying, cheating, stealing; and when we get to the end, covered with blood and dirt and sin and shame, and look back over the way we've come to a palace of our own, or the poorhouse, which is about the only possession we can claim in common with our brother men, I don't think the retrospect can be pleasing. . . . People are greedy and foolish and wish to have and to shine, because having and shining are held up to them by civilization as the chief good of life. . . . We can't help it. If one were less greedy or less foolish, someone else would have and would shine at his expense.

This economic chance world in which we live. A hundred years ago, the one thing that Howells—and Henry Adams and so many others—knew for sure was that a society with a tiny plutocratic class, a precarious middle class, and a large and immigration-fed proletariat simply could not go on. Now, at the turn of another century, we find it is the only thing that has gone on, in nearly perfect duplicate. August Belmont celebrated the last fin de siècle in a suit of golden armor; everyone who celebrated this fin de siècle in costume with the Soroses came away, we're told, with a bronze medallion embossed with the hosts' profiles. Three-star chefs are flown in from Paris for a night's diversion; ghost mining towns in Colorado are revived and fully peopled for two weeks each summer as "camps" where the rich can entertain their courtiers. Someone has just bought the International Center of Photography, a grand old mansion on Fifth Avenue, in order to turn it back into a private house, reversing the century-old process by which the mansions of the fin de siècle rich became institutions. The plutocracy has never been so plutocratic.

What makes it possible for the economic chance world to go on so peaceably now, with hardly a hint of the opposition that Howells took for granted? It is that a sense of Hazard has been replaced by Hope. It seemed to Howells that hazard and fortune were as right together as pride and lions, that risk and moneymaking were one. What's striking about this new Gilded Age isn't just that people are selling hope but that everyone is buying it. All the folk memories of busts and depressions past seem to have vanished; the rhetoric of hope has overcome even the romance of risk, the sinister glamour of greed.

The new tycoons are not in industry, like Howells's, or in asset stripping, like Tom Wolfe's. They don't look like old man Dryfoos, grasping and raw. They look, more often, like his son, Conrad, all quivering sensitivity and high-minded devotion to the future. The places of the new fortunes are not sweatshops or mines—not here, anyway—but ateliers reclaimed from the light-industrial Old New York the Marches knew. Six computers, a server, a wall of glass brick, a stamped-tin ceiling, a bright post-ironic attitude—these are the materials of a dot-com company, of the new fortunes. It is hope (and its Siamese twin, debt) that empties out the buildings on North Moore

Street and calls on you to extrapolate from the samples, hope that keeps you looking, that gets you to dramatize the whole thing. If it is a bubble—and common sense tells you that it must be—it has a bubble's bright, single highlight, and it encloses Manhattan from Ninety-sixth Street to the harbor. Hope is what gives this age its odd and original gleam, a strange ingenuous glow different from that of the Marches' age, a century ago, when even the people who had the gold knew the age was merely gilded. "Having and shining, having and shining": We still believe it. But now we shine first and assume that, if the glow is bright enough, we will all have later.

Howells, like Basil, was radicalized by his experience in New York in the 1890s. "I abhor it," he wrote to Henry James of American capitalism, "and feel that it is coming out all wrong in the end, unless it bases itself anew on a real equality." But, like Isabel, he also learned that New York is a city of accommodations. This double movement gives his masterpiece its pathos and its enduring moral. Later, he wrote of himself and his wife, "We are theoretical socialists, and practical aristocrats. But it is a comfort to be right theoretically, and to be ashamed of one's self practically." "Practical aristocrats": a lovely calling, nice work if you can get it.

It is at least a relief to discover that at the end of *A Hazard of New Fortunes*, the Marches find a place to live for good. If the explicit moral of the novel is radical, its dramatic point is liberal: Isabel's acceptance of New York domestic arrangements and her education in the irony necessary to accept them. Dryfoos, after the death of his son, goes off to Paris, selling *Every Other Week* to Basil and his publisher for a song. There is a big empty space on the second floor of the building, right above the editorial offices, and Basil and Isabel decide to live there with the kids. It is a sign of Isabel's transformation that this idea—in Boston, she thinks, fit only for Irish laundresses—is now acceptable to her. She has become as diffident and ironic as her husband, as someone seeing life pass by from the El. She has become a New Yorker, and she will live above the store. "In New York," she reflects at last, "you may do anything."

Man Goes to See a Doctor

Lately, a lot of people—why, I'm not entirely sure—have been sending me clippings about the decline and fall of psychoanalysis. Most of the reasons given for its disappearance made sense: People are happier, busier; the work done by the anti-Freudian skeptics has finally taken hold of the popular imagination, so that people have no time for analytic longueurs and no patience with its mystifications.

Along with those decline-and-fall pieces, though, I also got sent—and in this case I don't entirely want to know why—a lot of hair-raising pieces about mental illness and its new therapies: about depressions, disasters, hidden urges suddenly (or brazenly) confessed, and how you can cure them all with medicine. Talking is out, taking is in. Some of my friends seem to be layered with drugs from the top down, like a pousse-café: Rogaine on top, then Prozac, then Xanax, then Viagra. . . . In this context, my own experience in being doctored for mental illness seems paltry and vaguely absurd, and yet, in its way, memorable.

I was on the receiving end of what must have been one of the last, and easily one of the most unsuccessful, psychoanalyses that have ever been attempted—one of the last times a German-born analyst, with a direct laying on of hands from Freud, spent forty-five minutes twice a week for five years discussing, in a small room on Park Avenue decorated with Motherwell posters, the problems of a "creative" New York neurotic. It may therefore be worth recalling, if only in the way that it would be interesting to hear the experiences of the last man mesmerized or the last man to be bled with leeches. Or the last man—and there must have been such a man as the sixteenth century drew to a close and the modern age began—to bring an alchemist a lump of lead in the sincere belief that he would take it home as gold.

So it happened that on a night in October 1990, I found myself sitting in a chair and looking at the couch in the office of one of the oldest, most patriarchal, most impressive-looking psychoanalysts in New York. He had been recommended to me by another patient, a twenty-year veteran of his couch. The choice now presents itself of whether to introduce him by name or by pseudonym, a choice that is more one of decorum than of legal necessity (he's dead). To introduce him by name is, in a sense, to invade his privacy. On the other hand, not to introduce him by name is to allow him to disappear into the braid of literature in which he was caught—his patients liked to write about him, in masks, theirs and his—and from which, at the end, he was struggling to break free. He had, for instance, written a professional article about a well-known patient, in which the (let's say) playwright who had inspired the article was turned into a painter. He had then seen this article, and the disputes it engendered, transformed into an episode in one of the playwright's plays, with the playwright-painter now turned into a novelist, and then the entire pas de deux had been turned by a colleague into a further psychoanalytic study of the exchange, with the occupations altered yet again—the playwright-painter-novelist now becoming a poet—so that four layers of disguise (five, as I write this) gathered around one episode in his office. "Yes, but I received only one check" was his bland response when I pointed this out to him.

His name, I'll say, was Max Grosskurth, and he had been practicing psychoanalysis for almost fifty years. He was a German Jew of a now vanishing type—not at all like the small, wisecracking, scared Mitteleuropean Jews that I had grown up among. He was tall, commanding, humorless. He liked large, blooming shirts, dark suits, heavy handmade shoes, club ties. He had a limp that, in the years when I knew him, became a two-legged stutter and then left him immobile, so that our last year of analysis took place in his apartment, around the corner from the office. His roster of patients was drawn almost exclusively from among what he liked to call creative people, chiefly writers and painters and composers, and he talked about them so freely that I sometimes half expected him to put up autographed glossies around the office, like the ones on the wall at the Stage Deli. ("Max—Thanks for the most terrific transference in Gotham! Lenny.") When we began, he was eighty, and I had crossed thirty.

I've read that you're not supposed to notice anything in the analyst's office, but that first evening I noticed it all. There was the couch, a nice Charles Eames job. On one wall there was a Motherwell print—a quick ink jet—and, opposite, a framed poster of one of the Masaccio frescoes in Santa Maria del Carmine in Florence. I was instantly impressed. The two images seemed to position him (and me) between Italian humanism, in its first, rocky, realistic form, at one end, and postwar New York humanism, in its jumpy, anxiety-purging form, at the other. On a bookshelf beside him were nothing but bound volumes of a psychoanalytic journal, rising to the ceiling. (He had edited that journal for a time. "Let me give you some counsel," he said to me much later. "Editing never means anything.")

He was lit by a single shaded bulb, just to his left, in that kind of standing brass lamp with a long arcing neck. This put his face in a vaguely sinister half-light, but, with his strong accent and the sounds of traffic out on Park Avenue and a headlight occasionally sweeping across the room, the scene had a comforting European melancholia, as though directed by Pabst.

Why was I there? Nothing interesting: the usual mixture of hurt feelings, confusion, and incomprehension that comes to early-arriving writers when the thirties hit. John Updike once wrote that, though the newcomer imagines that literary New York will be like a choir of angels, in fact it is like *The Raft of the* Medusa—and he was wrong about this only in that the people on the raft of the *Medusa* still have hope. In New York, the raft has been adrift now for years, centuries, and there's still no rescue boat in sight. The only thing left is to size up the others and wait for someone to become weak enough to eat.

I spilled out my troubles; told him of my sense of panic, anxiety; perhaps wept. He was silent for a minute—not a writer's minute, a real one, a long time.

"Franz Marc was a draftsman of remarkable power," he said at last:

the first words of my analysis. His voice was deep and powerful, uncannily like Henry Kissinger's: not quacky, pleading Viennese but booming, arrogant German.

The remark about Franz Marc was not *quite* apropos of nothing—he knew me to be an art critic—but very near. (Franz Marc was the less famous founder of the German Expressionist movement called Der Blaue Reiter; Kandinsky was the other.) He must have caught the alarmed look in my eyes, for he added, more softly, "There are many worthwhile unexplored subjects in modern art." Then he sat up in his chair—swallowed hard and pulled himself up—and for a moment I had a sense of just how aged he was.

"You put me in mind," he said—and suddenly there was nothing the least old in the snap and expansive authority of his voice—"you put me in mind of Norman Mailer at a similar age." (This was a reach, or raw flattery; there is nothing about me that would put anyone in mind of Norman Mailer.) "*Barbary Shore,* he thought, would be the end of him. What a terrible, terrible, terrible book it is. It was a great blow to his narcissism. I recall clearly attending dinner parties in this period with my wife, an extremely witty woman, where everyone was mocking poor Norman. My wife, an extremely witty woman . . ." He looked at me as though, despite the repetition, I had denied it; I tried to look immensely amused, as though reports of Mrs. Grosskurth's wit had reached me in my crib. "Even my wife engaged in this banter. In the midst of it, however, I held my peace." He rustled in his chair, and now I saw why he had sat up: He suddenly became a stiff, living pillar, his hands held before him, palms up—a man holding his peace in the middle of banter flying around the dinner table. A rock of imperturbable serenity! He cautiously settled back in his chair. "Now, of course, Norman has shown great resourcefulness and is receiving extremely large advances for his genre studies of various American criminals."

From the five years of my analysis, or therapy, or whatever the hell it was, there are words that are as permanently etched in my brain as the words "E pluribus unum" are on the nickel. "Banter" and "genre studies" were the first two. I have never been so grateful for a mot juste as I was for the news that Mrs. Grosskurth had engaged in banter, and that Norman Mailer had made a resourceful turn toward genre studies. Banter, that was all it was; criticism, the essential competitive relations of writers in New York—all of it was banter, engaged in by extremely witty wives of analysts at dinner parties. And all you had to do was . . . refuse to engage in it! Hold your peace. Take no part! Like him—sit there like a rock and let it wash over you.

And then there was the wacky perfection of his description of the later Mailer, with its implications of knowing (not firsthand, certainly; Mailer, as far as I know, had never been his patient) the inside story: He had, under stress, found appropriate genre subjects. American criminals. The whole speech, I thought, was so profound that it could be parsed and highlighted like one of those dog-eared assigned texts you find on the reserve shelf in undergraduate libraries: Artists suffered from *narcissism,* which made them susceptible to *banter,* which they could overcome by *resourcefulness,* which might lead them to—well, to take up *genre studies.* ("Genre studies," I was to discover, was Grosskurthese for "journalism." He often indulged in strangely Johnsonian periphrases: Once, talking about Woody Allen, he remarked, "My wife, who was an extremely witty woman, was naturally curious to see such a celebrated wit. We saw him in a cabaret setting. I recall that he was reciting samples of his writings in a state of high anxiety." It took me days of figuring—what kind of reading had it been? a kind of Weimar tribute evening?—to realize that Dr. and Mrs. Grosskurth had gone to a nightclub and heard the comedian's monologue.)

I came away from that first session in a state of blissful suspended confusion. Surely this wasn't the way psychoanalysis was supposed to proceed. On the other hand, it was much more useful—and interesting—to hear that Norman Mailer had rebounded by writing genre studies than it was to hear that my family was weird; that I knew already. I felt a giddy sense of relief, especially when he added sardonically, "Your problems remind me of"—and here he named one of the heroes of the New York School. "Fortunately, you suffer from neither impotence nor alcoholism. That is in your favor." And that set the pattern of our twice- and sometimes thrice-weekly encounters for the next five years. He was touchy, prejudiced, opinionated, impatient, often bored, usually high-handed, brutally bigoted. I could never decide whether to sue for malpractice or fall to my knees in gratitude for such an original healer.

Our exchanges hardened into a routine. I would take the subway uptown at six-thirty; I would get out at Seventy-seventh Street, walk a couple of blocks uptown, and enter his little office at the corner of Park Avenue, where I would join three or four people sitting on a bench. Then the door opened, another neurotic—sometimes a well-known neurotic who looked as though he wanted to hide his face with his coat, like an indicted stockbroker—came out, and I went in. There was the smell of the air conditioner.

"So," he would say. "How are you?"

"Terrible," I would say, sometimes sincerely, sometimes to play along.

"I expected no less," he would say, and then I would begin to stumble out the previous three or four days' problems, worries, gossip. He would clear his throat and begin a monologue, a kind of roundabout discussion of major twentieth-century figures (Sigmund Freud, Albert Einstein, and, above all, Thomas Mann were his touchstones), broken confidences of the confessional, episodes from his own life, finally snaking around to an abrupt "So you see . . ." and some thunderously obvious maxim, which he would apply to my problems—or, rather, to the nonexistence of my problems, compared with real problems, of which he'd heard a few, you should have been here then.

For instance: I raised, as a problem, my difficulty in finishing my book, in writing without a deadline. I raised it at length, circuitously, with emotion. He cleared his throat. "It is commonplace among writers to need extreme arousal. For instance, Martin Buber." I riffled through my card catalog: Wasn't he the theologian? "He kept pornography on the lecture stand with him, in order to excite him to a greater performance as a lecturer. He would be talking about 'I and thou,' and there he would be, shuffling through his papers, looking at explicit photographs of naked women." He shook his head. "This was really going very far. And yet Buber was a very great scholar. It was appropriate for his approach. It would not be appropriate for you, for it would increase your extreme overestimation of your own role."

Mostly, he talked about what he thought it took to survive in the warfare of New York. He talked about the major figures of New York literary life—not necessarily his own patients but writers and artists whose careers he followed admiringly—as though they were that chain of forts upstate, around Lake George, left over from the French and Indian War: the ones you visited as a kid, where they gave you bumper stickers. There was Fort Sontag, Fort Frankenthaler, Fort Mailer. "She is very well defended." "Yes, I admire her defenses." "Admirably well defended." Once I mentioned a famous woman intellectual who had recently gotten into legal trouble: Hadn't she been well defended? "Yes, but the trouble is that the guns were pointing the wrong way, like the British at Singapore." You were wrung out with gratitude for a remark like that. I was, anyway.

It was his theory, in essence, that "creative" people were inherently in a rage, and that this rage came from their disappointed narcissism. The narcissism could take a negative, paranoid form or a positive, defiant, arrogant form. His job was not to cure the narcissism (which was inseparable from the creativity) but, instead, to fortify it—to get the drawbridge up and the gate down and leave the Indians circling outside, with nothing to do but shoot flaming arrows harmlessly over the stockade.

He had come of age as a professional in the forties and fifties, treating the great battlers of the golden age of New York intellectuals, an age that, seen on the couch—a seething mass of resentments, jealousies, and needs—appeared somewhat less golden than it did otherwise. "How well I recall," he would begin, "when I was treating"—and here he named two famous art critics of the period. "They went to war with each other. One came in at ten o'clock. 'I must reply,' he said. Then at four-thirty the other one would come in. 'I must reply,' he would say. 'No,' I told them both. 'Wait six months and see if anyone recalls the source of this argument.' They agreed to wait. Six months later, my wife, that witty, witty woman, held a dinner party and offered some pleasantry about their quarrel. No one understood; no one even remembered it. And this was in the days when *ARTnews* was something. I recall what Thomas Mann said. . . ." Eventually, abruptly, as the clock on the wall turned toward seven-thirty, he would say, "So you see . . . this demonstrates again what I always try to tell you about debates among intellectuals."

I leaned forward, really wanting to know. "What is that, Doctor?" I said.

"*No one cares*. People have troubles of their own. We have to stop now." And that would be it.

I would leave the room in a state of vague, disconcerted disappointment. *No one cares?* No one cares about the hard-fought and brutally damaging fight for the right sentence, the irrefutable argument? And: People have troubles of their own? My great-aunt Hannah could have told me that. That was the result of half a century of presiding over the psyches of a major moment in cultural history? And then, fifteen minutes later, as I rode in a cab downtown, my heart would lift—would fly. That's right: *No one cares! People have troubles of their own!* It's okay. That doesn't mean you shouldn't do it; it means you should do it, somehow, for its own sake, without illusions. Just write, just live, and don't care too much yourself. No one cares. It's just *banter*.

Sometimes his method of bringing me to awareness—if that was what he was doing—could be oblique, not to say bizarre. There was, for instance, the Volestein Digression. This involved a writer whose name was, shall we say, Moses Volestein. Dr. G. had once read something by him and been fascinated by his name. "What a terrible name," he said. "Vole. Why would a man keep such a terrible name?"

His name didn't strike me as a burden, and I said so.

"You are underestimating the damage that this man's name does to his psychic welfare," he replied gravely. "It is intolerable."

"I don't think he finds it intolerable."

"You are wrong."

Then, at our next meeting: "Your resistance to my discussion of Volestein's name at our last session is typical of your extreme narcissistic overestimation. You continue to underestimate the damage a name like that does to the human psyche."

"Doctor, surely you overestimate the damage such a name does to the human psyche."

"You are wrong. His family's failure to change this name suggests a deep denial of reality." He pursued Volestein's name through that session and into the next, and finally, I exploded.

"I can't believe we're spending another hour discussing Moses Volestein's funny name!" I said. "I mean, for that matter, some people might think my name is funny."

He considered. "Yes. But your name is merely very ugly and unusual. It does not include a word meaning a shrewlike animal with unpleasant associations for so many people. It is merely very ugly."

And then I wondered. My name—as natural to me as the sound of my own breathing? I had volunteered that it might be peculiar, out of some mixture of gallantry and point-scoring. But my hurt was enormous. My wife, who had kept her own name when we married—out of feminist principle, I had thought—said, "Yes, when we met, I couldn't believe it. I wouldn't go out with you for a week because of it." It was a shock as great as any I had received, and as salutary. Had he obsessed on Volestein with the intention of making me face Gopnik, in all its oddity, and then, having faced it, grasp some ironic wisdom? I had a funny name. And then the corollary: People could have funny names and go right on working. They might never even notice it. Years later, online, I found myself on a list of writers with extremely funny names—I suppose this is what people do with their time now that they are no longer in psychoanalysis—and I was, amazingly, happy to be there. So that was one score. Even your name could be absurd and you wouldn't know it. And the crucial addition: It didn't matter. Indifference and armor could get you through anything.

Sometimes Dr. Grosskurth would talk about his own history. He was born in Berlin before World War I, at a time when German Jews were German above all. His mother had hoped that he would become a diplomat. But he had decided to study medicine instead, particularly psychiatry; he was of that generation of German Jews who found in Freud's doctrines what their physicist contemporaries found in Einstein's. He had spoken out against the Nazis in 1933 and had been forced to flee the country at a moment's notice. One of his professors had helped him get out. (He was notably unheroic in his description of this episode. "It was a lesson to me to keep my big mouth shut" was the way he put it.) He fled to Italy, where he completed medical school at the University of Padua.

He still loved Italy: He ate almost every night at Parma, a restaurant nearby, on Third Avenue, and spent every August in Venice, at the Cipriani. One spring, I recall, I announced that my wife and I had decided to go to Venice.

He looked at me tetchily. "And where will you stay?" he asked.

"At this *pensione,* the Accademia," I said.

"No," he said. "You wish to stay at the Monaco, it is a very pleasant hotel, and you will have breakfast on the terrace. That is the correct hostel for you."

I reached into my pockets, where I usually had a stubby pencil, and searched for a stray bit of paper—an American Express receipt, the back of a bit of manuscript paper—to write on.

"No, no!" he said with disgust. My disorderliness was anathema to his Teutonic soul. "Here, I will write it down. Oh, you are so chaotic. Hand me the telephone." I offered him the phone, which was on a small table near his chair, and he consulted a little black book that he took from his inside right jacket pocket. He dialed some long number. Then, in a voice even deeper and more booming than usual—he was raised in a time when long distance meant long distance—he began to speak in Italian.

"*Sì, sono Dottore* Grosskurth." He waited for a moment—genuinely apprehensive, I thought, for the first time in my acquaintance with him—and then a huge smile, almost a big-lug smile, broke across his face. They knew him.

"Sì, sì," he said, and then, his voice lowering, said, "No," and something I didn't understand; obviously, he was explaining that Mrs. Grosskurth had died. *"Pronto!"* he began, and then came a long sentence beginning with my name and various dates in *giugno. "Sì, sì."* He put his hand over the receiver. "You wish for a bath or a shower?" he demanded.

"Bath," I said.

"Good choice," he said. It was the nearest thing to praise he had ever given me. Finally, he hung up the phone. He looked at the paper in his hand and gave it to me.

"There," he said. "You are reserved for five nights, the room has no view of the canal, but actually, this is better, since the gondola station can be extremely disturbing. You will eat breakfast on the terrace, and there you will enjoy the view of the Salute. Do not eat dinner there, however. I will give you a list of places." And, on an "Ask Your Doctor About Prozac" pad, he wrote out a list of restaurants in Venice for me. (They were mostly, I realized later, after I got to know Venice a bit, the big, old, fifties-ish places that a New York analyst would love: Harry's Bar, Da Fiore, the Madonna.)

"You will go to these places, order the spaghetti *vongole,* and then . . ."

"And then?"

"And then at last you will be happy," he said flatly.

He was so far from being an orthodox Freudian, or an orthodox anything, that I was startled when I discovered how deep and passionate his attachment to psychoanalytic dogma was. One day about three years in, I came into his office and saw that he had a copy of *The New York Review of Books* open. "It is very sad," he began. "It is very sad indeed to see a journal which was once respected by many people descend into a condition where it has lost the good opinion of all reasonable people." After a few moments, I figured out that he was referring to one of several much discussed pieces that the literary critic Frederick Crews had written attacking Freud and Freudianism.

I read the pieces later myself and thought them incontrovertible. Then I sat down to read Freud for the first time—*Civilization and Its Discontents, Totem and Taboo, The Interpretation of Dreams*—and was struck at once by the absurdity of the arguments as arguments and the impressive weight of humane culture marshaled in their support. One sensed that one was in the presence of a kind of showman, a brilliant essayist, leaping from fragmentary evidence to unsupported conclusion, and summoning up a whole body of psychological myth—the Id, the Libido, the Ego—with the confidence of a Disney cartoonist drawing bunnies and squirrels. I found myself, therefore, in the unusual position of being increasingly skeptical of the therapeutic approach to which I fled twice a week for comfort. I finally got up the courage to tell Grosskurth this.

"You therefore find a conflict between your strongest intellectual convictions and your deepest emotional gratification needs?" he asked.

"Yes."

He shrugged. "Apparently, you are a Freudian."

This seemed to me a first-rate exchange, honors to him, but I couldn't let it go. My older sister, a professor of developmental psychology at Berkeley, regarded Freud as a comic relic (I had told her about my adventures in psychoanalysis), and in the midst of the *New York Review* debate, she wrote one of the most devastating of the anti-Freud letters to the editor. She even made a passing, dismissive reference to the appeal of "figures of great personal charisma"—I knew what that was about—and then stated conclusively that there was nothing to be said in defense of psychoanalysis that couldn't also be said in defense of magic or astrology. ("She is very well defended, your sister," Grosskurth said.)

On behalf of his belief, Grosskurth would have said—did say, though over time, and not in these precise words—that while Freud may have been wrong in all the details, his central insight was right. His insight was that human life is shaped by a series of selfish, ineradicable urges, particularly sexual ones, and that all the other things that happen in life are ways of toning down these urges and giving them an "acceptable" outlet. An actual, undramatic but perilous world of real things existed, whose essential character was its indifference to human feelings: This world of real things included pain, death, and disease, but also many things unthreatening to our welfare. His project—the Freudian project, properly understood—was not to tell the story of our psyche, the curious drawing-room comedy of Id and Ego and Libido, but just the opposite: to drain the drama from all our stories. He believed that the only thing to do with the knowledge of the murderous rage within your breast was not to mythologize it but to put a necktie on it and heavy shoes and a dark blue woolen suit. Only a man who knew that, given the choice, he would rape his mother and kill his father could order his spaghetti vongole in anything like peace.

There was, however, a catch in this argument, or so I insisted in the third year of my analysis, over several sessions and at great length. Weren't the well-defended people he admired really the ones at the furthest imaginable remove from the real things, the reality, whose worth he praised so highly? Did Susan Sontag actually have a better grasp of things-as-they-are than anyone else? Would anybody point to Harold Brodkey as a model of calm appraisal of the scale of the world and the appropriate place of his ego in it? Wasn't the "enormous narcissistic overestimation" of which he accused me inseparable from the "well-defended, internalized self-esteem" he wanted me to cultivate? The people who seemed best defended—well, the single most striking thing about them was how breathtakingly out of touch they were with the world, with other people's feelings, with the general opinion of their work. You didn't just have to be armored by your narcissism; you could be practically entombed in it, so that people came knocking, like Carter at King Tut's tomb, and you'd still get by. Wasn't that a problem for his system, or, anyway, for his therapy?

"Yes," he said coldly.

"Oh," I said, and we changed the subject.

My friends were all in therapy, too, of course—this was New York—and late at night, over a bottle of red wine, they would offer one "insight" or another that struck me as revelatory: "My analyst helped me face the recurring pattern in my life of an overprotectiveness that derives from my mother's hidden alcoholism," or "Mine helped me see more clearly how early my father's depression shaped my fears," or "Mine helped me see that my reluctance to publish my personal work is part of my reluctance to have a child." What could I say? "Mine keeps falling asleep, except when we discuss Hannah Arendt's sex life, about which he knows quite a lot?"

His falling asleep was a problem. The first few years I saw him, he still had a reasonably full schedule, and our sessions were usually late in the day; the strain told on him. As I settled insistently (I had decided that if I was going to be analyzed, I was going to be analyzed) into yet one more tiresome recital of grievances, injustices, anxieties, childhood memories, I could see his long, big, partly bald head nodding down toward the knot of his tie. His eyes would flutter shut, and he would begin to breathe deeply. I would drone on—"And so I think that it was my mother, really, who first gave me a sense of the grandiose. There was this birthday, I think my sixth, when I first sensed . . ."—and his chin would nestle closer and closer to his chest as his head dropped further, so that I was looking right at his bald spot. There was only one way, I learned, after a couple of disconcerting weeks of telling my troubles to a sleeping therapist, to revive him, and that was to gossip. "And so my mother's relationship with my father reminds me—well, in certain ways it reminds me of what people have been saying about Philip Roth's divorce from Claire Bloom," I would say abruptly, raising my volume on the non sequitur.

Instantly, his head would jerk straight up, his eyes would open, and he would shake himself all over like a Lab coming out of the water. "Yes, what are they saying about this divorce?" he would demand.

"Oh, nothing, really," I would say, and then I would wing it for a minute, glad to have caught his attention.

Unfortunately, my supply of hot literary gossip was very small. So there were times (and I hope that this is the worst confession I will ever have to make) when I would invent literary gossip on the way uptown, just to have something in reserve if he fell asleep, like a Victorian doctor going off to a picnic with a bottle of smelling salts, just in case. ("Let's see: What if I said that Kathy Acker had begun an affair with, oh, V. S. Pritchett—that would hold *anybody's* interest.") I felt at once upset and protective about his sleeping. Upset because it was, after all, my nickel, and protective because I did think that he was a great man, in his way, and I hated to see him dwindling: I wondered how long he would go on if he sensed that he was dwindling.

Not long ago, I read, in a book about therapy, a reference to a distinguished older analyst who made a point of going to sleep in front of his patients. Apparently, Grosskurth—for who else could it have been?—was famous for his therapeutic skill in falling asleep as you talked. It was tactical, even strategic.

Or was he just an old man trying to keep a practice going for lack of anything better to do, and doing anything—sleeping, booking hotel rooms, gossiping, as old men do—so that he would not have to be alone? Either limitlessly shrewd or deeply pathetic: Which was it? Trying to answer that question was one of the things that kept me going uptown.

As we went on into our fourth and fifth years, all the other problems that I had brought to him became one problem, *the* New York problem. Should my wife—should we—have a baby? We agonized over it, in the modern manner. Grosskurth listened silently for months and finally pronounced.

"Yes, you must go ahead and have a child. You will enjoy it. The child will try your patience repeatedly, yet you will find that there are many pleasures in child rearing." He cleared his throat. "You will find, for instance, that the child will make many amusing mistakes in language."

I looked at him, a little dumbfounded—that was the best of it?

"You see," he went on, "at about the age of three, children begin to talk, and naturally, their inexperience leads them to use language in surprising ways. These mistakes can really be *extremely* amusing. The child's errors in language also provide the kinds of anecdotes that can be of value to the parents in a social setting." It seemed an odd confidence on which to build a family—that the child would be your own live-in Gracie Allen, and you could dine out on the errors—but I thought that perhaps he was only defining, so to speak, the minimal case.

So we did have the child. Overwhelmed with excitement, I brought him pictures of the baby at a week old. ("Yes," he said dryly, peering at my Polaroids, "this strongly resembles a child.") And, as my life was changing, I began to think that it was time to end, or anyway wind down, our relationship. It had been five years, and for all that I had gained—and I thought that I had gained a lot: if not a cure, then at least enough material to go into business as a blackmailer—I knew that if I was to be "fully adult," I should break my dependence. And he was growing old. Already aged when we began, he was now, at eighty-five or -six, becoming frail. Old age seems to be a series of lurches rather than a gradual decline. One week he was his usual booming self, the next week there was a slow deliberateness in his gait as he came to the office door. Six months later, he could no longer get up reliably from his chair, and once fell down outside the office in my presence. His face, as I helped him up, was neither angry nor amused, just doughy and preoccupied, the face of a man getting ready for something. That was when we switched our sessions to his apartment, around the corner, on Seventy-ninth Street, where I would ring the bell and wait for him to call me in—he left the door open or had it left open by his nurse, whom I never saw. Then I would go inside and find him—having been helped into a gray suit, blue shirt, dark tie—on his own sofa, surrounded by Hofmann and Miró engravings and two or three precious Kandinsky prints.

About a month into the new arrangement, I decided to move to Europe to write, and I told him this in high spirits and with an almost breathless sense of advancement: I was going away, breaking free of New York, starting over. I thought he would be pleased.

To my shock, he was furious—his old self and then some. "Who would have thought of this idea? What a self-destructive regression." Then I realized why he was so angry: Despite all his efforts at fortification, I had decided to run away. Fort Gopnik was dropping its flag, dispersing its troops, surrendering its territory—all his work for nothing. Like General Gordon come to reinforce Khartoum, he had arrived too late and failed through the unforgivable, disorganized passivity of the natives.

In our final sessions, we settled into a nonaggression pact. ("Have we stopped too soon, Doctor?" I asked. "Yes," he said dully.) We talked neutrally, about art and family. Then, the day before I was to leave, I went uptown for our last session.

It was a five-thirty appointment in the second week of October. We began to talk amiably, like old friends, about the bits and pieces of going abroad, visas and vaccinations. Then, abruptly, he began to tell a long, meandering story about his wife's illness and death, which we had never talked about before. He kept returning to a memory he had of her swimming back and forth in the hotel pool in Venice the last summer before her death.

"She had been ill, and the Cipriani, as you are not aware, has an excellent pool. She swam back and forth in this pool, back and forth, for hours. I was well aware that her illness was very likely to be terminal." He shook his head, held out his hands, dealing with reality. "As soon as she had episodes of dizziness and poor balance, I made a very quick diagnosis. Still, back and forth she swam."

He stopped; the room by now had become dark. The traffic on Seventy-ninth Street had thickened into a querulous, honking rush-hour crowd. He was, I knew, too shaky on his feet to get up and turn on the lights, and I thought that it would be indelicate for me to do it, they were his lights. So we sat there in the dark.

"Naturally, this was to be the last summer that we spent in Venice. However, she had insisted that we make this trip. And she continued to swim." He looked around the room in the dark—the pictures, the drawings, the bound volumes, all that was left of two lives joined together, one closed, the other closing.

"She continued to swim. She had been an exceptional athlete in addition to being, as you know, an extremely witty woman." He seemed lost in memory for a moment, but then, regaining himself, he cleared his throat in the dark, professionally, as he had done so many times before.

"So you see," he said, again trying to make the familiar turn toward home. And then he did something that I don't think he had ever done before: He called me by my name. "So you see, Adam, in life, in life . . ." And I rose, thinking, *Here at our final session—no hope of ever returning, my bag packed and my ticket bought to another country, far away—at last, the truth, the point, the thing to take away that we have been building toward all these years.*

"So you see, Adam, in retrospect . . ." he went on, and stirred, rose on the sofa, trying to force his full authority on his disobedient frame. "In retrospect, life has many worthwhile aspects," he concluded quietly, and then we had to stop. He sat looking ahead, and a few minutes later, with a goodbye and a handshake, I left.

Now I was furious. I was trying to be moved, but I would have liked to be moved by something easier to be moved by. That was all he had to say to me, *Life has many worthwhile aspects*? For once, that first reaction of disappointment stuck with me for a long time, on the plane all the way to Paris. All these evenings, all that investment, all that humanism, all those Motherwell prints—yes, all that money, my money—for that? Life has many worthwhile aspects? Could there have been a more fatuous and arrhythmic and unmemorable conclusion to what had been, after all, my analysis, my only analysis?

Now, of course, it is more deeply engraved than any other of his words. In retrospect, life has many worthwhile aspects. Not all or even most aspects. And not beautiful or meaningful or even tolerable. Just worthwhile, with its double burden of labor and reward. Life has worth—value, importance—and it takes a while to get there.

I came back to New York about a year later and went to see him. A woman with a West Indian accent had answered when I called his number. I knew that I would find him declining, but still, I thought, I would find him himself. We expect our fathers to take as long a time dying as we take growing up. But he was falling away. He was lying on a hospital bed, propped up, his skin as gray as pavement, his body as thin and wasted as a tree on a New York street in winter. The television was on, low, tuned to a game show. He struggled for breath as he spoke.

He told me, very precisely, about the disease that he had. "The prognosis is most uncertain," he said. "I could linger indefinitely." He mentioned something controversial that I had written. "You showed independence of mind." He turned away, in pain. "And, as always, very poor judgment."

In New York again, five months later, I thought, *I'll just surprise him, squeeze his hand*. I walked by his building and asked the doorman if Dr. Grosskurth was in. He said that Dr. Grosskurth had died three months before. For a moment I thought, *Someone should have called me, one of his children*. Yet they hardly could have called all his patients. ("But I was special!" the child screams.) Then I stumbled over to Third Avenue and almost automatically into Parma, the restaurant that he had loved. I asked the owner if he knew that Dr. Grosskurth had died, and he said yes, of course: They had had a dinner, with his family and some of his friends, to remember him, and the owner invited me to have dinner, too, and drink to his memory.

I sat down and began an excellent solitary dinner in honor of my dead psychoanalyst—seafood pasta, a Venetian dish, naturally—and, in his memory, chewed at the squid. (He liked squid.) The waiter brought me my bill, and I paid it. I still think that the owner should at least have bought the wine. Which shows, I suppose, that the treatment was incomplete. ("They should have paid for your wine?" "It would have been a nice gesture, yes. It would have happened in Paris." "You are hopeless. I died too soon, and you left too early. The analysis was left unfinished.")

The transference wasn't completed, I suppose, but something—a sort of implantation—did take place. The point of the analysis was, I see now, to prepare me for fatherhood by supplying a patriarchal model, however odd, and it did. In moments of crisis or panic, I sometimes think that I have his woolen suit draped around my shoulders, even in August. Sometimes in ordinary moments I almost think that I have become him. Though my patience is repeatedly tried by my children, I laugh at their many amusing mistakes in language—I have even been known to repeat these mistakes in social settings. I refer often to the sayings of my wife, that witty, witty woman. On the whole, I would say that my years in analysis had many worthwhile aspects.

A Purim Story

I suppose it is a sign of just how inadequate a Jew I am that when I got a letter from the Jewish Museum right after we got home this fall, asking me to be the Purimspieler at its Purim Ball in February, I thought there must be some kind of mistake. I don't mean that I thought there must be some mistake in asking me. I am enough of a ham that I would not be entirely surprised if a Hindu congregation had asked me to come forward and chant choice selections from the *Bhagavad Gita*. I mean that I was surprised because I thought the Jewish Museum was making a mistake about the date of Purim.

"Isn't that the one in the fall?" I asked my wife, Martha. "With the hamantaschen? And the little hut in the backyard?"

"No," she said. "No, it isn't. They have hamantaschen all year round. Even I know that."

"The thing that puzzles me," I went on, holding up the letter and reading it again, "is how they ever figured out I was Jewish."

She executed what I believe our fathers would have called a spit take. "That is the most ridiculous question I've ever heard. There's your name, for one thing, and then the way you use Jewish words in writing."

"What Jewish words have I ever used in writing?"

She thought for a moment. "Well, 'shvitz.' And 'inchoate.' "

" 'Inchoate' is not a Jewish word."

"It is the way you use it. You've got 'Jew' written all over you. It's obvious."

"It's obvious," my six-year-old son, Luke, echoed, looking up from his plate. "It's obvious." I was startled, though not entirely. We lived in Paris for the first five years of his life, and ethnic awareness is one of the first things he's been exposed to on coming home to New York. The lame and the halt, the meaning of Kwanzaa and the nights of Hanukkah—all the varieties of oppressed ethnic experience have become the material of his education. He sees the world in groups, or is beginning to. His best friend, Jacob Kogan, has a sister who was asked by her grandparents what she wanted for Hanukkah. "A Christmas tree," she said. Luke reported that with pleasure. He and Jacob have developed a nice line in old Henny Youngman–style jokes, which apparently circulate permanently in the lower grades of New York schools, like Mercury space-program debris circulating in outer space, getting lower and lower in its orbit each year: "Waiter, what's this fly doing in my soup!" "The backstroke."

I gave Luke a look. His birth was the occasion of my realizing just how poor a Jew I am. When he was born, at Mount Sinai Hospital in New York, almost every other baby in the nursery had Lubavitcher parents, and in the isolette they had proudly placed a little framed photograph of the Lubavitcher rebbe, Menachem Schneerson, so that the first thing the baby saw was the thin Russian eyes and the great Rembrandt beard of the rebbe. The Hasidic fathers clustered around the glass of the nursery, and I felt at once drawn to them and inadequate to their dark-suited, ringleted assurance. They looked wonderful, and I, another—if lost, or at least mislaid—member of the tribe, wanted, at least provisionally, to attach myself to them.

"He's crying from the circumcision," I explained to the father on my left, significantly.

He stared at me. With the hat and fringe, he looked at first very old and then, as my eye saw past the costume, very young. "He's been circumcised already?" he said. I hadn't known you were supposed to wait. Still, he grasped the gesture toward commonality. "What's his name?"

"Luke," I said proudly. "Luke Auden."

He backed away from me, really backed away, like a Japanese extra in a *Godzilla* movie when the monster comes into view, looming up above the power pylons.

I returned to the letter. It was a very nice, warm letter from the director of the museum, explaining that the "event takes the form of a masked ball in celebration of the Purim holiday, with approximately seven hundred guests gathered for a black-tie dinner-dance at the Waldorf-Astoria." The "highlight" was a "10–15-minute original Purimspiel—a humorous retelling of the story of Purim, Queen Esther's rescue of the Jews in ancient Persia." In a postscript, the director promised "to send some background information on the Biblical story of Purim."

Looking at the letter again, I began to realize that the Purimspieler barrel must have been thoroughly scraped before the museum people got to me, and also that, getting to me, they knew what they were getting. They had been able to deduce that, though Jewish, I was sufficiently ignorant about Jewishness to need "some background information on the Biblical story of Purim." If they had been asking me to talk on life in France, I doubted that they would have thought to send me a map of Paris.

"Daddy, did I tell you the new version?" Luke said suddenly.

"Which new version?"

"Man goes into a restaurant, he says, 'Waiter, waiter.' "

"No," I corrected him. "He should just say, 'Waiter!' It's the guy who goes to see a doctor who says it twice: 'Doctor, Doctor!' Just 'Waiter!' " What a thing, to be a pedant of one-liners.

"Oh. He says, 'Waiter, what's this fly doing in my soup?,' and the waiter, then the waiter says, 'There was no room left in the potato salad.' "

I laughed. "Of course I'm going to do it," I added.

"Is this going to be one of those things where you end up still skeptical but strangely exhilarated by the faith of your fathers?" Martha said. "Because if it is, I don't want you to do it. It's hard enough having you around morose all the time. It would be even worse if you were strangely exhilarated."

The next morning, a Saturday, I took down the Book of Esther from the shelf—or, more precisely, I took down the old King James

Bible, the only one I owned. It has all the words of Jesus picked out in red, as though highlighted by an earnest Galilean undergraduate. I was in charge of the kids, but I felt sure that I would have time to read. Luke was shut in the bedroom, watching Saturday-morning cartoons, struggling desperately to understand; I knew he would interrupt only occasionally, seeking clarification on some cartoon convention. Because of his time in Paris, he missed a lot of cartoon watching, and now he is frantically trying to catch up. He gets a worried look on his face as he runs into the room and asks about what he has just seen: "Why, when people go through walls in a cartoon, do they leave holes exactly the same shape as them?" "Why, when someone touches electricity in a cartoon, do you see his whole skeleton? But only for a second?" The rules of an alternate universe, what there is to laugh at and what is just part of life, remain mysterious.

Meanwhile, the baby, Olivia, was happily occupied at the window, dog-spotting. "Dog! Dog!" came the occasional shout. Breakfast and dinner, she will not stay in her high chair but insists on scanning the skies, or streets, like a scientist in a fifties sci-fi movie, searching for life forms she has identified as alien. She is endlessly excited, then wildly agitated whenever she spots one, which, given the density of dogs on Upper East Side streets, she does, predictably, twice a minute.

"Good girl," I said absently, and went back to my Bible. The story of Purim, I learned, takes place in Persia, mostly in the court of King Ahasuerus. Ahasuerus, who reigned over 127 provinces from India to Ethiopia, has a wife, Vashti, who hosts a "banquet for the women" and then refuses to come when the king commands. The king overreacts, and his advisers tell him to divorce the queen and hold a beauty contest to choose a new one, which he does. He chooses a Jewish girl named Esther. Esther's cousin, an ambitious fellow named Mordecai, then saves the king's life by exposing a plot against him, though the king doesn't know that Mordecai has done it. But the king gets bored with Esther, and meanwhile, his chief councillor, Haman, decides to start a pogrom against the Jews, for all the usual reasons: They are tight and clannish and obey only themselves. He gets the king's approval, and Mordecai, hearing of the plan, goes out in sackcloth and ashes to protest. He tells Esther that she ought to protest, too, and she says, "Well, what can I do?" "Do something," he tells her. She gets dressed up in her best clothes and goes to the king, who, thinking she looks nifty, listens to her. He suddenly learns how Mordecai saved his life, and orders Haman to be hanged on the scaffold he had prepared for Mordecai. The Jews, about to be pogromed, massacre Haman's followers, including all ten of Haman's sons, who are hanged or, depending on the translation, impaled on stakes. Then everybody celebrates.

I stopped reading. Send this up? I couldn't even grasp it. I knew that the thing to get was Esther's rescue of the Jews, but that seemed almost incidental to this general story of competitive massacre and counter-massacre and bride shopping. The trouble, I realized, was not that I did not know how to read in the text but that I did not know, had never been taught, how to read past it. Like Luke with the electrified cat, I did not know what was significant and what was merely conventional—I did not know what were the impaling practices of ancient Near East culture, and what was, so to speak, the specifically Jewish point. Although all our official school training in reading is in reading *in*—in reading deeply, penetrating the superficial and the apparent to get to the obscure and hidden—a lot of the skill in reading classics actually lies in reading *past* them. The obsession with genetic legitimacy and virginity in Shakespeare, the acceptance of torture in Dante—these are not subjects to be absorbed but things you glide by on your way to the poetry. You have to feel confident saying, "Oh, that's just then," with the crucial parallel understanding that now will be then, too, that our progeny will have to learn to read past sentences like "After the peace demonstration, they stopped at Joe's for veal scallopini," or perhaps "In their joy, they conceived their fifth child," or even "They immunized the children." Obviously, it was necessary to read past the impaling of Haman's sons, the ethnic pogroms, to some larger purpose—otherwise, there would not be Purimspiels and happy Purim balls—but I did not know how to do it. I saw impaled Iranians where I needed to see a fly doing the backstroke in the soup.

I walked over to the baby at the window seat. Out the window, in the near distance, we could see a synagogue. Even now, I thought, people were being taught in there to read past the scaffold. "Dog,

dog!" the baby cried, as a dog walker came up the street, six or seven dogs on leashes held in one hand. Olivia began to cry out in delight. So many dogs! I closed the book and hoped glumly that a spiel, that whole leashfuls of them, would come before Purim did.

The next day I decided to return to the only Jewish tradition with which I was at all confident: having smoked fish at eleven o'clock on Sunday mornings. Every Sunday morning throughout my childhood, my grandfather would arrive with the spread—salty lox and unctuous sable and dry whitefish and sweet pickled salmon. Sometimes he took me with him to shop; he always had a pained, resigned look as he ordered: "Yeah, I guess . . . give me some of the whitefish." But when he got home, he would be pleased. ("He has very nice stuff, Irving," he would say to my father.) For Purimspiel purposes, I thought, I had better get into Jew training and eat as my fathers had.

Every Sunday morning for the next few weeks, Luke and I went together to Sable's, the extraordinary smoked-fish and appetizer store at Second Avenue and Seventy-eighth Street. Sable's is the only place in my neighborhood where my grandfather would have been entirely comfortable—with the hand-lettered signs and the Dr. Brown's and the mingled smell of pickles and herring—and yet it is owned and staffed by Asians who once worked as nova slicers at Zabar's, on the West Side, and who walked out to claim their freedom. (I imagined them wandering, in their aprons, through Central Park for years before arriving at the promised land.) They sell Jewish food, and with the same bullying, ironic Jewish manner that I recalled from my childhood trips with my grandfather, but they do it as a thing learned.

"They got nice stuff, anyway, Irving," I said to Luke as we walked over.

"Why are you calling me Irving?" he asked.

"My grandfather always called me Irving when he took me shopping for smoked fish. He had me confused with Grandpop, I guess."

"Oh. Is Grandpop's name Irving?"

"No," I said. "His name isn't actually Irving, either. But your great-grandfather could never remember what his name really was, so he called him Irving. I think he thought all small Jewish boys should be called Irving."

Luke wasn't interested. "Oh," he said. I could see he was looking inward. Then, in a rush: "Why in cartoons, when someone touches electricity, after you see their whole skeleton for a second, do they go all stiff and straight up in the air and then their whole body turns black and then it turns into dust and then it crumbles while they still look out and smile as if they were feeling sick? Why?"

I said it was just a convention, just the way cartoons are, and was meant to be funny.

"Why is it funny?" he asked.

We walked on in silence.

Later that day I sat down with a piece of paper. I had one mildly derivative comic idea, which was to adapt the Purim story to contemporary New York. Ahasuerus was Donald Trump: dumb as an ox, rich, lecherous, easily put out, and living in a gaudy apartment. So Vashti must be Ivana—that was easy—and Esther was a Russian Jewish model who had immigrated from Odessa, a beauty, but hardly aware that she was Jewish save for the convenience of immigration. Haman—what if you said that Haman . . . But I couldn't focus. How was it, I wondered, that I could know nothing of all this? For the truth is that "Jew" *is* written all over me. If, on my father's side, they were in wholesale food, on my mother's side, they were dark-skinned Sephardim who had stayed in Palestine—so busy squabbling that they actually missed the bus for the Diaspora. One of my maternal great-grandfathers, family lore has it, was the rabbi sent from Hebron to Lisbon at the end of the nineteenth century to call the Jews out of hiding and back into the synagogue.

And yet, when I think about my own upbringing, the best I can say is that the most entirely Jewish thing about us was the intensity with which we celebrated Christmas: passionately, excessively, with the tallest tree and the most elaborately wrapped presents. Coming of age in the fifties, my parents, like so many young intellectuals of their generation, distanced themselves from the past as an act of deliberate emancipation. My parents were not so much in rebellion against their own past as they were in love with the idea of using the values unconsciously taken from that culture to conquer another—they went from Jewish high school to Ivy League college and fell in love with English literature. Like so many others, they ended in that queer, thriving country of the Jewish-American possessor of the Christian literary heritage: They became Zionists of eighteenth-century literature, kibbutzniks of metaphysical poetry. The only Bible-related book I can recall from my childhood was in my father's office, an academic volume called *The Bible to Be Read as Living Literature;* the joke was, of course, that in those precincts it was literature that was to be read as the Bible. (We didn't have a Christian Christmas; we had a Dickensian Christmas.) The eradication left an imprint stronger than indoctrination could have. We had "Jew" written all over us in the form of marks from the eraser.

What was left of overt, nameable Jewishness was the most elemental Jewish thing, and that was a style of joking. My grandfather, who ran a small grocery store in a black neighborhood, lives in my memory, apart from Sunday-morning fish, mostly in his jokes, a round of one-liners as predictable as the hands on a clock, and yet, weirdly, getting funnier by the year: "Joe Banana and his bunch? The music with appeal." And "I used to be a boxer. In a shoe store." And "I used to sing tenor, but they traded me in for two fives." And "Feel stiff in the joints? Then stay out of the joints."

The first time I had a sense of Jewishness as a desirable state rather than as background radiation, humming in a Christian cosmos, was when I was thirteen and, turned on to the idea of New York, saw that it was made up of Jewish comedians; of jokes. I discovered the Marx Brothers and then Woody Allen. I bought a book of old comics' routines and learned the telephone spiels of Georgie Jessel. ("Mom, why did you cook that bird? He was a valuable bird; he could speak six languages!" "Oh . . . he shoulda said something.") *The Ed Sullivan Show* fascinated me: Corbett Monica and Norm Crosby and Jackie Vernon, and, hovering above even them, Myron Cohen, the mournful storyteller, and Henny Youngman, genuinely the funniest man, who looked exactly like my grandfather, to boot. The greatest generation. I read interviews with obscure Jewish comedians, old and young—really obscure ones, Ed Bluestone and Ben Blue—and noticed with a rising thrill that none of them talked about "jokes" that you "told." Instead, they talked about "bits" that they "did"—and killed "them" doing them. That, for me, explained everything, life and art: Life was stuff that happened, art was bits you did. It was the first religion that had ever made sense to me.

I came to New York to practice that faith, do bits, be a Purim-spieler, only to find that world was gone. Sometime in the decade after my arrival, the Jewish comic culture dried up. The sense, so strong since the beginning of the century, that New York was naturally Jewish and, by an unforced corollary, naturally funny had gone. Of course, there were stand-up comics, many of them Jewish, but the particular uneasiness, the sense that talking too fast might keep you alive, the sense that you talked as a drowning man might wave his hands, the whining, high-pitched tone and the "R"-less accent: All that had gone. Paul Reiser, Jerry Seinfeld, much as I enjoyed and even identified with them, were as settled and as American as Bob and Ray or Will Rogers. This was an event with a specific date, marked in the work of the last great New York Jew comedian. Between 1977 and *Annie Hall*, in which being a Jewish comedian is a slightly weary and depressing obligation to be rebelled against, and *Broadway Danny Rose*, just seven years later, when the black-and-white world of the comics shpritzing at the Carnegie Deli is frankly presented as a Chagall world, a folk-tale setting, the whole thing vanished. Even Jackie Mason, a rabbi in training and ostensibly a master of the style, was quite different; in the eighties, when he returned from obscurity, his subject wasn't the unsuspected power of being a loser but the loss of power in the face of all those new immigrants.

New York Jewish comic manners were still around, only they were no longer practiced by Jews, or were practiced by Jews as something learned rather than as something felt. What had replaced the organic culture of Jewish comedy in New York was a permanent pantomime of Jewish manners. The fly doing the backstroke in the soup was part of a kind of chicken-soup synchronized-swimming event, as ordered and regulated as an Olympic sport: Jewish New York manners were a thing anyone could imitate in order to indicate "comedy."

One sensed this at Sable's, where Jewish traditions of shpritzing were carried on by non-Jews, and in television commercials, where New York taxi drivers were still represented as wise guys, even though they had not been for a generation or more. But it was true in subtler ways, too. On *Seinfeld,* which I had missed while living abroad but now could watch in reruns every night, everything is, at one level, shockingly Jewish, far more than Sid Caesar or Mel Brooks was ever allowed to be, with mohels and brisses and whining fathers who wait all week for their copy of *TV Guide*—but the unstated condition is that there be absolutely no mention of the "J" word, while the most Jewish character, George, is given an Italian last name, Costanza. This is not because Jewishness is forbidden but because it is so obvious. Jewishness is to *Seinfeld* what the violin was to Henny Youngman: the prop that you used between jokes, as much for continuity as for comedy. The Jewish situations are mimed by rote, while the real energy of the jokes lies in the observation of secular middle-class manners. In the old Jewish comedies, it had been just the opposite: The manners of the middle class were mimed by rote—the suits and ties, the altered names, Jack Benny's wife called Mary—while the energy of the jokes lay in the hidden Jewishness. (The comedy of Phil Silvers's great Sergeant Bilko almost scandalously derives from the one thing that no one on the show is allowed to mention, which is that Bilko is a clever New York Jew dominating a kind of all-star collection of dim Gentiles.) New York Jewishness was now the conscious setup rather than the hidden punch line.

One Sunday morning, Luke and I walked over to Sable's and bought even more than usual; we were having company. But the Cambodian cashier and the Chinese slicer were unimpressed. The cashier looked over our order.

"How many people you having?" he asked.

"Eight."

"From out of town?"

"Yes."

He sighed. "Me, I would be ashamed to put this on the table."

"You would?"

He looked at the ritualized bits of cured sable and salmon and shrugged again—my grandfather to the life!

"This is not worth putting on the table. I would be ashamed."

"What do you think I should do?"

"Get a pound of herring salad. Pound of whitefish salad. Pound of bluefish salad."

I did. "Now I proud to put this on the table," he said. "Now I no longer ashamed for you."

He had learned to do it at Zabar's, I realized as I left—the permanent pantomime of Jewish manners with wings on! Though it cost me nearly a hundred dollars, it was worth it for the lesson. The combination of an Asian sense of face with a Jewish sense of guilt may be the most powerful commercial hybrid in history.

So, see, I have an Esther in my family, too. The matriarch of my family. She dominated her sisters, in a grasping way, and then came to die of emphysema in my grandparents' apartment in Florida. We went to see her in—this is in about 1993, I guess. Wheezing and pained, she said, 'People tell me you are doing well, but I lie here in bed at night and worry, oh, I worry about you. How I worry. So now tell me, tell me, so your aunt won't lie here as she is dying and worry . . . tell me . . . how much are you really making?' "

"You can't possibly tell that story," Martha said. "It's anti-Semitic."

"It's true," I said.

"Of course it's true," Martha said. "It's just not appropriate."

I was trying out possible spiels on the more Jewish of our many Jewish friends. We have a certain number of friends who, though coming from backgrounds not unlike my own, have recommitted themselves to Jewishness in a serious way. While Yiddishkeit as a practice had nearly disappeared from New York, one of the things replacing it, paradoxically, was Judaism. A number of our friends are what I have come to think of as X-treme Jews, who study Kabbalah or glory in the details of the lives of Jewish gangsters and even like to call themselves "Hebes," in the manner of young black men calling each other "niggas."

I envied my friends the seeming clarity of their Jewishness, just as I envied, a little, the clarity of the family of observant Jews who live down the hall from us. On warm Friday evenings, one or two of the adolescent boys in that family will come knocking at our door, galumphing in heavy shoes and with pale faces, and, looking woeful, say, "Could you come and turn on the air conditioner in our apartment? We can't, 'cause we're Jews." I admired the simplicity of their self-definition: "We can't, 'cause we're Jews." We are unashamed of our essence, even as it makes us sweat.

But whatever the appeal of that plain faith, I can't say I was inclined to follow them. It seemed to me that my contemporaries, in contrast to the boys down the hall, had chosen Jewish—they were *majoring* in Jewish, just as my father had majored in English—when the force of the tradition was that it was not elective. And since the choice of what to consider properly Jewish was always interpretive—nobody except the very simple or very faithful actually believed or followed it all, seven days of creation and the rules of animal sacrifice in the temple—there were only competing styles of Alexandrianism, of Jewishness rather than rote Judaism, some recognizing themselves as such.

I decided to sit down and read what I imagined was the Bible on the subject of New York Jewishness, Alfred Kazin's memoir *New York Jew*, a book that, over the years, I had neither read in nor read past but simply not read, thinking, unforgivably, that I already knew its contents. (The forties, boy! The fifties, joy! The sixties, oy!) In fact, it's an unpredictable, rhapsodic, uncontentious book—but for all the starkness of its title, its premise is that Jewishness is the board from which one springs, rather than the ground one must dig. To be a New York Jew is, for Kazin, like being a New York tree. It is what you are.

Reading Kazin, I became a little impatient with my own apologetic attitude toward the poverty of my Jewishness. Wasn't it the invigorating inheritance of the self-emancipation of my parents? My father had done the deracinating, to become a devotee of Pope and Swift, Molière and Shakespeare, and to reracinate was to be disloyal to him, to the act of emancipation from tribal reflexes that, with a considerable effort of will and imagination, he had pulled off. What is bracing about Kazin is not his Jewishness but that he makes no effort to pretend he is something else. His liberation lay in not pretending to be Van Wyck Brooks; the liberation for us surely lies in not pretending to be Alfred Kazin.

In the midst of these bitter-herb thoughts, Luke came in.

"Here's the new version," he said. "Man says to a waiter, 'What's this fly doing in my soup?' 'Shhh,' the waiter says, 'everyone will want one.' " It broke me up. Whether or not there are Jewish essences, there are surely some essentially Jewish jokes. That was one, and I was in the middle of another.

I was about to call the Jewish Museum and give it all up when a friend suggested, "Go see Rabbi Schorsch. He's the chancellor of the Jewish Theological Seminary. He's a terrific guy, and I'm sure he'd be glad to help you out with the spiel thing." I vaguely remembered hearing Rabbi Ismar Schorsch on the radio once or twice, so I made an appointment—it felt like making a date with a dentist—and on the day I took the subway up to 125th Street.

The rabbi's secretary showed me into his office, and after a couple of minutes, there was Rabbi Schorsch.

"Rabbi," I began, "I was not raised as an observant Jew, but I am nonetheless of a Jewish background, and I am naturally concerned to show some grasp of a tradition that, though familiar in spirit, is still alien to me in many ways." I don't know; that's how I thought you ought to talk to a rabbi. Anyway, I eventually explained that I couldn't make head or tail of the Book of Esther.

"It's a spoof, a burlesque, really," he almost mumbled. He picked up my Bible, riffled through it as though there were a kind of satisfaction just in touching the pages, and then frowned. "This is a Christian Bible," he said, genuinely puzzled.

He was the kind of hyper-alert elderly man who, instead of putting on weight around the middle, seemed to have drawn all his energy upward into his eyes and ears, which gleamed, outsized. "Yes. It's a kind of comic chapter, not to be taken entirely seriously," he went on, holding my King James Version in his hand as though it might be loaded. "It's a light book with a serious message. You see, Scripture, the Bible, one of the remarkable things about it is that it contains a chapter about every form of human experience. There's a book of laws and a book of love songs. A book of exile and a book of homecoming. A skeptical and despairing book in Job, and an optimistic and sheltering book in the Psalms. Esther is the comic book, a book for court Jews, with a fairy-tale, burlesque spirit."

You could see my whole skeleton underneath my jacket; my hair stood on end; I turned into a pile of black ash, smiling sickly as I slowly crumbled.

"It is?" I said.

"Yes. You see, Mordecai is a classic Jew of the Diaspora, not just exiled but entirely assimilated—a court Jew, really. It's a book for court Jews. Why doesn't he bow down to Haman? Well, it might be because of his Judaism. But I think we have to assume that he's jealous—he expects to be made first minister and then isn't. Have you noticed the most interesting thing about the book?" He looked at me keenly.

"I hadn't even noticed it was funny."

"It's the only book in the Bible where God is never mentioned," he said. "This is the book for the Jews of the city, the world. After all, we wonder—what does Esther eat? It sure isn't kosher. But she does good anyway. The worldliness and the absurdity are tied together—the writer obviously knows that the king is a bit of an idiot—but the point is that good can rise from it in any case. Esther acts righteously and saves her people, and we need not worry, too much, about what kind of Jew she was before or even after. She stays married to the Gentile king, remember. This is the godless, comic book of Jews in the city and how they struggle to do the righteous thing."

I was stunned. This was, as they say, the story of my life. A funny book about court Jews . . . I had been assigned to burlesque it when the text was preburlesqued, as jeans might be preshrunk.

We talked for a while longer, about the background of Haman as a Jew hater, and of how the most startlingly contemporary thing in the book was the form of anti-Semitism; even twenty-five hundred years ago in Persia, the complaint against the Jews was the same as it is now. In the end, the rabbi gave me a signed copy of the Bible, the Jewish Bible, the Tanach. (Signed by him, I mean.)

We got together a couple of times after that, and eventually I decided to try and go ahead with the Purimspiel. He said, "Why not? What have you got to lose?"

What have you got to lose? It was, I reflected, like the punch line of a Jewish joke.

In the ballroom of the Waldorf-Astoria, hundreds of people in dinner jackets and sequined dresses were wearing masks, although this made them look less festive than vaguely embarrassed, as though they were worried about being seen by their friends. I had forgotten the look and feel of a New York benefit: the ballroom made to look like a gym; the chicken stretched out, mortified, on its plate, with the Indisputably Classy Ingredient—the quince, or sun-dried tomato, or preserved lemon—laid on top of it; the fiftyish women, sexy and intimidating in sports clothes, wilting in their fancy gowns. The only difference was that at this benefit, there was a giant video-projection screen at either end of the hall and one above the podium, and the speakers—who included Rabbi Schorsch, saying the blessing—were projected on them. I gulped. I had thought it would be like a nightclub, where I could play with a microphone in the manner of Rodney Dangerfield. This was more like a political convention. I was an impostor, even though I had bits to do. I heard my grandfather's voice: *Feel stiff in the joints? Then stay out of the joints!*

At last, just before dessert, I got up and went to the podium. Out of the corner of my eye, I could see my own image on the giant screen.

What did I tell them? Well, I did the "New York as Persia, Donald, and Ivana" bit, and then I did a bit I'd made up that afternoon on Haman. That got a modest laugh, and, encouraged, I went on to do the "man goes to see a rabbi" bit. I said that, once I'd thought of transposing the story to New York, I had gotten stuck on Mordecai. Who could Mordecai be in the modern city? I had gone to see a rabbi, and the rabbi had told me that the Book of Esther was in part a spoof, a burlesque: a comedy in which worldly people took risks and did unworldly things, and that Mordecai, if he was anyone, was us—the assimilated court and city Jews. And this was sort of amazing to me, since the idea that the man of the world might be the honest man was an idea that was central to the comic tradition I revered—Molière says it, for instance, just like that—but was not one that I had known had a place in the Jewish tradition. The Jewish tradition, I had always thought, proposed that the honest man was the man out of the world, the prophet crying in the wilderness. But I saw now that there was a connection between a certain kind of comedy, the comedy of assimilation, and a certain kind of courage, the courage to use your proximity to power, bought at the price of losing your "identity," to save your kinsmen. The real moral center of the story, I saw now, lay in the tiny, heartbreaking, and in many ways comic moment when Esther—trayf-eating, dim-witted, overdressed, sexy Esther—appears before the king, who hasn't found her particularly sexy lately. I could see her in her Lacroix pouf dress, gulping for breath and showing up, so to speak, at Donald Trump's office in the middle of a busy day, saying that she had to speak to him. But she did, and the Jews were saved, for once.

It went over okay. I didn't kill them, but I didn't die, either. They were expecting something more consistently amusing, I suppose, but no one minds a little moral sententiousness in an after-dinner speaker. "Congratulations, that was unusual" or "You obviously spoke from the heart" or "I knew that when we asked you to do the Purimspiel, we would get something different!" or just "Thank you for your interesting remarks" was the general tone when I got back to the table. (I still meet people who were there. They give me exactly the look a father might have after seeing his daughter topless in a progressive-college production of *A Midsummer Night's Dream;* he respects the sincerity of the intention, but it was extremely embarrassing to be there nonetheless.) I had fund-raising-benefit dessert—something soft and white interspersed with something red and juicy—and went home. As a thank-you present, I was given a little silver grogger, a rattle, meant to be shaken when you heard the name "Haman."

Though I am not strangely exhilarated by my experience as a

Purimspieler, I did find something significant in the Book of Esther, and I am certainly glad I did it. In one way, it was no different from any other exposure to an ancient, irrational belief-culture. I suppose I would have felt about the same if I had been a young Athenian who finally went to Delphi and heard the oracle: Even if it didn't change the future, it was nice to make the trip. But if there is something particularly Jewish about the experience, it may lie in the odd combination of a narrow gate and a large gathering; the most exclusive and tribal of faiths, Judaism is also the one that sustains the most encompassing of practices, from Moses to Henny Youngman, from Esther to Sammy Davis, Jr., and all of us Irvings. Whether it sustains this because, as the rabbi believes, it is in its nature narrow but infinitely various, or because, as I sometimes suspect, anything ancient and oppressed must be adaptable, still it is so. At least for a certain kind of court Jew, being Jewish remains not an exercise in reading in or reading past but just in reading on, in continuing to turn the pages. The pages have been weird and varied enough in the past to be weird and varied in the future, and there is no telling who will shine in them. The Jewish occasion lay in rising to the occasion. Even if it was too late to be an everyday, starting Jew, one could still be, so to speak, Jewish in the clutch.

We celebrated our own Seder this past spring and are thinking of joining the synagogue we can see from our window, in part because we want to, in part because there is an excellent nursery school there for our daughter. That is the kind of things Jews do in Persia. I gave the silver grogger to the baby, who holds it at the window and shakes it in warning when she sees a dog. I believe that she now has the first things a Jewish girl in exile needs: a window to see from and a rattle to shake.

First Thanksgiving: Densities

New York still looks best in fall. ("April in Paris" is a fiction, but "Autumn in New York," by the same songwriter, is a glorious fact.) Thanksgiving—not just the holiday, I mean, but the sweep of days it superintends, the long autumn that begins in October and runs, festively, through the Jewish holidays, to Halloween and beyond, with Christmas peeking around the corner—has always been the best time of year in New York. Abroad, I often thought about the lines at Ottomanelli's in the Village the day before Thanksgiving, where everybody who ordered a turkey has his name misspelled in black marker on brown paper—and I thought about the absence of evident warmth combined with the come-one-come-all brown-paper democracy of the scene, the weary procedural dutifulness of the butchers—and I then felt a rush of something like patriotism. These months are nearly perfect in New York, the slow roll up to the great secular feast of shopping and feeling at Christmas. After that comes dread, the winter with shoes in the trees and unbiodegradable plastic bags blowing at your feet, the Lenny-Bruce-in-Times-Square sordidness of the place.

To inventory the holidays, Jewish and Christian and creedless, each with its little burst of merchandise and ritual, is to expose the intermingling of the sacred and the secular. But that is our city, and it fits somehow. In London, where they invented the idea of Christmas as middle-class mass ritual, there is still some sense that the festival overflows from the spiritual side; Dickens makes his dutiful, sober asides to the religious holiday before he gets on with the games. In Paris, the old Catholic hardness one hears in French baroque Christmas music, the premonition of tragedy that is so much a part of Christmas for the believer, still reigns. But in New York, heroic materialism is all the heroism we've got, and it goes on: Thanksgiving, secular and greedy, balloons pumped up with helium, leading to the coronation of the department-store Santa Claus.

The first few weeks back from France are precious, because naive vision is a capital sum, quickly depleted, and for a few months, New York—the Great Home, Our Place—can be seen again. On our first morning back, woken early by the jet lag, I took Luke for a long dawn walk down Fifth Avenue, past the University Club and St. Patrick's Cathedral and Saks. *This is all from another place,* I thought, shocked by the derivativeness of Fifth Avenue architecture. I felt, I *saw,* for the first time ever, the adolescent absurdity of so many Manhattan monuments—the sad, wilderness, opera-house-in-the-Arctic and Amazon pathos of copying old European styles in a New World city. *This isn't a true Gothic cathedral,* I thought, staring at St. Patrick's. *There are such things, I've seen them, and this is just a . . . copy, a raw inflated thing thrown up in emulation of a far-off and distant thing! That Renaissance palazzo on Fifty-fourth Street is no Renaissance palazzo—it's a cheap stage-set imitation!*

This perception—of New York as a blown-up Inflato city, aspirational rather than achieved, gawkily imitating its models, the proper cities of Europe—which was once so obvious and embarrassing (to Henry James, much less to Tocqueville), has faded away now, and I no longer see it that way. For that single early morning, though, it seemed that the architecture of New York was not quite real, not organic, coming from elsewhere and imposed, a delirium of old styles and other people's European visions: the Gothic vision of sublime verticality, or, for that matter, the Bauhaus vision of the glass tower. For a moment New York seemed unnatural, the anti-matter city. "You're not real!" I wanted to cry out, to the city. *"Yes, we are,"* the buildings cried back blankly. *"It is the old thing that is the lie; the true thing is our re-creation of it."* But the moment passed quickly, and now New York just looks like New York: old as time, worn as Rome, mysterious as life.

. . .

The children are flying above our heads, the neighbors are sighing below our feet, and between them we are trying to return to a life we thought we knew already. A full life is what we said we wanted when we left Paris, and full it is, in moments already too full. We fill our eyes and heads with things already seen and known, and try to see them and know them again.

The city looks wonderful no matter how you squint at it, there's no denying that: the park restored, the shops freed from their goalie masks of protective cages, even Times Square, through which I had to trudge by night twenty years ago to extract Martha from seedy out-of-the-way film-cutting rooms. Where we once threaded our way among Dumpsters in which bodies turned up is now gleaming, but the cutting rooms have become condos, and the film editors have fled to some other place, as yet unknown.

The children are even happier to be here than I'd hoped. On that first morning, once the stores were open (the coffee shops, I had forgotten, never close), I bought Luke the one thing he wanted: a Razor-brand scooter, the kind that was invented while we were away and that now fills the streets here. (They have not yet made it to Paris.) They are one of those simple, amazing things that make you wonder enviously why no one—why not you!—had thought of it before: three pieces of hinged aluminum, a pair of plastic wheels, and you're whooshing off down the avenue to the delight of other children and to the doom of the calves of a thousand old ladies on Madison.

As he rushes down the streets, Luke's ears are still attuned to the new sounds of the city. I see him stop his scooter and leap from it in ecstasy: "Those girls are speaking English," he informs me. "I think I'll talk to them." This delivery to his long-dreamed-of paradise, the English-speaking city, is still beyond his comprehension. The density of space produces, famously, a wild variety of people. Luke, hostage to Parisian food, cannot believe the range of cheap takeout, the empire of menus. You press a button, and all the world's spices come obsequiously to your door: Indian food, Chinese food; the baby loves chicken in pancakes, the boy loves steak fajitas, and without saying so, I see that he likes the sweetness of New York food, the way that, as I had forgotten, Americans put sugar in everything, in ketchup and mustard and cereal and bread. The incidental sweetness of American life is, to an unaccustomed palate like his, overwhelming and quickly addictive.

We took him to Luke's Bar and Grill, a hamburger joint on Third Avenue, because we thought he would like the idea of a place with a name the same as his own.

"Hey," I said as he searched the menu and then the room. "Do you see why I brought you here?" I point to the menu: his place. "Yes," he said solemnly. "Because you wanted me to know a place where, if I got lost, I could go where everybody speaks English."

T*hey all speak English here*. It is one of the things that makes life so full and then so dense. Every exit from the house threatens to become an encounter, and every encounter threatens to become an entanglement. The joy of isolation is hard to find. Coming home has been strange and hard for Luke's parents, even though, or perhaps because, it is home. The taxi wars and rituals, for instance, are so odd. In France, we became accustomed to the rigorous conventions of taxi hailing. You walk to a corner, you see the blue sign, TAXI, and you wait in line, uncomplaining, however long it takes. (You can send for a taxi by telephone, and if there's one available, you will get one. But if there isn't one, the phone line goes dead. You don't even get to whine about it, much less talk to the supervisor.) If, on your own, you find a taxi on the boulevard, you may hail it; but the driver may choose not to stop, and he may not be allowed to stop at all if he is anywhere near a taxi station.

Here at home, I am shocked, amazed, searching for a taxi to get us to a dinner or to take the children to the doctor, to rediscover what I once knew: It's every man or woman for himself or herself, and no rules at all. A man—or, more often, a woman—steps right in front of you half a block away, back turned but entirely conscious of your presence (the New Yorker knows that sly half-look around), hand raised in taxi-hailing salute.

And there is nothing to be done: no reproach, no appeal to fairness, no pointing to the implicit social contract the philosophers love to write about, whereby we, in the ideal city, would grant one another a full city block of taxi-hailing rights, or at the very least adhere to some grandfather clause: We cannot cut in front of another human being who is late for the pediatrician and had his hand raised already.

The rule is not even conflict aversion. Perpetually hotheaded in life if not on the page, I often grumble and mutter impotently, "That's piggish behavior," or the like. The Other just stares or even smirks. The rule is combat avoidance. We won't actually come to blows over this taxi, but apart from that, anything goes. Absolute anarchy is a rule regulated not by the state but by a kind of wary understanding that fistfights have costs in the long term and should be avoided. Financial prudence about the outcome of lawsuits sometimes seems to be the only moral arbiter left in New York.

Yet not entirely so. The impressive thing, on reflection, is that even nonviolent confrontation is almost always evaded, and not by following rules but by following social instincts. When you do see conflict—one taxi driver yelling at another, a cop yelling at a trucker—it is rare enough to, well, stop traffic. What an unbelievable concord of invisible trust is required to live in the city at all! This is true of every city, but in New York, it somehow has the force of a daily miracle. Even more amazing than the taxi truce is the car compact, the social contract grumbling at you from every car engine stopped at this light for this moment but still ready to launch. *Thousands* of tons of metal crash down the avenues, while thousands of pedestrians play a wary game of chicken with them, and all that holds one back from destroying the other is a kind of minimal trust between the reckless walker and the reckless driver. There are no zebra crossings, as in London, and not many scowling traffic policemen, as in Paris; there is simply an understanding, like the understandings among neighbors, that though we may hate and resent one another, we will not kill one another, at least no more often than we have to. Untune that string, and New York would become what by all rights it ought to be, what it was: hell, a place of absolute anarchy, the Hobbesian universe.

But who tuned the string? Cities are self-organizing, but they also once seemed self-devouring. Even at its most Hobbesian, New York was never entirely so (more Wellsian, actually, with the Eloi on one side and the Morlocks down below). Even then the cascading, flowing trust that enabled the city to go on was there. Coming home, though, I am overwhelmed not just by the fact that the city doesn't explode into murderous conflict more often than it does, but by the sedation, the domestication, of the place. A city of cars and strollers; even the subway is cleaner now, shocking as that may be. A strenuously considerate male voice regularly announces, "Stand clear of the closing doors!"—a voice of benevolent oversight, like the celebrity voices urging you to buckle up in the backseats of the taxis. Pedestrians cross the street even earlier than I recalled, treating Second Avenue as a country lane: One peek, nothing oncoming, and you walk. And yet all the cars wait for the light to change, even when the pedestrians, crazily, don't.

And I can see how everything is reversed, like coming back through a mirror, and not being able to adjust to seeing things the right way round. At the gym we went to inspect, there are actually screen monitors on every stationary bicycle, where you can read your e-mail as you pedal, and check your stock market quotations as you pant. I took the children on the carousel in Central Park. It whirls and heaves at a truly frightening speed. It makes music at its center, old-fashioned wheezing fairground organ music, from the turn of the last century. The children hang on for dear life, where in Paris they turned in stately time to the cranking of the ancient motor and chain, with silence all around.

Martha still has dreams of another place. She tells me she has the New York dream, as common among New Yorkers as the student-anxiety nightmare in which you are facing the final exam for a class that you registered for but then forgot all about (I still have that one). In the New York dream, you discover that your apartment has one more room than you remembered, one more room than you realized when you moved in. You open a closet door, and there it is—another room! She has it every other night.

She dreams of escape, too, of flying away. As she always has, when we have a long way to go downtown at night, Martha will ask cabdrivers to take the "East Side Highway"—and no matter how often, or how obnoxiously, I tell her that there is no East Side Highway, that it is called the FDR Drive, or just the Drive or the FDR, she persists. The East Side Highway is a sacred place for her somehow, the Yellow Brick Road of her mind and heart, never really settled in New York, still dreaming of Canada or Paris and a road to take you there.

She also always gives the cabbies intense, complicated local information: "We're going to ABC Carpet? At Nineteenth Street? But not the old building on the east side of Broadway; the other one, across the way." Or she tells them to take her to Bergdorf's, "men's-store side." The drivers give her patient, wary, opaque looks. Her mental map of New York is still so minutely drawn, so realized in intricate curlicues of familiar places and imaginary retreats, that even after years away, it is hard for her, as for all of us, to realize that her map is only hers, hers uniquely, and that the little sign that says YOU ARE HERE! points only to the place that she is standing, all alone.

Combat is avoided, but conflict cannot always be, it seems, not if the irritant is sufficiently small. We are already at war with our downstairs neighbors because, they say, we are too loud. They complain that the children's footsteps drum into their consciousness, giving them broken days and sleepless nights (though how could they? The kids are asleep by eight or nine, sometimes ten). The neighbors send us letters, they knock on our door, they call the doorman, and they complain.

We write back; they write again. A correspondence, almost eighteenth-century in its variety and viciousness, ensues. The solution—carpeting and tolerance—is obvious, just as the solution to the Middle East problem is two states. It's getting there that's hard, requiring a road map and a leap of faith. To concede anything would be to concede everything; it would make the other side's story the true story. We shop for carpet, sufficiently thick to absorb all sound, sufficiently lovely to avoid any obvious sign of concession. I write long, ornate, indignant, elaborately Madisonian letters, full of "notwithstandings" and "urge you to remind your clients."

I feel the need for the intercession of some other, more mordantly combative sensibility—S. J. Perelman, say. ("Laughing gaily at the implication that our offspring—a light-footed lad of some twenty stone and a bright-eyed sylph of a girl, banished from ballet class not, as rumored, as a danger to the other performers but out of the sheer spite of her teacher, Madame Offenskoff—could be causing them to lose sleep, I dashed off a quick feuilleton of indignation, a screed to rival for length *The Federalist Papers* and for satirical verve the collected works of H. L. Mencken, and that would have caused them to abandon their petty plaints like the French government abandoning Paris in 1940—had I not, as my doxy pointed out, chosen in my haste to write it with the secret-spy pen from the young lad's Intelligence play set, leaving it readable only to those specially equipped with a plastic decoder ring and Bunsen burner . . .") High-spirited comic indignation, the old sensibility.

"Tell them to move to the suburbs," a friend at the office says flatly, shrugging it off. My indignation, which is real and absolute—children have a right to be children, especially good ones like ours—wars with my liberal guilt, or at least with my liberal urge to see everything from two sides: Just how loud *are* the children's footsteps? (The liberal always asks if he might be wrong, on his way to asserting that he knows he's right. This is better than being a radical, who asserts his righteousness without asking if he might be wrong, but the cash value is about the same.) When we left New York, it was the rats in our loft, as much as anything, that helped drive us away. Now *we* are the rats, and I see things from the rats' perspective: We are here and will remain what we are. It is our nature.

Shaken by the conflict, we raise it with the other neighbors, with other friends. Everyone has a noise dispute story. People sue each other; they measure the neighbors' racket in decibels with noise meters. The cartoon image of the city deep inside everyone's mind is that of the man with the broom banging on his ceiling, which is his neighbor's floor—and this turns out to have actually happened to our friends the W's. Their boy ran across the floor, and a neighbor, right on West End Avenue, started banging their floor, his ceiling, with a broom. We were stunned to hear it, the cartoon made real, as though, after having paid his taxes, someone was actually obliged to walk down Third Avenue in a barrel.

Noise is *the* New York issue, yet why should it be so? Surely all cities are equally noisy, but I have never heard anyone in Paris complain about the noise, and in San Francisco, my sister's family seems to thrive unnettled by other people's noises. Yet Paris is as loud as it gets: the streets with traffic, the families with dogs; and in San Francisco, they play the stereo all night long. Noise in New York is, must be, a symbol, a referred pain, for something else. It is an issue on which no compromises seem possible. The anger comes from elsewhere, even if (as they claim, and as we refute at length) the noise comes from upstairs.

As our neighbors complain about the children's footfalls, I think of saying to them, "We will teach them to fly!" Because we will. The kindergarten production in Luke's class is to be *Peter Pan*—the full musical, complete with the wonderful Moose Charlap music. They do it every few years, apparently, with incredible aplomb, under the direction of the saintly, energetic, all-seeing teacher.

The entry-level musical is a tradition at Artists & Anglers, as I'll call it, the school where we have enrolled Luke. In a move that is no surprise to his mother, though extremely puzzling to the other mothers, Luke has been cast as Peter. But the other children have all been given good parts; there are, as we point out tumidly, no really *bad* parts in *Peter Pan*—a five-year-old Hook and a six-year-old Smee and several Wendys, to share the uplift and the nightgown. But soon our more or less common parental pleasure turns to anxiety. For how will they fly?

"This year the children have to fly," said one of the businessman fathers, and he meant business. In previous productions of *Peter Pan,* we were told, the children had flown mostly by assertion, as in Elizabethan theater: They said they were flying, so they were (as people in Shakespeare travel to Bohemia: "Here we are in Bohemia," they say, and there they are). Their parents clapped, but they clapped alone, within an otherwise silent gym. So this year we are determined to make the children fly: to lift them physically off the ground, however briefly, out the nursery window, to hover for a moment above London.

Some of this urge, this insistence, is, I think, due to the general buoyancy of the age—everything else is flying, stocks, real estate prices, why not the children?—and some (given the cast of characters, a lot) is due to the competitive nature of New York parenting: We'll show all the earlier, earthbound parents.

But some of it, too, comes from a genuine desire to please the children. They had seen dinosaurs walk and roar and toys talk, by *someone's* so potent art. Why couldn't they fly? We formed an ad hoc flight committee. When Martha told me about it, I imagined it as one of those political lobbying groups with a misleadingly wholesome name, the Committee to Make Our Children Fly. At Artists & Anglers, the parents fall into two groups, those who make symbols and those who price them. There are writers and dancers and media people, one painter and half a sculptor (he sculpts part-time these days), and then there are people—the copyright lawyers, book publishers, agents, and computer software programmers—who traffic in the little bits of equity that can be wrung from all that raging creation. Each class seems beautifully devised—a core of creative people's children, a sample of richer children, a frosting of minorities.

When we were brooding about what to do with our lives, we decided to come back to New York in large part because of Artists & Anglers. Although Luke's school in Paris had been just fine, there were everywhere suggestions of the sterner French schools yet to come—dark shadows of an education with its frowning absolutes and frigid hours were looming all around the boy, and he knew it. The New York school seemed, by comparison, like heaven. The children's band played Bernstein, and the second-graders illustrated the books of E. B. White. There were absurdities; the children have to take an entrance exam, an SAT for four-year-olds, but it all seemed worth it, more than worth it, a paradise where curiosity and self-fulfillment would be welcomed. A public school kid myself, I balked a little at the thought of sending them to private or "independent" schools. But Martha was firm, it is what people do here, and though I believe that the best possible law that could be passed in the city would compel everyone to send their kids to public school, that law has yet to be passed and the ancient dilemma of the first mover reigns.

And then the school is so good. After his first day, I asked Luke what he thought.

"The teachers are too nice," he said, a little frightened. "What do you mean?" I asked. "The teachers are too *nice*," he repeated. "I drew a picture of me on my scooter, and I got it all wrong—I made the ears too big and the wheels too small—but they said, 'It's perfect! We're putting it up!' They're too nice, Dad." Nothing in France—nothing in life—had prepared him for the embrace of American progressive education.

"What would they have said in France?" I asked him.

"Oh, you know. *N'importe quoi, n'importe quoi . . .*" "Whatever. No matter what, you do it wrong." In the French philosophy, all education begins in the recognition of perpetual error; here it begins in the recognition of universal good, or at least universal niceness. Now Luke is in a place where, no matter what, you do it right, and even are supposed to fly while you are doing it.

Martha meets and e-mails the other parents on the ad hoc committee, and methods of flight are scrutinized. It is Kitty Hawk and Hogwarts, wizardry and aeronautics joined, with knowing nods to invisible wires and vague hopes of helium. Many proposals come our way (or rather, Martha's way, as she is the point person for child flight, since I am away most of the fall, traveling from one bookstore and lecture hall in America to another to keep the kids in these schools, in flight to let them fly).

The first and most obvious idea, she tells me, was to attach the children to ropes on pulleys and hoist them up. The look of delight on the faces of the "creative" parents at this notion was equaled only by the flush that spread like a contagion, like a bobbed apple being passed from chin to chin, across the faces of the lawyers. Pull them up to the ceiling—and then let them drop and *dangle* them there? Legal history might be made; little Sophie sure isn't covered for *that*.

Another idea was a limited, modified hanging. The children might be put on a high ladder—or why not a series of ladders, one for each to climb?—to give, through the fact of loft, the illusion of flight.

"That won't give the illusion of flight. That'll give the illusion of their being housepainters," one mother said. Then someone else proposed (brilliantly, I thought) having grown-ups, dressed in black clothes and masks, whisk onstage at the key moment and lift the children up; these are kindergarten kids, after all, not Kate Smith. A mother who has been doing her yoga and Pilates could lift even the larger ones right up over her head for a moment.

But someone else pointed out that having unknown grown-ups with their faces covered run out and grab the children would cause panic and fear. "Emma can't deal with clowns at birthday parties, much less with ninja assaults," one mother said.

Someone else proposed building a riser on the stage that would slowly move up, bringing the children aloft on a platform. The hydraulics and mechanics of the riser haven't been worked out, but the magic words "Oh, put them on a riser" had for a moment held everyone taut.

Martha also reports—and this is the interesting, unexpected thing—that everyone, symbol makers and symbol pricers, is good at this: The parents are all would-be carpenters and scene painters and lighting designers. No one suggests, as they would in a bad movie about New York schools, that we ought to hire someone, pay someone else to do the job. The willingness of New York parents is bracing compared with the aloofness of French parents, or even of earlier generations of American parents. *They will do anything to make their children fly.*

But do the children really *want* to fly? This is kindergarten, after all; they're doing well just to tie their shoes and use the bathroom. Is the whole elaborate apparatus we construct "to keep from disappointing them" for us or them? Will they be any happier, or wiser, or less likely to turn on us in fifteen-year-old rage—"You never let me do anything I wanted to do!"—if we make them fly? Or will they turn on us anyway: "You made me fly, and there I was, so happy on the ground."

The flying children haunt us; we see them hovering overhead at night, free of wires and entanglements, launched without obvious trickery or cheap effects. We see them aloft, above. They are flying, off above—London, in this case. Unlike us, they are free to fly, while we remain below in the sublunary city, arguing about the noise and just who made it.

Ah, the children, the children! Has any place ever been better contoured to them than Manhattan is now? We take them out on fall Saturday mornings—Paul Desmond saxophone mornings, as I think of them, lilting jazz sounds almost audible in the avenues—to go to the Whitney or the park to look dutifully at what remains of the avant-garde in Chelsea, or to shop at Fairway, a perfect place, more moving than any Parisian market in its openness, its joy, a place where they have cheap soap lets you taste of six different olive oils. I prefer Fairway to any Paris market: its openness, its ironic self-consciousness—GREAT COFFEE! UGLY AS HELL PACKAGING! reads a sign—its democratic mixture of six kinds of goat cheese and six kinds of discount toilet paper, for the way that suspicious elderly immigrant men in cloth caps bump elbows, carts, and temperaments with starting couples and four-part families. A fugue of appetites rather than a counterpoint of classes. Even the implicit rules, as well understood as those about crossing streets and hailing cabs, are beautiful to observe in action. The endless lines waiting for the cashiers are broken in half to give people space to get by. The first three in line wait by the cash register; everyone else waits back in the aisle behind, with the interrupted intersection between. In Paris, a rule this instinctive and complex would be debated, doubted, deplored, transgressed, and enforced only by a sign saying THIS RULE WILL BE ENFORCED; here, everyone enforces it not through goodwill, exactly, but through suspended ill will, through glances of mutual suspicion. The line at Fairway, like the city, is ultimately self-forming and self-regulating. Regulated not by forces of the free market, exactly—you couldn't pay a premium to break the line—but by a cumulative force of bare repressed mutual suspicion. Keep the line and we'll keep our peace; break the line and we'll break you.

We have formed a club, the children and I—or a klub, rather, the Krispy Kreme Klub. We meet on Saturday mornings, sneaking out of the house before their mother has woken up, and going—one scooting, one walking, one being pushed—to the Krispy Kreme donut shop on Third Avenue. We buy three Classic Glazed and sit at a table in the window, staring at the early risers on the weekend avenue and the health food store across the street. (When we get home, we tell Mom, "We've been out to breakfast on Third Avenue near Eighty-fourth—you know, where the health food store is." The children think that this is hilarious, as does their quietly unfooled mother.) The donuts are even more intensely sweet than all the other American commercial food we are getting reaccustomed to, and a small moment of regret, of longing, for a Paris café and a strong cup of coffee and a sober *tartine* crosses my mind. But not for long, really. The abundance of this place, and the generosity of its sweetness, a kind of American optimism, fills the little franchise as much as does the smell of frying donuts coming from the elaborate Rube Goldberg donut machine kept behind glass in the rear of the store. New York is so easy, so fresh-baked yet funky: You can walk around in your jogging pants and baseball cap, and no one will look at you twice, or funny.

Olivia, just one, watches the donut machine soberly. She could stay here for hours. When the squads of donuts come down from the fryer on their automated conveyor belt, one or two always fall to the side, and she gasps. She identifies with the abandoned donut, empathizes with the circle of yeasty dough that has lost its way.

Other children come in with other weary, early-rising dads and moms. They have a city of their own, whose map we are learning, with the American Museum of Natural History as its St. Peter's and the countless places where birthday parties are held as its chapels. Yet we see already that the attention deadens—that they risk losing the alert light one sees in the eyes of French children, the sensitivity that comes from recognizing that there are unappeasable powers in the world who must be placated and avoided. The art of child rearing, of parenting, is to center the children and then knock them off center; to make them believe that they are safely anchored in the middle of a secure world and somehow also to let them know that the world they live in is not a fixed sphere with them at the center; that they stand instead alongside a river of history, of older souls, that rushes by them, where they are only a single small incident. To make them believe that they can rule all creation, while making them respect the malevolent forces that can ruin every garden: That is the task. (It crosses my mind, blasphemously, that this was exactly the dilemma, the twin task, of that greatest father of them all in his one unfortunate episode in parenting. He didn't manage it that well, either.)

I had thought Martha was a crazed lunatic when it came to her children, only to discover that in New York, she was a completely normal mother, that a constant obsessive-compulsive anxiety about the children—their health, their future, the holes in their socks, and the fraying of their psyches—is taken entirely for granted here. Child obsessiveness is a substitute for status obsessiveness, to which the mothers seem quite indifferent. Clothes, bags, shoes, all of that Capote and Dawn Powell stuff seems to have vanished from them, as martinis and prime ribs have largely fled from us, their husbands. (The martini drinkers now are the ironists downtown.) They love these things, of course, but they love them as recreation or escape, not as elements of their own. Child possession itself is a form of status, some anthropologist or novelist might argue, but it produces exhaustion so quickly that the ritual game is over by the time you have made the opening move.

And then there is something so beautiful about the lists of children's names posted outside the classrooms, children who didn't even exist six years ago—the mix of Celtic, Hebrew, African, with the proviso that the Celtic names are likely to belong to the Jewish children and the Jewish names to the Asian ones. We have a beautiful slant-eyed Noah and a Dylan who looks like my cousin—well, like that other Dylan, the generational bard.

Money and power are everywhere, and the sense of a bubble, a perfect glass dome that extends over the city, is palpable—one can almost see its highlight, its gleam. As we walk through the park, sharing a muffin, Kirk Varnedoe—who seems well again, thank God, after cancer and chemo—talks about the speed with which money came together for the new building for the Museum of Modern Art, the institution he oversees. He has the *Times* in his hands as we leave for breakfast, and he says with wonder, "Somewhere, somewhere in these pages, there's the little piece of news that will end all this—some story about a virus or an oversold Internet stock that will precipitate the crash. It has to happen. It always has. But the amazing thing is that we don't know which page that piece of news is on, and we can't know."

When it comes to grass and gardens, Central Park remains another kind of miracle. I always knew this, but in your twenties, parks and trees are just part of the decor, like the backgrounds in an Astaire musical. Now I walk to work through the park and am amazed by it all over again, the retreat of it and the liberal illogic of it. In Paris, I had idealized it: its liberal open-endedness, its absence of grand allées, its endless adaptability. Now I take Luke on long walks there, and we look at Belvedere Castle, where the dealers used to congregate, whispering, "Smoke, smoke," and I tell him the castle in the park once belonged to a great king who dominated the city when Central Park was a separate country, who invented brunch and flew his flag from the top of the Belvedere battlements. The king was lost, and ever since, Central Park has been without a leader. But the king of Central Park will return someday; it could be any one of us. Luke watches and listens with his serious squint, his mother's almond eyes.

Then, on his scooter, he swoops down the hills above the Ramble and disappears, he is lost to me in a second, as the path takes an Olmstedian romantic bend. I have never lost him before! After years of watching him trike down the straight allées of the Luxembourg Gardens, I am in a liberal parent's panic. Having identified the paths of Olmsted with the free play of liberalism, I am its typically panicked victim. People vanish in this park! Their identity is unstable! Where the hell has he gone? The children are free here—*too* free, they whiz around corners, and they're gone. They know so much. They get away too soon in this country. People are too damn nice here. They sing, and they are praised for their singing. They draw, and they are praised for their drawing. They scoot. They fly. And they are gone—I call out his name . . .

Then I see him at the bottom, at the foot of an unexpected hill, looking back and waiting for me.

We go down and out into the Great Lawn, where we find a raptor festival being held: hawks and falcons and eagles hooded in cages, tenderly lifted out by their keepers, who hold them on immensely thick gauntlets. The raptors have blank, indifferent killer eyes. ("Could you keep a hawk as a pet?" one New York child asks. "No," the man with the birds says flatly.) He does let one small hawk free, though, just so we can see how it soars. The hawk flies toward the bank of trees on the east side of the lawn, and before he gets there, a thick, panicked gray cloud of pigeons rises from inside the trees and flies off, a single dense flock, back across the park to the west-side bank of trees. The hawk turns and then flies west, and the pigeons intelligently panic again and fly back, all together, the other way, a dingy gray flapping crowd across the blue sky, heading home. The keeper, nettled, calls back his bewildered raptor. I realize that I am rooting for the pigeons, real New Yorkers, dense, plain, panicky, and acting as a unit only when they have to, when there is a criminal nearby. They fly as New York children really ought to, all together, and only at need.

Other ways to make the children fly race around by e-mail, are sought on the Internet, are whispered over egg-white omelettes (no toast, *no* potatoes or carbohydrates of any kind) at the coffee shops (not cafés, God knows, nor coffeehouses) near the school. Pull them up on harnesses or (I like this one) make mock children made of papier-mâché and rubber. Flick the lights off, flick them back on, and then fly these "children" from the wings. Who cares if *they* fall?

"Why don't we just push them off a high place? They might fly," someone said ironically. But for a half second, a nanosecond of possibility, the smile that went around the room was not a mordant one of knowledge but a happy one of promise: *Our* kids just might.

While Martha is in charge of flight, I am still the defense counsel for noise, the Perry Mason of my own family, defending them with rancor, sarcasm, and evidence. In other American cities, I discover, no matter how hard I probe, noise stories are hard to find. (Instead, car stories—parking stories, carpooling stories, intense NPR-inflected debates about the ethics of SUVs—are everywhere.) But the moment I am back in Manhattan, I hear noise stories. They seem to have a set form. The herd of elephants, to begin with. "It sounds like a herd of elephants," everyone says, though how could anyone in a New York apartment know what a herd of elephants sounds like one floor above?

The rote forms, the familiar aggravation, must point to something, even if not to anything concrete. Is it noisier here than it is elsewhere? I listen on the street and think that, yes, it is noisy here, though I had never really noticed before. The situation can even be said to have improved somewhat, for everything has gone indoors, inside, been internalized. Once there were kids with boom boxes, declaring the strength of their shoulders and their indifference to middle-class opinion by hoisting huge radios to create insulating, almost visible clouds of defiant sound. Now everyone walks with headphones, merely earbuds; when I walk around Manhattan with my old Walkman and large headphones on, I look, I'm sure, like an air traffic controller in a sixties disaster movie.

The only noisy talkers are the people with those cell phones that slip around their necks, enabling them to talk directly, disconcertingly, to the air as they walk. You cannot know whether you are dealing with a schizophrenic, or a Realtor trying to talk sense into a disbelieving client, or a man trying to talk love to a disbelieving girl. Yet the background noise, like the incidental sweetness, is overwhelming: the rumble of buses, the constant whistles, a kind of white hush very different from that in other places. No hushed Sunday-morning moments when church bells ring from a distance.

The noise is a symbol, I see now, and what it signifies is *crowding*, the this-cheek-to-that-cheek, on-top-of-one-anotherness that is the defining New York phenomenon. For that is the undeniable, the inevitable, the overwhelming fact of life here. Eight million people squeezed into a space that might accommodate a couple of aboriginal tribes, screaming about sound when what they are feeling is the press of density, more humanity per square inch than humanism can bear.

A fight over noise is a displaced fight over space. You struggle so hard to claim a few hundred, a bare thousand, square feet that anything intruding—a take-out menu, a neighbor's piano—becomes an affront to your privacy, to your selfhood. The dancing overhead, the barking down below, however harmless, encroach on your dearly bought and long-fought-for solitude. We fight about noise as people in Venice might have fought—did fight—about water rights at the Palazzo. As we do, they blamed the malice of their neighbors for the fact of their circumstances. The annual flooding, the damp mold creeping into your basement, the certain fatality of wet; it all got referred to an argument with your neighbor about where he left his gondola.

Even the building where we have been accommodated is enormous, dense with so many kinds. The building is a layer cake of the original inhabitants, who began as renters back in the sixties, were part of the original co-op, and now are the stunned (and imprisoned, really; where can they go?) inheritors of million-dollar apartments, schoolteachers and cookbook writers who contribute the odd recipe to the

Wednesday *Times* and really believe in City Opera; true yuppies of the eighties generation, still in sneakers and skirts, upwardly mobile; single men in studios and lonesome Eleanor Rigbys who have occasional shouted telephone conversations with distant children, audible at seven o'clock in the morning and then again at the same time that night.

There is an impossibly elegant older couple, a veteran television anchor and his perfect European wife, up in the penthouse, with vast views, and then there is Sally, our favorite neighbor, the writer who lives above us and comes down, like a character in an old radio comedy, every day around six as I cook dinner, to consult and crack wise. She in turn lives just below a strange woman who complains every day about a noise that the catlike and solitary and unmusical Sally is incapable of making. The family of Orthodox Jews lives down the hall, sweating on Saturdays; a solitary stockbroker lives alongside. As on some huge, improbable advent calendar, you could not open a door without finding a Type, and could not peel back the Type without finding something more. We live within spitting—within shouting—distance of all of these, and the miracle is that we manage, save for our neighbors below, with whom we war.

The other night I had a dream that Sally and I walked from apartment to apartment searching for my door, looking for the children. Door after door, floor after floor, we knocked and buzzed: happy neighbors, sad neighbors, poor men, rich men, vast apartments and tiny sad studios . . . and then we realized, to Sally's satisfaction, to my growing and gnawing panic, that the building had no end. I had forgotten what floor we lived on, as one does in dreams, and that we were living not just in the Colossal Co-op but in the Infinite Apartment House; like the library of Babel in Borges, in which every possible book has been shelved, the dream version of our apartment building was one in which every possible interior decor, every possible neighbor, every possible New York life, existed. We would knock forever and see infinite numbers of coffee tables and couches, and I would never find my way home. I woke up bewildered and frightened and then listened for a minute to the sounds—the *Today* show in the next apartment, the skittering of the child above us getting ready for school—of the building waking up.

Yet density has its gaieties, too. Halloween—this is our first real one in years, the Paris version being entirely ersatz—has become a Manhattan festival of neatly encoded exchanges of privileges. Downtown Halloween had kept some of its ancient charge of the pagan and the simply weird—"Why do we need another holiday celebrating how bizarre life can be here?" Martha had said plaintively, when still a girl with the snows of Canada in her hair—but uptown Halloween has become as American as *Meet Me in St. Louis*, with a fillip of class difference, which in New York is always property difference.

It is beautiful: The children walk up and down the streets and dart into the townhouses. Once there was something kind of sad about the parade of Halloween children we witnessed in the buildings of friends with kids, racing up and down in elevators to designated apartments; in our own building, you have to put a sign, a pumpkin, on the door to let people know that you are child-friendly. The new Halloween, though, is like the old Halloween of my Philadelphia childhood, outside and door-to-door, with a slight air of unspoken condescension to greet us.

On the Upper West and Upper East sides, it is the wealthy in their townhouses on the side streets who really make the holiday. They decorate their beautiful reclaimed brownstones with dangling skeletons and witches' silhouettes and reams of spray spiderweb. There are cut-paper pumpkins taped to the windows; there are real jack-o'-lanterns, each carved with a different style of grin, terraced on the flagstone staircases.

We visit them in wonder, with a peasant's sense of privilege Just to Be Allowed. In the October dusk, the children walk up and down the avenues in their costumes, grim reapers and witches, and many of them still just ghosts. (The primal force of the sheet with two holes punched in it remains quite startling, stunning the way that the triangle and two circles of fabric on the mannequins in the lingerie store down the street are; that simple, that powerful.) There are store-bought costumes—Spider-Man and Wonder Woman, her lasso trailing behind her, her skintight unitard paired with a light but sensible coat—and then there are creative costumes made at home by the more poetically minded parents: Charlotte and Wilbur, a man without a head, a figure from Dante, one child made by a nimble-fingered mother to look like the Thinker. Luke, with some of the old-fashioned gold dust of Paris lingering in his eyes for just another month, decided to go as Zeus, with thunderbolts made of cardboard wrapped in aluminum foil. Olivia went as a witch, a baby witch, in peaked cap.

My own childhood Halloweens still resonate. Apart from the artistic ambition of my mother—who would dress us as a Chinese dragon, as Poseidon and his court, and would have had us parade naked and painted blue, like Picts, if we could have won the neighborhood costume contest that way—Halloween had, I would insist, a significant air of ritual about it: We shouted, "Trick or treat!," and the grown-ups oohed and ahhed at our costumes. Now, in New York, it is a much more jaded exchange of incidental sugar for deference. The children walk up the stairs to the houses for candy, but no one admires the children; the children admire the houses. Since the people in the townhouses are, as a rule, older, people who either bought early and smart or else graduated upward after selling the old apartment at some immense profit, there is also a generational exchange of display signs. No one even asks the kids the obvious question: "And who are you supposed to be?" Instead, we, the trick-or-treaters, are expected to ask the houses what *they* are supposed to be. "My goodness, you've done a beautiful job this year," we say to the owners as they come to the door, carefully encouraging the kids, "Look at the skeletons up there; do you see how they hang on the sill? That ghoul in the window. It looks so scary!" (Why do the richest New Yorkers all live in sunless brownstones, while so many who live in middle-sized buildings get some light?) Our possession of the children, of the burgeoning future and present, is real, but it is not the trump. *We've got the kids,* we announce as we knock; *yes, but we have the real estate,* they say as they open the door. It is unanswerable. In other cities, they congratulate the children on their disguises; here, we congratulate the houses on their costumes.

. . .

The next morning, the march of the children to private schools is the same kind of Veblenian parade on the same streets, though this one happens every day. The Catholic schoolgirls wear uniforms that for some reason feature kneesocks with pleated skirts at Mary Quant length, which, on a gamine fourteen-year-old, look as though they were designed by Al Goldstein. A scene of absolute privilege, but anxious—privilege without a secure sense of entitlement on the part of the parents. Howells's great secret, his great discovery, registers here, too: New York knocks the comfortable down to the anxious, the anxious to the indigent, the indigent to the criminal, and only the truly rich find true comfort. Howells's line between Fifth Avenue and the rest still holds.

Class distinction in New York is more complicated and subtle than any simple taxonomy of bourgeois and bohemian, or rich and middle-class and poor, can encompass. In New York, as Howells was the first to grasp, the professional classes are the middle classes; here, that great bulk of people between the extremes has more money but less security than its counterpart in the rest of the country. Professional people outside New York have always been, or believed themselves to be, essentially comfortable, so that F. Scott Fitzgerald and Booth Tarkington's midwesterners (hardly more than burghers, really) think of themselves as lords. The professional classes of Manhattan live as middle classes used to do, pushing themselves to send their children to school and afford their housing.

Precarious privilege is the rule. Professional life here, then, acquires an unusual air both of entitlement and of embattlement. This affects politics; people with interests to protect expect to be challenged and demand the right to assert themselves, to hold guns and fear minorities, and they call it liberty. People on the bottom who expect to be sat upon value solidarity and protection, and they call it fairness. New Yorkers in the middle, however well-off they may actually be, feel as if they're being sat upon, or might be, by the rich or squeezed together by the poor and so abide laws—rent protection, equal housing—that they suspect might be in their interests, too, or that they feel might offer some protection from those nearby who really *are* being sat on.

Once again, density is fate, and liberalism the organized wariness of the precariously well-off.

Density has its own pattern of serendipity, its happy accidents. On one of the most beautiful mornings of this beautiful fall, Martha tells me, she was walking home, up the street, and saw, or thought she saw, Olivia at her usual spot, with me as I type, in the corner window, searching the streets for dogs and intimates. (Martha didn't have on her glasses.) She waved violently, extremely, to me. The figure in the window waved back, just as passionately, with all his heart—and Martha realized that she had miscounted floors, and the figure in the window was our downstairs neighbor, the one who writes letters about the noise. She had mistaken him for me, defender of her perfect children; he must have mistaken her for a friend or maybe his own good wife, coming home to endure the noisy neighbors.

They waved, and then, as Martha approached and recognized the mistake and—reluctantly but almost inevitably, from necessity more than affability, from some semi-articulate Manhattan Zen impulse that says when you begin to wave, you must go right on waving until the other waver disappears from sight, from some semiconscious impulse of decency that rises from the decorum of density—they kept on waving to each other, the wave losing some of its enthusiasm, but only some, until Martha crossed the street and was out of view. It felt, Martha said, precariously happy, a bit like the Christmas truce in 1914 on the Western Front.

On Thanksgiving morning, friends invited us to their apartment on Central Park West to watch the parade roll down the avenue. I sold it very big to Luke: the giant balloons, the highly trained rope holders—I exaggerated that expertise, I suspect—and the sheer scale of the thing. As he looked out the window, Luke seemed more bemused than impressed, crowding up against it with another ten kids. The balloons, I realized, are at once too big and too small—too big to be cute yet smaller than they promised you, smaller than you had hoped. The *scale* of Manhattan unscales everything else. The buildings are already so much bigger than you can imagine or understand that even a giant caped dog or a massive cartoon moose passes blithely in their shadows, just another event. I could sense Luke's polite disappointment. Even things they tell you really fly don't fly; they just float below the cornice line of the buildings. They don't attain the sky—just the fifth floor.

A musical family, our hosts sit down to sing to the quickly bored children. Someone checks a watch, noting the morning hour. "Don't play the piano," she says. "*You* know. The neighbors." And the music stops.

On an airplane over middle America, I sit down to read *Peter Pan,* which we saw once but I have never really read. Maybe, I think, I can find some secret flight formula buried in the Original Text. I read with pleasure, if not with illumination. *Peter Pan,* I see, is about escape, outward motion, the flight beyond to Neverland. For J. M. Barrie, the townhouse, very much like those we envy on Halloween, represented the thing to fly *away* from, the little prison of bourgeois bedtimes. It wasn't that Barrie didn't like the houses he knew; he tried to build one like the one in his book for the real boys who inspired the story. It was that he took the fifth-floor window for granted, as part of the bourgeois entitlement, even though there are no servants in this house, just the dog. (Reading *Mary Poppins* to the children, we were startled to discover that the embattled, harried Banks family has *four* full-time servants before the Divine Nanny even arrives.)

But to us, the house in *Peter Pan* looks like an unobtainable idyll of domestic pleasure, a place to fly *to,* just as Cherry Tree Lane is the place you want your children to be, not the one you need the magic nanny to lead them out of. The Edwardian-Georgian London, which sits just before and just after the great warning disaster of liberalism, the Great War, nonetheless casts its spell as a place for children's books to come out of.

There is an untieable knot at the heart of child raising: We want both a safe house with a garden and a nursery, and the world beyond, stars and redskins and even a plank to (harmlessly) walk. Unlike our great-grandmothers, we worry less about our children having the power to escape us—our children are more or less forced out in flight by the propulsions of commerce before they know how to walk—than we do about their having a window to fly out of. For the truth is that our own flights are inward; what is beguiling about *Peter Pan* now is the image of the children safe in the house in London. I see that it is what Martha and all the other mothers want for the children, with a passion so ferocious that it transcends all selfishness. They want the children to fly off and then to fly home.

That these two hopes are irreconcilable—that, having flown, they won't fly home, save as we fly home now to our parents, preoccupied with our own lives and pitying theirs—does not alter the pathos of the hope. There's a lovely instance of it in *Macbeth,* of all places. "How will you live?" the mother asks a small boy with gentle mockery, and the boy answers, "As birds do, Mother." It is the exchange of the generations, the exchange of the, well, the ages: The parents say, "How will you live?," and the child says that it's really no problem. Birds eat, and so will I. (Jesus, whom Shakespeare was sampling, was on the side of the kids; the lilies of the field get by, sparrows get by, you'll get by.)

We want our children to fly, and we want them to be tethered. We believe in freedom for them, but freedom within narrow channels of liberty, parent-tested and precut. We want them to fly, but we want them to fly as kites do, as Macy's balloons do, safely on the ends of strings, not freely, as birds do, Mother.

Peter Pan opened at last. It was wonderful! The force of the story, the children longing to be free, the songs, the sword fights . . . a great show! Everyone was delighted. And the children flew! *How* they flew! Or, rather, how *did* they fly? Someone had had an inspiration: As the first act ended and the children approached the window with Peter, our Peter, leading, the lights dimmed and then flickered, and then there appeared a small-scale model of the London skyline, the steeple of Big Ben and the cupola of St. Paul's—and the flying children in their nightclothes around it. Above it, around it, leaning over it, they were . . . not flying, exactly, but flying enough, certainly running and dancing above the skyline of London. That surely counted, fulfilled the mission: It was dark, they were in clouds, and they were above the city. If it was not flying, it was indubitably flight.

We all gathered around afterward for congratulations and pizza and photographs. It was only later on that one of the parents, in an e-mail we chose to ignore or delete, touched gently on another point: "We didn't really raise the children," she wrote equably. "We simply lowered the heavens and told them they were flying, as we always do."

Our downstairs neighbors put their apartment on the market and fled to a loft downtown, the place where I, funnily enough, had wanted to be in the first place.

Coming home from work on the same day that *Peter Pan* premiered and the children flew, at a time while they were still looking for a buyer, I actually found myself in the elevator with the man of the house: a decent, serious, sensitive-seeming man. I could not say anything; he could not say anything. We pressed our buttons, too-touchy five and too-noisy six, and then faced front, still as rocks, unmoving, unbreathing, unconnected, eyes fixed tight on the blinking lights of passing floors, as still as cat burglars holding their breath in the presence of a motion sensor alarm in a caper movie. He got off and I watched his herringbone tweed coat recede into the infinitude of apartments. I realized that together we had accomplished the hardest of all New York things. We had at last achieved a moment of perfect silence.

Power and the Parrot

The city of New York sits on a power grid. This is not the power grid one reads about in magazines, where rich men reassure one another of their existence by eating the same food in the same place at the same time. It is an honest-to-God grid, consisting of thousands of miles of cables and wires and pipes, all carrying electrons—organized into do-with-me-what-you-will currents and let-me-tell-you-what-I'm-thinking pulses—and it runs on just about every street in the city, below the ground in Manhattan and mostly aboveground outside it. Strange animals and objects erupt on the grid, and two of the strangest of these are the feral parakeets of Flatbush and the switch hotels of lower Manhattan. Feral parakeets are (probably) pet birds that have escaped and gone to live in the wild or, anyway, on the power poles of Flatbush. They are flourishing, and their presence has raised interesting ornithological, and even legal, issues, not to mention a hell of a racket in Flatbush. A switch hotel—often called a carrier or telecom hotel—is a great big building that eighteen months ago might have been filled with people and is now inhabited exclusively by switches, both servers and routers, who rent small locked rooms in which they exchange electrons, making dreamy machine love to other machines all night long, and sucking more power from the grid below than any tenants ever have before. Both the birds and the buildings resonate to the deepest, alligator-in-the-sewers myth of New York—to the notion that we have introduced strangers among us who not only have made themselves at home but have actually moved out on their own.

The parakeets can be found in a couple of different places and approached in a couple of different ways. There is a large colony of them in Green-Wood Cemetery, but the densest concentration, according to Jen Uscher, a Columbia graduate student and bird lover who is working on a thesis about New York birds, is right on and around the campus of Brooklyn College, at the end of the number 2 line. The neighborhood there, apart from the parakeets, is an outer-borough mixture of long-established African-Americans, new East Indian immigrants (whose stores dominate the shopping streets), and Orthodox Jews (whose small shuls are set along the residential avenues).

In the early morning, Jen often takes the number 2 out from Park Slope, where she lives, to look at the parakeets, and she is often with her boyfriend, Jason. Jen is a birder but a democratic one. As a girl in Fairfax, Virginia, she kept pigeons—real city pigeons. She is a small, intently pretty young woman who has the eager eyes, quick mind, and you'd-be-amazed-how-much-fun-the-subway-can-be avidity of the new New Yorker.

As she and Jason turned down Avenue I toward Twenty-eighth Street one recent Friday morning, she said, "The parakeets were supposed to be eradicated in the early seventies, but here they are. Can't you hear them already?" First there was nothing, then a distant static-electricity crackle, and finally, an intense chattering, like a chorus line shaking maracas in a forties South American musical. The sound filled the quiet street of one-family houses with napkin front yards. "You *hear* them first, but they're not hard to see," Jen went on. "These birds are so bold. They're real New Yorkers. They have so much attitude. I'm amazed they don't drive more people crazy. They're tough, social birds who live in colonies. Look right there!" She pointed to a flock of about ten feral parakeets sitting on the wires running between power poles.

The term "feral parakeet" calls to mind a furtive escaped songbird, perky but vulnerable, its small heart fluttering, a hunted look in its eye. This image does not apply to the feral parakeets of Flatbush. What they got in Flatbush are not feral parakeets. What they got in Flatbush are wild parrots. (Technically, a parrot is just a big parakeet; there is no sharp line between the species.) Filling the trees and power lines along

Avenue I are great big bright green pirate-ready parrots, with sharp, hooked beaks and blue wing feathers and raucous, jeering voices, tens and tens of tens of them, chattering like Mike and the Mad Dog after a Giants game. Their nests, of twigs and sticks, are immense hanging *trulli*, with multiple entrances—only slightly smaller than the spaces that are usually rented in the city to people like Jen and Jason for nine hundred dollars a month.

"They usually build their nests on high-voltage power poles—there's something about power entrances—and if their nests catch on fire, they can cause outages," Jason said. "There's even a website that offers solutions for infestations. The power companies regard them as a major pest."

Jen watched the birds fly back and forth, calling to one another from tree to tree, going in and out of the many entrances and exits to their communal nest. "They don't even look that cold, you know?" she added. "I used to keep parrots, and when they got loose, they were all fluffed up. I like to see pet birds that have gone wild. It's like they're getting the last laugh."

A Hasidic woman walked by. She was wearing sneakers and a shawl. She did not even look up at twelve big parrots that were cawing in her front yard. She stopped to read a poster, though, that someone had pasted on the power pole: JEWISH WOMEN, it read in part. FIND OUT THE KABALIST SECRETS OF WHAT MAKES WOMEN TIC. ONLY AT HILLEL THIS WED. 12–2 PM. FREE CHINESE FOOD LUNCH!

One parrot gave a shot to another with his beak—playfully, but he did it. "They're very aggressive," Jen said solemnly. "There's one report that they killed a house sparrow in Pittsburgh."

The feral parakeets of Flatbush have given rise to a certain amount of affection (there's a playground in Flatbush decorated with a frieze of metal parrots), a certain amount of resentment (Con Ed, in particular, sees them as rats with wings in drag), and a lot of theorizing. The theorizing turns on the question of how big green parrots got loose in Brooklyn in the first place, why they don't mind the cold, and why every attempt to get rid of them has failed. Here is pretty much all that is known about the feral parakeets of Flatbush: They come from South America. They are a subtropical bird, native mostly to Argentina, genus and species *Myiopsitta monachus*. In the wild, they're usually called Monk parrots; pet owners refer to them as Quaker parrots. They are highly intelligent. They are good talkers—they have at least eleven different vocalizations—and excellent imitators. They are unique among the 330 or so species of parrots because they live in co-ops. Their nests can contain from one to six pairs, each with a separate chamber and entrance hole.

The folk explanation of how they got here is that a crate carrying Monks broke open at Kennedy Airport in 1968, and the birds got free and started a local settlement. (They were first seen that year, and were first observed breeding in Valley Stream, Long Island, in 1971.) Among serious bird theorists, though, the crate-broke-open-at-Kennedy theory of the origins of the feral parakeets is about as well regarded as the vegetables-just-fell-in-the-pan theory of the origin of pasta primavera around the same time. One strong argument against the theory is that a colony of Monks exists in Hyde Park, in Chicago, near the campus of the University of Chicago—an even colder climate—and the Chicago parrots were also seen for the first time in the late sixties. This would seem to demand a crate-broke-open-at-O'Hare-right-around-then-too theory. The best guess seems to be that both colonies are the consequence of Monk escapees. ("I've never known a pet bird who didn't get away sooner or later, and they don't always come home," Jen points out.)

The Monk parrots, like so much that comes north to us, manage to be both illegal and expensive. At least ten states won't let you own them as pets, partly out of fear that they will go feral and drive the local birds crazy. The parrots are also said to carry psittacosis. At first New York State tried to kill them off, and by 1975 they were all thought to be dead. They were not. Although they may live outside the law, Monk parrots have a street value in the pet trade of around two hundred dollars a bird. It is said that one local pet-store owner tried to climb the poles of Flatbush to capture them and cash in but came away empty-handed and pecked.

No one has a very good explanation of how the birds survive the harsh winters here. One theory, popular among people who have actually lived in Argentina, is that the climate in Argentina is not all that temperate. Another is that the parrots are adaptable. This theory is circular, of course—they survive because they're good at surviving—but then so are most theories about how immigrant groups thrive in New York. (Nobody thought that Koreans had a particular affinity for fruit, or, for that matter, the Irish for police work, before they came here.)

A theory popular among pigeons is that the parrots survive because they're pushy. Jen and Jason like to watch the parrots around the playing field of Brooklyn College. They have nested high up in the light stanchions that circle the field; beneath the lights, on little platforms made for upkeep, are nests, and the parrots swoop down to the field to wander around and dis the sparrows. On this cold morning, some parrots had flown down to the ground and were out walking on the tired gray snow, searching for birdseed near a chain-link fence.

"I've never seen that, parrots walking on snow," Jen said.

Three or four sparrows were feeding greedily with the parrots. Nearby, though, a couple of pigeons were giving them a sour, disconsolate, Archie Bunker, who-let-the-element-in? look.

"Well, *they're* strangers, too," Jen said. "All the common birds of New York are exotics. Pigeons, house sparrows, starlings . . . They all came from outside North America and got introduced to the continent."

"Maybe parrots are the next pigeons," Jason said.

"I've read lots of good scientific reasons why they can't be," Jen said carefully. "For one thing, unlike pigeons, the Monk parakeets don't breed all year round. But people said they couldn't survive here, and they did, and people said they were eradicated in the seventies, and they weren't, and here they are in winter."

The bright green parrots were walking in the snow. They were chattering wildly, telling one another about the last thing that sparrow said in Pittsburgh. The two pigeons stood on the sidewalk and watched them, furious.

I've never seen a mouse here, not once, never," the night watchman was saying that night, up on the tenth floor of what was once a warehouse, at 325 Hudson Street. The windows of 325 Hudson are not dark at night, nor do they have the soulful checkerboard pattern—this one working late, this one gone home—of most office buildings late at night. The windows all glow faintly, and the building hums. This is because 325 Hudson is a switch hotel. Switch hotels, which real estate people prefer to call carrier hotels, are the cleanest buildings in New York—security-conscious, sterile, airtight, and animal-free. They are buildings that are filled with very heavy, very expensive, very power-thirsty telecom equipment, which allows computers to talk to one another on telephone lines. Switch hotels have been in existence for only about five years, but in the commercial real estate boom, they have boomed the loudest. There are at least seven switch hotels in Manhattan: 325 Hudson, 60 Hudson, 32 Avenue of the Americas, 111 Eighth Avenue, 636 Eleventh Avenue, 75 Broad Street, and 85 Tenth Avenue. They exist because behind the paper ballerinas of the virtual and the light-footed electronic lurk, unseen, the steadfast tin soldiers of heavy machinery. A switch hotel is the place where the tin soldiers and the paper ballerinas sleep together, and since each pair couples a little differently, it does not want the others to see exactly what it's doing. This is why a switch hotel is called a switch "hotel"—because the space in it is rented out to different companies, and each tenant jealously guards his privacy.

Now the night watchman shone his flashlight along the floor. It caught a little kitchen that had been set up when the tenth floor was renovated for the "collocation" room of a company called Net2000. It had a blue terrazzo floor, brushed-aluminum cabinets. Inside the cabinets were tiny packets of instant coffee, lined up in perfect rows, untouched by human hand. "O brave new world," a man from Cushman & Wakefield, which manages 325 Hudson Street, said in awe. Just to the right, behind a wall of glass, in a space that not long ago was a warehouse for Century 21, seven-foot racks of switches winked rapid little red lights at one another.

Switches come in two kinds, servers and routers. Servers hold on to things—Web pages, most often—while routers take people who are searching for things on servers and send them somewhere else. Only the eye of love can tell a router from a server. The rooms that hold the switches are noisy, and they are hot. The hum of the giant air-conditioning units that are needed to cool them, even when there is a chill in the air and snow on the ground for parrots to walk on, is as loud as the subway. Big orange pipes filled with fiber-optic cable reach down to them. At the entrance to the bedroom where Net2000 keeps its routers and servers, which it rents out to high rollers for high prices, there is a handprint ID check, the kind you see in James Bond movies. You can get in to service the switches only if they recognize the touch of your hand. (Some of the rooms in a switch hotel use retinal identification: You have to look the switches sincerely in the eye to be allowed in.)

Switch hotels are generally owned or managed by real estate developers, who convert warehouses that have high ceilings, strong floors, and ugly fronts. They need to have high ceilings to hold the seven-foot vertical switch racks and the ducts that run above them; strong floors to hold the heavy machinery; and ugly fronts, because if they didn't, they would be turned into lofts where people who work with switches live. Then the developer rents out space, at about sixty dollars a square foot, to telecom companies, which specialize in trafficking data and information, and which install the racks and equipment. Then the company rents out space on the machines to AOL or Yahoo! or whoever wants it. Each tenant—it is part of telecom-hotel etiquette—makes a point of keeping separate from the other tenants. In particular, each has an emergency two-megawatt generator on the roof, entirely its own, no sharing. "They want to be completely independent," the real estate man said. "Everybody else in the building will go down, but we'll still be running."

It is often said that switch hotels are in Manhattan because it is necessary to reamplify fiber-optic signals every mile or so. The real reason that big telecom companies like to keep their switches in dark rooms in Manhattan is that they think it's sexy. "It's a marketing issue as much as anything," said James Somoza, a broker at Cushman & Wakefield who is the Alice Mason of the switch hotel. "It's a fit-and-finish issue; they want to come and be able to see their equipment. They want to show their clients a nice facility. And there are back-haul-charges issues—the closer you are to the user, the cheaper it is. Also, having the switches in Manhattan makes it easier to have a self-healing loop." A self-healing loop is one in which, if a section of the network breaks down, the electronic traffic reverses flow and runs in the opposite direction, bypassing the break. "But there's no absolute reason why the switches couldn't be kept in Long Island City or New Jersey. That people can afford Manhattan rents to keep machines in the dark—well, I guess it's just a sign of how much money there has been in telecoms in the past decade."

The interior of a switch hotel on a Friday night in 2001 looks exactly like the interior of a Soho gallery on a Saturday afternoon circa 1985: the same tiny, cryptic lettering, the same inexplicable arrangements of racks and liquids and bolts and electric cells, the same pervasive air of sterility and airless ominousness. The battery boxes for the emergency generators, which are kept in bright side chapels near the dark switch rooms, are translucent tubs half filled with liquid, with copper buses above as shiny as pennies, and as deadly as power lines. (They are alive with electricity and hold no insulation.)

Most people who develop and rent out switch hotels are aware of the paradox they suggest, which is that the more virtual the world gets, the heavier the machines are to get it that way, and the more space they take up in Manhattan. "That was the one thing no one really thought about the New Economy," James Somoza said. "How much power you would need to run it. A telecom hotel demands a hundred watts per square foot." A normal office needs, at most, around six watts per square foot. "I mean, this is the Internet," he said, standing among the chattering switches. "You're looking at it. It smells like an old Lionel train set. It weighs a ton. It sits on the floor on Hudson Street. Virtual reality depends on the strength of this floor."

Late that night, the watchman was talking excitedly about the ID equipment, the New Economy, life among the switches. The night watchman in a switch hotel is actually more of a concierge and knows something about his guests. He continued his rounds.

"It's the only place in 2001 that looks like 2001," the real estate man said, looking over the rows and rows of red blinking lights that fill the busy, empty building, and shaking his head.

. . .

New York itself can sometimes seem to be a giant switch, taking in improbable immigrants and routing them out as ideal tenants. If the parrots recall our ethnic origins, the telecom machines are, from a real estate agent's point of view, the perfect renters of the future. They have everything: They are clean, intelligent, and reliable, don't own pets, and spend a lot of their own money on improvements. Each tenant spends as much as half a million dollars for generators and batteries, in case of a blackout, which, until recently, no one thought could ever happen. Now the men who own the switches wake up in their beds to contemplate all those things which were surely never meant to happen: the bankruptcy of a state power corporation; an earthquake on the Upper East Side; a fire in Flatbush; and a sudden flurry of green feathers.

That Sunday

Things in New York begin either six flights up or one flight down and then just vanish. All the wonders that Henry James wondered at a century ago—the Waldorf-Astoria, the Metropolitan Opera—are gone, and the wonders that he didn't wonder at but that we know enough to wonder at now—say, Albert Ryder's room in the Village—are gone, too. The past, even the immediate past, in New York is organized more or less like the cemetery in Venice: The skeletons are buried and then, after a dozen years, dug up and evicted and thrown onto a second island in a mixed-up heap of remembrance. New Yorkers live on that second island and sort through crazy heaps of memory to find a past. There are compensations for our indifference, though. Freed from its connection to its origins, the past has more carry. Nothing calls it home, and the picture or the poem or the piano part often just keeps on traveling, past the original audience and into the world, the way that, though the Polo Grounds are gone, Bobby Thomson's home run is still traveling over that fence.

Exactly forty years ago this summer, on June 25, 1961, three young jazz musicians—the piano player Bill Evans, the bass player Scott LaFaro, and the drummer Paul Motian—went down to a New York basement, smoked, yawned, joked a bit, and got to work. The trio played thirteen songs, most of them slow: "My Romance," "I Loves You, Porgy," and even a waltz from the Walt Disney movie *Alice in Wonderland*. The music they made was recorded, and was released later that year by a small independent label called Riverside. The album's title was *Sunday at the Village Vanguard*. Later in the year, another record from that afternoon was released, called *Waltz for Debby*, after one of the songs. Since then the same two and a half hours have been repackaged and rereleased and remastered and reconsidered, in albums called, among other things, *The Village Vanguard Sessions* and *At the Village Vanguard*.

It is easy to cite worshipful jazz-crit passages about them, concerning intonation and modal passages and singing tones, though none of the writing itself has the least emotional force. It is difficult to explain the force the music does have, since it is not particularly forceful. People who don't respond to it are puzzled that anyone hears anything in it at all. They say that it sounds like "background music," or like cocktail music. Philip Larkin, acerbic but sound, said that it had a Pierrot-in-moonlight quality, and how you feel about it, perhaps, depends on how you feel about Pierrot in moonlight. As the jazz critic Ira Gitler pointed out in the original liner notes, Evans was at the time an aficionado of Zen Buddhism, and the music he made was meditative and tuneful, between Suzuki and Snow White.

If you are vulnerable to this music, however, you are completely vulnerable to it. Bill Evans has no casual fans. After that afternoon, his name became synonymous with a heartbreak quality that is not like anything else in music. It is not little-boy-lost or blue, like Miles Davis, but transparent and wistful. Evans's solos on "Alice in Wonderland" and "My Foolish Heart" and, especially, "Porgy" begin with a mother-of-pearl tone, singing and skipping, as though they were being played on the celesta or the xylophone, and then suddenly turn dark blue, a sad and resonant music. They are as close to pure emotion, produced without impediments—not at all the same thing as an entire self poured out without inhibitions, the bebop dream—as exists in music. His music hints at the secret truth that New York is sad before it is busy, and that it is a kind of inverted garden, with all the flowers blooming down in the basements.

This particular basement, the Village Vanguard, still stands, or cowers, under Seventh Avenue. And three of the people who were there that particular afternoon—the producer, the drummer, and the club owner—were in town. On June 24 and 25 of this year, it was possible to speak to them, and to get them to ruminate a bit on how the afternoon happened, why so many people now remember it, why earnest French and Japanese scholars and collectors brood and argue over and analyze it, and what it all has to do with the still-potent romantic formula of city lights, early death, and the piano.

The facts of Bill Evans's life, and of the events leading to that afternoon, are easy to find. Bill Evans was born in 1929 in New Jersey, into a Russian Orthodox family. He studied music at Southeastern Louisiana College and graduated playing flute and piano and violin—a prodigy. He was one of the first jazz musicians who knew Schubert and Nat King Cole equally well, and he thought that he could get more of the spirit of Schubert by playing like Nat Cole than by playing like Arthur Rubinstein. He came to New York in 1955, scuffled around, and then was taken up by Miles Davis. In 1958 Evans joined Davis's group for eight months—the only white musician in the sextet—and then played piano on Davis's *Kind of Blue,* for which, by most accounts, he collaborated on many of the basic tunes. Davis gave him noise—a sudden credibility in the suspicious jazz world—but he gave Davis quiet. He sounded "like crystal notes or sparkling water," Davis said.

Evans recorded a few albums with bass players and drummers around New York and then, in 1959, discovered the young bass player Scott LaFaro, who played the bass as if it were a guitar, freely and melodically, rather than dutifully and as a blue-collar obligation. Paul Motian, a poetic brushes-and-silver-high-hat drummer, joined them, and what is usually called "the first trio" was born. They made a very good record together, *Portrait in Jazz*—all their album titles tried to hit a slightly Lane Coutell, suede-elbow-patches note then seen as "intellectual"—and in 1960 they went on the road.

Orrin Keepnews produced both Vanguard records, and on June 25 forty years later, he happened to be staying at the Algonquin (jazz impresarios of his vintage maintain a high regard for the Algonquin), and he settled down in the lobby to talk. In his late seventies, he lives now in San Francisco, where he still produces jazz recordings. He is a small, burly bear of a man, still wearing a fifties bongos-and-beatniks goatee. He is also a world-champion digresser, sending out long skeins of words that bend back and dissolve into the previous ones.

"To understand that day, you have to understand this about the time: Jazz was a prevalent music, but it wasn't a popular music," he said. "People read about it and talked about it and it got written about, and you could hear the occasional hit—a 'Take Five'—on AM radio, but basically, it didn't sell. If a record sold a few thousand copies, we were quite pleased. On the Sunday, I was working dials and worrying about power outages—we had one early—and the rest of the time I was worrying about Bill. What was striking about Bill from the beginning wasn't the quality of his playing—there were a lot of good players—but the quality of his self-criticism. He was always genuinely ready to learn. The trouble with Bill—and, as much as anything, that was the cause for our deciding to record him live—was always persuading Bill to play at all. He had very low self-esteem. That's what drew him to Scott. Scott was already a rumor even before he was a whisper—everyone had heard of this phenomenal bass player, and when they started working together, what was clear from the first was that Bill had something very different in mind from the normal interplay of piano with bass. Most so-called trio records are just an accompanied piano player—the bass player's function is to emancipate the pianist's left hand. Bill was looking for something very different—a joined-together kind of thing.

"We chose Sunday because we knew that we had two shows, the afternoon matinee and the evening show, and we would have both. Live recording was pretty much in its infancy. Today you'd have a van with a studio inside, but we just had portable Ampex equipment, which I think we lined up by the banquette. Bill was tough, of course. Even after we had made the first record with the trio, he didn't believe that he had enough to express. He was brutally self-critical. I used to joke about forming a Demon Band of musicians who never thought they were good enough, never thought they had got it right. The Demon Band would have included Sonny Rollins on sax, J. J. Johnson on trombone, Wes Montgomery on guitar, and Bill on piano. It seemed to have an inordinate number of my musicians. Finally, I realized that the Demon Band could never really exist, because we could never find a drummer. No drummer suffers from self-doubt."

Paul Motian is a drummer. Though he is seventy, he looks twenty-five years younger, kept limber, it seems, by constant doses of the hipster skepticism proper to a jazz musician of his generation. He still plays regularly and will have a date at the Vanguard this month, and is looking for a publisher for his autobiography, *We Couldn't Find Philadelphia*. He has kept his "gig books," recording where he played and how much he got, for the last forty-five years.

"We were great," he said that weekend at a Hungarian strudel-and-coffee spot on Amsterdam Avenue. "But look at this—I got one hundred and thirty-six dollars for the famous legendary record, one hundred and ten for the gig, and one hundred and seven for the second record.

"Look at the gig book: Here we are at the D.C. Showplace. That's where Bill said, first night, second night, 'Ladies and gentlemen—I don't feel like playing tonight. Can you understand that?' And they kind of did. Bill was sincere, and he had a great sense of humor. He was good, but I was good with him, you know, because I listened. We listened to each other, and you can still hear us listening when we play. Scott was tough on Bill. He was the one man who could be tough on Bill. Like if he didn't think the music sounded right—if it was great but not perfect—he'd say to Bill, 'Man, you're just fucking up the music. Go look at yourself in the mirror!' He'd even say it to me, when he didn't think I was playing right. And he had only been playing the bass for a few years.

"Okay, here's May, two weeks in Detroit, then in Toronto, and then here comes June, and there we are, booked at the Vanguard. Then I remember we were in Philadelphia and somebody said to us, 'Hey, you know, they're imitating the way you guys sounded in Detroit!' Imitating the way we sounded in Detroit! I knew then something was happening. Imagine people imitating the way you sounded in Detroit!"

. . .

Paul Motian and Orrin Keepnews had a clear memory of the afternoon, but what they remembered was work, not art: dials that rose and fell, and money counted out in three figures. Lorraine Gordon is the widow of Max Gordon, who invented the Vanguard. She helped run it then and still takes reservations for the club, and on the anniversary Sunday, she was where she ought to be, and that was on the phone. "Vanguard. Yes, reservations are recommended. What if you have to cancel? You have to cancel." She hung up. "We're blessed, you know, because a Japanese tourist service makes regular visits. They love the idea of the Vanguard and, of course, they love jazz.

"In 1961 everything was changing because of television," she said. "When Max opened the Vanguard, it was a place for poets. It was a speakeasy, a theater after that, but it always had the same wedge shape. It was only in the late fifties that it became a jazz club. Sundays for us was a time when we had a relaxed crowd. And Max had a Steinway, which was replaced by a Yamaha, which Bill loved. Of course, I remember, was it that gig or the next, when Bill's left arm was paralyzed and he played anyway, balling a fist and bringing his hand banging down from the force of gravity."

Lorraine Gordon did not have to explain this image. Evans was, for most of his life, a drug addict. Lorraine Gordon saw him banging the left side of the keyboard with a paralyzed hand because he had been shooting up heroin and hit a nerve. "He'd been a junkie for a couple of years by then, and I had to slip him a few dollars," Keepnews said later. "I'm his friend, I'm his record company, I'm his producer. People say to me, 'Why couldn't you refuse him?' Look, he was going to find the money, junkies do, and I wasn't worried about him mugging someone in an alley. I was worried about him owing money to someone who would break his fingers if he didn't pay it back. So I advanced him money, and I refuse to think that I was doing anything wrong."

Paul Motian says, " 'I think I could play better'—that was what you always heard him saying, whatever he was thinking of trying, a hypnotist, a psychotherapist. Maybe he took drugs because he thought it made his music better." It is even sadly possible that the dreamy, otherworldly quality of Evans's playing that day had something to do with what was flowing in his veins.

On that Sunday afternoon in New York in 1961, the trio played five sets, about two and a half hours' worth of music. The numbers ran between five and ten minutes a turn. In the first three sets, knowing that the machines were running, they didn't repeat numbers, playing a lilting "Waltz for Debby," a hushed "My Foolish Heart," a floating "Alice in Wonderland," and an up-tempo "My Romance." Then, for the first time that day, Evans played "I Loves You, Porgy." In the last set, they ran back over numbers from the first few sets. By then it was late, a long day's hard work, and they finished with a number by LaFaro, a strange 9/8 Zen thing called "Jade Visions." Throughout the recordings, you hear the crowd noise: Glasses tinkle and conversation goes on, a counterpoint of forty-year-old flirtation and talk. Orrin Keepnews said, "I remember listening to the tapes and saying, 'There's nothing bad here!' Normally, you can cut one or two things right away, and there was nothing bad."

Two weeks later, on July 6, 1961, Scott LaFaro was driving up Route 20, a back road in those days, to his parents' place in Geneva, upstate. The car skidded and hit a tree, and he was killed instantly. "I was sleeping and the phone rang, and it was Bill," Paul Motian recalled. "He said, 'Scott's dead,' and I said, 'Yeah,' and I went back to sleep. And the next morning I said to my wife, 'Man, I had the weirdest dream last night. I dreamed that Bill called me and said that Scott had been killed!' So I called Bill right away at that apartment over on West Eighty-something to tell him about the dream."

After Scott LaFaro's death, Bill Evans became numb with grief; it took him months to recover, and there are people who think that he never did recover. Paul Motian: "Bill was in a state of shock. Look at my gig book: nothing, nothing, nothing with Bill, until December. Bill was like a ghost."

"All jazz records," Orrin Keepnews said, "have two lives, one in their time and another twenty-two years later. What no one could have imagined was that the second life would be so large."

Why has that afternoon lasted so long? "You know what I like best on that record?" Paul Motian asked. "The sounds of all those people, glasses and chatter—I mean, I know you're supposed to be very offended and all, but I like it. They're just there and all." Perhaps that's it, or at least, in a complicated way, part of it. Though we're instructed to search for "timelessness" in art, it is life that is truly timeless, the same staggeringly similar run of needs and demands and addictions, again and again, that blend one year into the next and one day into another and February's gig in Detroit into March's in Toronto. It is art that puts a time in place. Art is the part of culture that depends most entirely on time, on knowing exactly when. The emotions it summons belong to the room they were made in, and the city outside the room when they were made. Not a timeless experience of a general emotion but a permanent experience of a particular moment—that is what we want from jazz records and Italian landscapes alike. The gift the record gives us is a reminder that the big sludgy river of time exists first as moments. It gives us back our afternoons.

One of the mysteries of Evans's career is that, after that Sunday, he continued to play "Porgy" over and over again, almost obsessively—but almost always as a solo number. Paul Motian gave this some thought. "I don't think there was any reason—no, wait, I remember something now. While we were listening to that number on the tape, Bill was a wreck, and he kept saying something like 'Listen to Scott's bass, it's like an organ! It sounds so big, it's not real, it's like an organ, I'll never hear that again.' Could that, his always playing it without a bass afterwards, have been a sort of tribute to Scott? I kind of doubt it, but then again, maybe so." When we hear Evans play "Porgy," we are hearing what a good Zen man like Evans would have wanted us to hear, and that is the sound of one hand clapping after the other hand is gone.

The City and the Pillars

That morning the city was as beautiful as it had ever been. Central Park had never seemed so gleaming and luxuriant—the leaves just beginning to fall, and the light on the leaves left on the trees somehow making them at once golden and bright green. A bird-watcher in the Ramble made a list of the birds he saw there, from the northern flicker and the red-eyed vireo to the rose-breasted grosbeak and the Baltimore oriole. "Quite a few migrants around today," he noted happily.

In some schools, it was the first day, and children went off as they do on the first day, with the certainty that this year we will have fun again. That protective bubble that, for the past decade or so, had settled over the city, and that we had come home to with a bubble's transparency and bright highlights, still seemed to be in place above us. We always knew that that bubble would burst, but we imagined it bursting as bubbles do: No one will be hurt, we thought, or they will be hurt only as people are hurt when bubbles burst, a little soap in your mouth. It seemed safely in place for another day as the children walked to school. The stockbroker fathers delivered—no, inserted—their kids into school as they always do, racing downtown, their cell phones already at work, like cartoons waiting for their usual morning caption: EXASPERATED AT 8 A.M.

A little while later, a writer who happened to be downtown saw a flock of pigeons rise, high and fast, and thought, *Why are the pigeons rising?* It was only seconds before he realized that the pigeons had felt the wave of the concussion before he heard the sound. In the same way, the shock wave hit us before the sound, the image before our understanding. For the lucky ones, the day from then on was spent in a strange, calm, and soul-emptying back-and-forth between the impossible images on television and the usual things on the street.

Around noon, a lot of people crowded around a lamppost on Madison, right underneath a poster announcing the Wayne Thiebaud show at the Whitney: all those cakes, as if to signal the impotence of our abundance. The impotence of our abundance! In the uptown supermarkets, people began to shop. It was a hoarding instinct, of course, though oddly not brought on by any sense of panic; certainly no one on television or radio was suggesting that people needed to hoard. Yet people had the instinct to do it, and in any case, in New York the instinct to hoard quickly seemed to shade over into the instinct to consume, shop for anything, shop because it might be a comfort. One woman emerged from a Gristede's on Lexington with a bottle of olive oil and said, "I had to get *something*." Mostly, people bought water—bottled water, French and Italian—and many people, waiting in the long lines, had Armageddon baskets: the Manhattan version, carts filled with steaks, Häagen-Dazs, and butter. Many of the carts held the goods of the bubble decade, hothouse goods: flavored balsamics and cappellini and arugula. There was no logic to it, as one man pointed out in that testy, superior, patient tone: "If trucks can't get through, the army will take over and give everybody K rations or some crazy thing; if they do, this won't matter." Someone asked him what was he doing uptown? He had been down there, gotten out before the building collapsed, and walked up.

People seemed not so much to suspend the rituals of normalcy as to carry on with them in a kind of bemusement—as though to reject the image on the screen, as though to say, *That's there, we're here, they're not here yet*, it's *not here yet*. "Everything turns away quite leisurely from the disaster," Auden wrote about a painting of Icarus falling from the sky; now we know why they turned away—they saw the boy falling from the sky, sure enough, but they did not know what to do about it. If we do the things we know how to do, New Yorkers thought, then what has happened will matter less.

The streets and parks were thinned of people, but New York is so dense—an experiment in density, really, as Venice is an experiment in water—that the thinning just produced the normal density of Philadelphia or Baltimore. It added to the odd calm. "You wouldn't put it in a book," a young man with an accent said to a girl in the park, and then he added, "Do you like to ski?" Giorgio Armani was in the park—Giorgio Armani? Yes, right behind the Metropolitan Museum, with his entourage, beautiful Italian boys and girls in tight white T-shirts. *"Cinema,"* he kept saying, his hands moving back and forth like an accordion player's. *"Cinema."*

Even urban geography is destiny, and New York, a long thin island, cuts off downtown from uptown, west side from east. (And a kind of moral miniaturization is always at work, as we try unconsciously to seal ourselves from the disaster: People in Europe say "America attacked" and people in America say "New York attacked" and people in New York think "Downtown attacked.") For the financial community, this was the Somme; it was impossible not to know someone inside that building, or thrown from it. Whole companies, tiny civilizations, an entire zip code vanished. Yet those of us outside that world, hovering in midtown, were connected to the people dying in the towers only by New York's uniquely straight lines of sight—you looked right down Fifth Avenue and saw that strange, still, neat package of white smoke.

The city has never been so clearly, so surreally, sectioned as it became on Wednesday and Thursday. From uptown all the way down to Fourteenth Street, life is almost entirely normal—fewer cars, perhaps, one note quieter on the street, but children and moms and hot-dog vendors on nearly every corner. In the flower district, the wholesalers unpack autumn branches from the boxes they arrived in this morning. "That came over the bridge?" someone asks, surprised at the thought of a truck driver waiting patiently for hours just to bring in blossoming autumn branches. The vendor nods.

At Fourteenth Street, one suddenly enters the zone of the missing, of mourning not yet acknowledged. It is, in a way, almost helpful to walk in that strange new village, since the concussion wave of fear that has been sucking us in since Tuesday is replaced with an outward ripple of grief and need, something human to hold on to. The stanchions and walls are plastered with homemade color-Xerox posters, smiling snapshots above, a text below, searching for the missing: "Roger Mark Rasweiler. Missing. One WTC, 100th floor." "We Need Your Help: Giovanna 'Gennie' Gambale." "We're Looking for Kevin M. Williams, 104th Fl. WTC." "Have You Seen Him? Robert 'Bob' Dewitt." "Ed Feldman—Call Ross." "Millan Rustillo—Missing WTC." Every lost face is smiling, caught at Disney World or Miami Beach, on vacation. Every poster lovingly notes the missing person's height and weight to the last ounce and inch. "Clown tattoo on right shoulder," one says. On two different posters, there is an apologetic note along with the holiday snap: "Was Not Wearing Sunglasses on Tuesday."

Those are the ones who've gone missing. On television, the reporters keep talking about the World Trade Center as a powerful symbol of American financial power. And yet it was, in large part, the back office of Wall Street. As Eric Darton showed in his fine social history of the towers, they were less a symbol of America's financial might than a symbol of the Port Authority's old inferiority complex. It was not the citadel of capitalism but, according to the real order of things in the capitalist world, just a come-on—a desperate scheme dreamed up in the late fifties to bring businesses back downtown. In later years, of course, downtown New York became the center of world trade, for reasons that basically had nothing to do with the World Trade Center, so that now Morgan Stanley and Cantor Fitzgerald were there, but for a long time, it was also a big state office building where you went to get a document stamped or a license renewed. No one loved the buildings save children, who took to them because they were iconically so simple, so tall and two. When a child tried to draw New York, he would draw the simplest available icons: two rectangles and an airplane going by them.

Near Washington Square, the streets empty out, and the square itself is beautiful again. "I saw it coming," a bicycle messenger says. "I thought it was going to take off the top of that building." He points to the little Venetian-style campanile on Washington Square South. The Village seems like a village. In a restaurant on Washington Place at ten-thirty, the sous-chefs are quietly prepping for lunch, with the chairs still on all the tables and the front door open and unguarded. "We're going to try and do dinner today," one of the chefs says. A grown woman rides a scooter down the middle of La Guardia Place. Several café owners, or workers, go through the familiar act of hosing down the sidewalk. With the light pall of smoke hanging over everything, this everyday job becomes somehow cheering, cleansing. If you enter one of the open cafés and order a meal, the familiar dialogue—"And a green salad with that." "You mean a side salad?" "Yeah, that'd be fine. . . . What kind of dressing do you have?"—feels reassuring, too, another calming routine.

Houston Street is the dividing line, the place where the world begins to end. In Soho, there is almost no one on the street. No one is allowed on the streets except residents, and they are hidden in their lofts. Nothing is visible except the cloud of white smoke and soot that blows from the dense stillness below Canal. An art critic and a museum curator watched the explosions from right here. "It was a sound like two trucks crashing on Canal, no louder than that, than something coming by terribly fast, and the building was struck," the critic said. "I thought, *This is it, mate, the nuclear attack, I'm going to die*. I was peaceful about it, though. But then the flame subsided, and then the building fell." The critic and the curator watched it fall together. Decades had passed in that neighborhood where people insisted that now everything was spectacle, nothing had meaning. Now there was a spectacle, and it *meant*.

The smell, which fills the empty streets of Soho from Houston to Canal, blew uptown on Wednesday night and is not sufficiently horrible from a reasonable distance—almost like the smell of smoked mozzarella, a smell of the bubble time. Closer in, it becomes acrid and unbreathable. The white particulate smoke seems to wreathe the empty streets, to wrap right around them. The authorities call this the "frozen zone." In *The Narrative of Arthur Gordon Pym of Nantucket*, spookiest and most cryptic of Poe's writings, a man approaches the extremity of existence, the pole beneath the South Pole. "The whole ashy material fell now continually around us," he records in his diary, "and in vast quantities. The range of vapor to the southward had arisen prodigiously in the horizon, and began to assume more distinctness of form. I can liken it to nothing but a limitless cataract, rolling silently into the sea from some immense and far-distant rampart in the heaven. The gigantic curtain ranged along the whole extent of the southern horizon. It emitted no sound." Poe, whose house around here was torn down not long ago, is a realist now.

More than any other city, New York exists at once as a city of symbols and associations, literary and artistic, and as a city of real things. This is an emotional truth, of course—New York is a city of wacky dreams and of disillusioning realities. But it is also a plain, straightforward architectural truth, a visual truth, a material truth. The city looks one way from a distance, a skyline full of symbols, inviting pilgrims and Visigoths, and another way up close, a city full of people. The Empire State and Chrysler buildings exist as symbols of thirties materialism and as abstract ideas of skyscrapers and as big dowdy office buildings—a sign and then a thing and then a sign and then a thing and then a sign, going back and forth all the time. (It is possible to transact business in the Empire State Building and only then nudge yourself and think, *Oh, yeah, this is the Empire State Building.*) The World Trade Center existed both as a thrilling double exclamation point at the end of the island and as a rotten place to have to go and get your card stamped, your registration renewed.

The pleasure of living in New York has always been the pleasure of living in both cities at once: the symbolic city of symbolic statements (this is big, I am rich, get me) and the everyday city of necessities, MetroCards and coffee shops and long waits and longer trudges. On the afternoon of that day, the symbolic city, the city that the men in the planes had attacked, seemed much less important than the real city, where the people in the towers lived. The bubble is gone, but the city beneath—naked now in a new way, not startling but vulnerable—seemed somehow to increase in our affection, our allegiance. On the day they did it, New Yorkers walked the streets without, really, any sense of "purpose" or "pride" but with the kind of tender necessary patriotism that lies in just persisting.

New York, E. B. White wrote in 1949, holds a steady, irresistible charm for perverted dreamers of destruction, because it seems so impossible. "The intimation of mortality is part of New York now," he went on to write, "in the sound of jets overhead." We have heard the jets now, and we will probably never be able to regard the city with quite the same exasperated, ironic affection we had for it before. Yet on the evening of the day, one couldn't walk through Central Park, or down Seventh Avenue, or across an empty but hardly sinister Times Square—past the light on the trees, or the kids on their scooters, or the people sitting worried in the outdoor restaurants with menus, frowning, as New Yorkers always do, as though they had never seen a menu before—without feeling a surprising rush of devotion to the actual New York, Our Lady of the Subways, New York as it is. It is the symbolic city that draws us here, and the real city that keeps us. It seems hard but important to believe that city will go on, because we now know what it would be like to lose it, and it feels like losing life itself.

Urban Renewal

Last week you could walk almost anywhere you wanted to in New York if you had the sneakers and the time, and what you saw when you were walking looked different from what you saw when you watched television. Things looked older and, on the whole, better. The Wall Street canyon on Monday morning, just before the market opened, for instance, looked as though it had come from another time—several other times, in fact. It was as if the urban landscape, the look of the city itself, had collapsed back into its historical parts, gone searching in another time for a new meaning. The ruins of the Trade Center, glimpsed from the corner, looked like the ruins of a Gothic cathedral, Reims, in World War I. The Gothic tracery that had been the towers' one concession to ornament had dignified them in death. On the other hand, the narrow valleys of streets, emptied of cars and caked with white dust, looked as if they belonged to the early part of the last century. The dust caught the light and turned it into beams, and filled the canyons in searchlight columns, making the buildings behind look like old photographs of themselves. Even the music playing seemed to belong to another time. Someone had, weirdly, placed loudspeakers outside the Federal Reserve Bank building, and all morning they were blaring out martial music—American martial music, the marches of John Philip Sousa. First came "The Stars and Stripes Forever" and "Hands Across the Sea," but then came "The Liberty Bell March," which has been known for the past thirty years exclusively as the theme from *Monty Python's Flying Circus.* For three or four minutes, the Monty Python theme dominated the streets of lower Manhattan.

Everyone in New York is desperately looking for a way out of mourning, a path toward healing, and the sign of "healing," we are told, is "normalcy"—but, like an unstable compound, normalcy tends to break down quickly into its component human elements of routine and absurdity and fatuousness, which, when they appear, seem like an insult to mourning. And so, as people catch themselves smiling or laughing at the wacky music or just walking along and humming, they return, guiltily, to mourning—which in turn demands healing, whose sign is normalcy, which shows itself in routine and absurdity and fatuousness, those insults to mourning. . . . It is a strange cycle, and New Yorkers were riding it up and down this Monday morning like a wave.

The reporters who crowded the streets had three stories to tell: Life Goes On, Life Does Not Go On, and Does Life Go On or Not? "Are there weddings going on in there?" one reporter asked, gesturing at the Municipal Building and seeing images of recuperation and paper carnations, life in the midst of loss. But there weren't, and she kept plugging down Broadway toward Wall Street. A crowd of onlookers, an anonymous sneaker-and-windbreaker crowd, followed the first ranks of stockbrokers and messengers and reporters as they surged downtown. Peddlers sold T-shirts: five-fifty for one that showed the towers and an American flag waving; two-fifty for a hat with just the flag. In a way, people were there to gawk, and as they came downtown through the beautiful morning light, they were judiciously allowed one gape each at the corner of New and Wall, where you could see the ruins. "Okay, move along there, you've seen it, let's just move along," the cops said peaceably. The people looked down the street at the place where the towers had been—not seeing much, just the fencelike facades that still stood at odd, expressionist angles—and then walked on. Photographers turned toward the crowd and took pictures of the people looking at the ruins, and the people looking at the ruins looked back over their shoulders, trying to figure out what the photographers were taking pictures of. In another way, people had come not to gawk but to see—to see if life would go on or not, and what was reassuring was that they were not allowed to gawk. The cops sounded neither more nor less emotional than they ever do—sounded, in fact, like the salesladies on the eighth floor at Saks on the day the Christmas tree is lit, letting the nightgown shoppers stare for a moment into Rockefeller Center. Officiousness is one more form of normalcy.

What is so difficult is the scale of the disaster: both greater than you can imagine and smaller than you can believe. There is so much left, so many tall glass towers, that if you didn't know something vital was missing, you would never guess it. The huge pile into which the towers crumbled looks like what it is, a vast and terrifying graveyard. But just across the street, not fifty feet from the site, stands a building with an ad for E*Trade painted on it: FINALLY, A PLACE ON MADISON AVENUE WHERE YOU CAN INVEST MONEY, INSTEAD OF SPEND IT. It's as though the sinking of the *Titanic* had taken place right beside a subway station and been watched by a frightened or curious crowd who saw something unbelievable, the great ship listing and rising up and breaking in two and the people falling from the funnel, and then walked home from the disaster and showed their families that their hands were still cold from touching the iceberg.

Although you were officially required to show that you worked on Wall Street to get there, a less than intrepid reporter wandered around, found himself following a group of National Guardsmen along William Street, talked to them briefly (they wanted a beer), and then, meandering up the first big street he came to, found himself directly beneath the big flag on the front of the Stock Exchange. Brokers in blue jackets were standing there, taking a cigarette break. "Your shoelace is untied," a cop said, disgusted, and moved him along. At some semiconscious level, the decision had been made to let life go on. Normalcy is basically incompatible with security. Either life will go on or it won't, and if it does, it will go on as life, with its shoelaces untied and an unexpected back way to the destination.

Inside, the brokers were saying what their country was worth, and the country was asking them not to. As you talked to brokers coming out of the exchange, they would begin by telling you the truth—"Well, we were headed downhill already, and so this is really just . . ." And then they'd stop themselves and say, "This is a great day for America. The fact we're open." Though a stock exchange is part of civil society, it is not a civic-minded place in the conventional sense of the term: It is not about people pulling together for the common good but about people pulling apart to pursue their own interests in the long-term faith that the common goodwill eventually emerge someplace out there, in the form of buildings and wealth. A stock market exists to make bets on what will happen, and since what has happened has for so long been what we want, the idea of hope has gotten stuck on it like a decal. On Monday, though, the brokers knew that a disaster had been made to happen within a few feet of where they were standing by people who hated everything they stood for. We were asking them that morning to bet it wouldn't make a difference to what would happen next. They decided to bet it would.

At the Javits Center, where the Federal Emergency Management Agency (FEMA) and the National Guard are keeping their spirits up, the vast main atrium is empty. But there are to be a couple of press conferences downstairs, where someone has found the only cramped and dingy-seeming room in the huge well of light and space. A lectern has been placed up on a dais, with a blue cloth behind it and American and New York City flags all around. National Guardsmen hover at one side of the stage, men in their forties and fifties (the younger ones are downtown) who, in combat fatigues, look costumed for a G.I. Joe party. State troopers with Smokey Bear hats have created a hangout on the other side; they, too, look incongruous indoors. "You keep expecting them to pull you over for speeding," someone says.

The first press conference turns out to be an announcement by Governor George Pataki that the penalty for aiding terrorists will now be raised in New York, and is followed by a press conference for "Auction for America," on eBay. Even though the mayor—who has, in a week, become an international figure, the Churchill of the moment—is to be present, the press conference is sparsely attended, with the rows of bridge chairs only half full. Governor Pataki, a very tall man, says that spirits in the city are higher now than they've ever been, and then he introduces the head of eBay and executives of Visa and MasterCard, who have promised the "waiving of the fees" for the eBay auction. The auction will be a hundred-day event intended to raise $100 million. The executives get up and speak in the new language of the disaster. They offer their deepest sympathies for the victims of the atrocious event, along with their thoughts and prayers, and congratulate those involved with the auction for their great team effort. They use the expression "waiving of the fees" again and again, as though it came from the Bible.

When Rudy Giuliani arrives, the temperature changes. Seen up close, the mayor seems to have collapsed in on himself, becoming stooped and gray; his shoulders hunch, and in repose he has not the fed-on-organ-meat look of a man of power, as Governor Pataki does, but the bowed and nervous look of an earlier generation of politician. In his round wire-rimmed glasses and baggy suit, he is like a figure from the era before charisma. He stands with his hands clasped in front of him, rocking a little. It is possible, in this moment, to sense the real source of his authority: He lacks imagination, genuinely does not care about appearances, is not self-conscious about the effect he is making, and has the crucial ability to know just how grave things are and, at some decent level, not be overwhelmed. Where the governor carefully modulates his voice, trying to deepen it when he mentions the families and find a note of rueful optimism when he is being ruefully optimistic, Giuliani rises to the occasion because he is not ruled by a sense of occasion. He is not a good actor. He is just a public man, a mayor.

Someone asks the mayor about the costs of rebuilding, and he says simply, "They're incalculable. We've never had an attack of this dimension." For a moment the smell of the white soot from downtown seems to fill the room. Another reporter asks what the mayor will donate to the auction, and he stops to think and brood. "Let me see," he says. Then his face brightens. "I know! I'll donate my Yogi Berra baseball. He gave it to me on his day at Yankee Stadium, at the last perfect game." Someone passes him a piece of paper, and he brightens even more. It seems that someone is "donating the 1999 baseball that was the final out of the Series—it was the final out of the twentieth century!" Happily, he repeats, "The final out of the twentieth century."

. . .

There has been a rash of street poetry pasted up on walls. At least two pastiches of *How the Grinch Stole Christmas* have appeared. One, called "How the Binch Stole Christmas," tells how a Binch decided to stop the singing in Uville:

> *"I must stop that singing," Binch said with a smirk.*
> *And he had an idea—an idea that might work.*
> *The Binch stole some U airplanes in U morning hours*
> *And crashed them right into the Uville twin towers.*
> *"They'll wake to disaster," he snickered so sour.*
> *"And how can they sing when they can't find a tower?"*
> *They do, of course.*

At a higher level, W. H. Auden's poem "September 1, 1939" has been circulating in the city like a text by Nostradamus. It was quoted on the editorial page of the *Post* (in the same issue that offered readers a "Wanted Dead or Alive" poster of Osama bin Laden), posted in a forum on the Academy of American Poets website, and read aloud on NPR. (One writer says that he received it as an e-mail six times within the week.) This is the poem about the onset of World War II. The poet, in exile from London, sits "in one of the dives / On Fifty-second Street" as the hopes of a "low dishonest decade" expire and "The unmentionable odour of death / Offends the September night." He sees an enemy gone mad in the worship of a psychopathic god, confronts

> *the lie of Authority,*
> *Whose buildings grope the sky,*

and decides that "we must love one another or die." Composed "of Eros and of dust," he prays to "show an affirming flame."

Auden, whose "Funeral Blues" became the semiofficial poem of AIDS in the eighties, seems confirmed as the preeminent elegist of our time. Yet "September 1, 1939" was one of the poems that he banished from his collected works, as too sonorous and false (we are all going to die whether we love one another or not). The poem, as Joseph Brodsky once pointed out, is really about shame—about how cultures are infected by overwhelming feelings of shame, their "habit-forming pain," and seek to escape those feelings through violence. What drives men mad—drives them to psychopathic gods—is the unbearable feeling of having been humiliated. The alternative, the poem says, is not to construct our own narrative of shame and redemption, which never really comes in any case, but to follow our authentic self-interest, which means being in touch with the reality of what is and is not actually possible in the world. Although a lot of people have said that the attack marks the end of irony, this poem of the moment is actually in favor of irony. That affirming flame begins, ironically, as "ironic points of light," meaning the skeptical clarity that sees the world as it is, rather than as our fears would make it. The crucial movement in the poem is not from decadence to renewal but from symbols to people and from rhetoric to speech. "All I have is a voice," the poet says, "to undo the folded lie."

The dive in the poem, as it happens, was a gay bar and cabaret on Fifty-second Street called Dizzy's, once, apparently, a wild place. If you go at night, after many hours on foot, and stand on West Fifty-second Street where Auden imagined the poem, you find that Dizzy's is gone, and so is the townhouse it was in. Now there is just another mute lit tower groping the sky, and hoping the sky won't grope back.

Second Thanksgiving: Intensities

It is hard to explain how much the sounds have changed in meaning. The small, constant din of density that we noticed all last year—the cars snorting at intersections, the harrumph and burst of a motorcycle, the helicopter hovering, the three-in-the-morning sound of the bus rushing up the avenue, heaving and rumbling—all have altered in possible meaning, in what they could portend. You wake up at night, hear the bus, and think, *Is that a bus, or a plane, or a . . . ?* We scan the skies for low-flying aviation, sudden experts on cruising altitudes. Anxiety is a stimulant; fear is a hallucinogen and a paralytic—it makes you imagine things that aren't happening and then freeze in the face of your own imaginings.

We had two parties for the two children; one on September 10, for Luke, and one on September 11, for Olivia. The one on the tenth was better. Luke has now read Harry Potter, so we had a Harry Potter party. We had been planning for it all summer.

"Are there any wizards in *Harry Potter*?" Martha, a *Potter* non-reader, asked innocently. Luke and I paused in wonder and then broke up in cruel guffaws. "Are there wizards in *Harry Potter*!" we said.

It had been a wonderful summer, the best. There were fireflies in the air and black seals in the ocean water. The fireflies had been out in force near the park all summer long. If you took a walk up Fifth Avenue alongside the park, they were everywhere: floating in and out of the twilight along the cobbled sidewalk near the park, resting invisibly among the twigs in the gutters, hovering around the doormen at epaulet level. They were out elsewhere, too, of course: Everywhere in and around Central Park was dense with them. But there was something piquant about their presence on Fifth. They were the only creatures living there who have not had to seek approval first. They were this year's Razor scooter, the thing that every child wants. Luke set off for Fifth Avenue in the Nineties one night, jar in hand—actually, it was a plastic receptacle that had held take-out chicken vindaloo the night before—and stalked his prey. (It was not very good sport, since fireflies are almost ridiculously easy to catch: You can pluck them out of the air gently with your hand and hold them there.) The summer's fireflies glowed green, and only when they wanted to. The green was a strange X-Men kind of green, the color of the aureole that comic-book artists used to draw to suggest mutancy, radioactivity—the chartreuse glow that engulfed Bruce Banner as he became the Incredible Hulk. The folk explanation for the abundance of fireflies was that they were here because the mosquitoes were not. Last summer's West Nile spraying, the legend goes, had eliminated the bloodsuckers and left a niche for the fireflies. Last summer's bug was the whine in the ear of an imperial city, reminding us how vulnerable we are. This summer's was a consolation, and all the things we would still like to be: sexy yet reticent, and bringing its own gilding to a drier season.

And then, on our two weeks by the sea, there were seals—real honest-to-goodness big black harbor seals that would come within ten or fifteen feet of the shore. They would just sit there and watch you, mustachioed and skeptical, looking like the uncles in turn-of-the-last-century photographs. You almost expected them to be wearing bathing costumes, like in a Chaplin film: striped suits with long pant legs and bare arms.

We took pictures of our family and our friends all summer, and planned the Harry Potter party. I would play—I was drafted into playing—Dumbledore, the head of Hogwarts, and I'd do a little magic show. I have my doubts about Dumbledore. Although he is relentlessly good and wise, he seems strangely lax in his administration. He allows the Slytherin house nearly free reign in Evil; tolerates the malicious Professor Snape; and generally intervenes only at the very last possible second when Harry is facing a hippogriff or a basilisk or the all-evil Voldemort. I am instinctively a religious conservative: I want God, Dumbledore, just to take care of it, to intervene before the evil takes place. But he can't, or won't.

The party was fine. The kids played pin the snitch on the Quidditch broom, and pass the broomstick, and lots of other games, and there was a green Ridgeback dragon piñata. I failed rather grandly as Dumbledore, doing magic, sweating through the artificial robe and unbelievably scratchy white beard. The kids all knew how the tricks were done and let me know it—not aggressively, but sore with boredom. Sorry, Luke's Dad, I've seen that one. I felt a little exasperated with New York children, their knowingness and their knowing too much too soon—their lacking, at times, the sensitivity that goes with being a little fearful of the world, that look you see in French kids' eyes that reflects their knowledge that the world is a difficult and demanding place.

We went to bed thinking, *God, this two-birthday business is a marathon.*

Olivia slept through the whole thing, taking her morning nap. We stumbled out onto the street with half a crazy thought of laying in provisions. I ran into David Del Guiso, a friend in wordless shock who happened to be carrying a big brown paper package, which I knew was the framed version of a French etching of a white woman stretched out on a blanket in the forest of Fontainebleu, her back turned. I had bought it for Martha one Christmas. He had framed it for us, and now he handed it to me, and, perplexed and cheerless and robotic, we hung it up. It looked wonderful; she looked wonderful. Then I walked downtown. The pile of presents stood on the table. Later, we got back the summer snapshots and found that there was something wrong with the camera; all of them, all, had a black band cutting the picture in three, two thirds cheer and then a marked black stripe cutting off the image of good times. Everyone forgot about the fireflies.

. . .

Early Thursday morning, a friend brought me into the Emergency Operations Center, which had been set up on Fifty-fourth Street, right by the river. The intended command center had been, with an irony that was almost unbearable, in 7 World Trade Center and had been destroyed. People who had seen it before said that it was very fine, with light-up maps and signals that told you the condition of every traffic light in the five boroughs. The city people had been given two days to create a new center from scratch.

They have been mapping every day, the mapmaker tells me, flying over the site, taking pictures, and then translating them into schematics. "It's a very dynamic site," he says drily. It is hard to give a sense of how virtuous they seem. These are the city men who live in a world where it is always 1961. Every morning they send out an aerial camera to see exactly how the destruction lies and what lies beneath. They treat it as a challenge in mapping. Only they know the precise, impossibly intricate pattern of cables and pipes and sewers and tunnels and lines. They don't stop; they don't grieve or mourn or melodramatize. They just work.

These, of course, are the bureaucrats, the deadwood employees of a socialized state for whom everyone had contempt, and who were being made obsolete, we were told, obsolete by the forces of the New Economy. Now, as that world cowers, or at least is paralyzed, it is the City Men, of all improbable people, who come to the rescue. The infrastructure of New York has turned out to be solid and resourceful, which one would have guessed if one had spent time with the mapmakers in the first place. The firemen first, and then the policemen—but it was the mapmakers and the engineers and all of the anonymous bureaucrats in loosened ties and white shirts and gray flannels, the women in suits, who held us together and stitched up the wounds when everything was coming apart. Alan says to me, "I never want to meet another guy who talks about deadwood in the bloated city bureaucracy," as he looks out over the vast, hastily assembled, room full of energy. The public had come to the rescue of the private and, to its credit, did not jeer at the private's incapacities or impotence or weakness, as the private had so often done to the public.

Later that day, I bump into F.A., the Arabist, and we have a talk about What Is to Be Done. I ask him if there is anything we can do about madmen who worship psychopathic gods. And he says something obvious but interesting: that there's nothing to be done about the core, the real nuts, but they exist, as human beings must, within concentric circles of culture: an immediate circle of murder-minded sympathizers and financiers; a circle just outside that of sympathizers who would not do such things themselves but will not stop them from happening; a circle beyond that of people who choose not to know what is being done but sympathize with the radical purpose; a circle beyond that one of the fearful and even sentimentally sympathetic—on and on, each circle of culture outside the actual nucleus of evil a little larger and a little less regular in its orbit than the one before, and therefore able to be dried up, reduced, set loose. Attack and persuade the outer circles of culture to abandon the inner circles, and eventually, the core will be all alone, isolated and futile.

It occurred to me, going home—taxicab responses, the New York version of the *esprit d'escalier*—that the city men, the firemen and policemen and city workers, live in concentric circles of culture, too. The simple, unimaginable bravery—going up the stairs toward the fire while everyone else was going down, away—was possible only because of the other firemen, who could not be let down, and then the brothers and fathers and sisters who shared their job and expected them to do this and would have been let down if they hadn't, and then the still wider circle of New York working-class culture, with its odd combination of skepticism and solidarity, on and on, circles saying, in this case, *Yeah, we do this.* It was a moment of self-definition: a true hero doesn't *want* to be one, he just is one. Their culture turned out to be far stronger than anyone would have known or guessed.

All the little rituals of New York are enacted more mindfully now: from the breakfast special in a coffee shop to pizza on Saturday night to the way people never know how to pay when they get on a bus to the way they pull out tables in their living rooms to dine. I've always liked Howells's comparison of New York and Venice but thought it a sport, a conceit. Now it seems suddenly real: It's amazing, this city as dense as that city is wet, and you can imagine it engulfed by water.

We try to control the uncontrollable through small acts of organization and domestic continuity. We have dinner every Saturday night with friends, the M's, as reliably as any family might have had dinner in Winesburg, Ohio, a standing date for a covered-dish supper. All across the city one hears about such retreats, though one also hears, enviously, that among the preparental group, it takes the form of passionate, unimpeded coupling, "terror sex," sex made more exciting by fear. The child-laden instead have terror dining. Perhaps there is a lucky couple somewhere having both, terror sex with terror dining afterward; we make do, as our class cohort always has, with food alone.

But what do you tell the children, what do you do with the children, what do you do *for* them? Do you level with them, protect them, or engage them? Our dear Deb K. decided to act. She took Luke's friend Jacob to Pakistan to deliver in person the money that their class had collected on behalf of Afghan refugee children. Admirable courage and proper aplomb. But we refused to send Luke along—Martha won't let him cross the street alone, much less send him halfway around the world on a mission of emergency relief. And there are parents who want . . . *nothing,* no news, no fright, only insulation and postponement. There was a prayer meeting, though not called so, in the church around the corner, where the firemen paraded down to a standing ovation from the children and the parents. The firemen looked embarrassed, but the children seemed glad to have someone to applaud.

In the end, the children figure it out for themselves. They find their own models and formulate their own hypotheses, theories of the immediate world that might explain the larger and perplexing one outside. They are mindful but not careworn. After the towers fell, for instance, Luke became absorbed in playing chess, and then he became a Yankees fan, and I watched him use both these things, in different ways, to steady himself, to seek and grope and understand, and even to steady us.

How much he grasped, how much he knew, I couldn't be sure. Did he play chess in "reaction"? I don't know. He is a seven-year-old boy in a school where chess has a large, perhaps overlarge, place; but I do know that he was frightened, a little, and was glad to have a game, to have anything, that he could control. We had, in the end, tried, as every parent did, to soft-pedal the disaster without sweet-talking it; to let him know what had happened without letting him see too clearly the unthinkable abyss of malice and nihilistic hatred that could produce it; to let him know that something terrible had happened in the city without making him think that something terrifying had permanently entered his world. We tried to conceal from him our fears, so different from our anxieties, which, like any child, he has long ago learned to notice and discount. (Children don't mind if their parents are worried; they expect it—parents are there to worry. But they notice at once if their parents are afraid, for that is what parents are never to be.)

Luke looks soberly at us, as all children do now, in part for reassurance: "Like, if there's a war, they have no chance, right? Our army is much bigger than their army?" "Well, they don't really have an army," the father begins, before recalling that what is wanted here is reassurance, not a page on asymmetrical warfare from Foreign Affairs. Dr. Spock, not Tom Friedman.

So: "Whatever happens, it will all happen far away from here." "How do you know?" "Well, because we're going over there to try and get the bad guys." "Why are we going over there?" "Because that's where they bad guys are." "Well, didn't the bad guys come here?" Well, they did. But the father says only, "We're going to go over there and stop them from being dangerous." "You mean they'll have the war *there*?" "Yeah. I mean, obviously." "Oh," he says, greatly relieved, "I thought it was, like, they would *choose* where to have the war."

And I realize that he knows both far more than I imagine and far less than I realize. He thinks it is a tournament, like a baseball play-off, home and home series. (And, terrifying fact, this may not be so far from the terrible truth; it *is* home and away games.) As he presses the questions, harder and harder, the father is left, finally, with the one-size-fits-all parental explanation: "Don't worry. I know I'm right about this. You just have to trust me."

. . .

Just trust me! Half the time, more than that, as a parent, at the end of long, rational argument, you end up saying, "It's okay. Just trust me." Are we safe? Yes. *Just trust me.* Is there a wolf in the closet? There isn't. How do you know? I know. *Trust me.* Are there tsunamis in New York? Not really. How do you know. Well . . . (long explanation of wind currents and weather patterns, at least half of which the parent knows he's getting wrong). But that doesn't mean there could *never* be a tsunami? No, it doesn't. But there won't be. Just trust me.

"Just trust me" means, first of all, You don't have to worry about this—I know. Or, we shouldn't argue about this—I know. But it means more, too; it means not just, I know more, but I've lived longer, and, most of all, it means something vaguely Dumbledoreish: I can see a small way into the future. It really means not, *I know* . . . but *chances are.* It is a short-term guess disguised as a long-term certainty.

And to some degree a parent *can* see into the future better than a child, although the future the parent can see into isn't often more than a week further: I really do know that there are no monsters in that closet, I really do know that there is morning coming, I really do know that no one has died of a toxic yo-yo and that your mother's back won't break if you step on a crack. But though the parent's guesses about the world and its regularities are reasonably good, pretty solid, and a bit more mature than the child's, the truth is that violence and madness can alter everything and everyone, that the complicated structure of trust on which the liberal city depends—all those cars I wondered at just last year, waiting patiently at the intersection for the tiny light to change color—can be violated in the morning. *Trust me,* the big universal statement, is really a short-term statement, hoping to pass as something larger. *I know there is no monster in that closet* has to be expressed as *I know there are no monsters.* But what if there are?

One part of the parent thinks, Well, I'll level with the child, give him a sense of the landscape of probabilities and odds that are out there governing his anxieties. And the other part thinks, no, the question, after all, isn't *What are the odds?* but *Are you looking out for me?* Not, Are there hidden reefs in this river? but, Are you a reliable pilot in the bridge? And the degree to which you know that you are not reliable—that it is a long confusing river, and the night is dark, and who knows how the hidden landscape has changed overnight—is not something that you can talk about. The children don't trust in your knowledge; they trust in *you,* because, basically, they have to trust in someone. It is not a calculation, but a variant of Pascal's gamble: I better believe in God, because I have nothing to lose if he doesn't exist, and imagine the advantages if he does! The child reasons, If I accept that Dad knows what he's talking about, at least I'll feel safer, for now. What Pascal doesn't say is how God feels about the gambler, which is partly gratitude, and partly love, but also something close to panic. Hey, don't ask me how this universe runs, pal. I'm a stranger here myself. It explains why Dumbledore is so sloppy. *Just trust me* means not *I know* but *I'm trying.*

The impulse within a broken world is to build a small safe place. Chess and chess tournaments offered this, and then, oddly, so did the Yankees. I think Luke would have liked chess in any case, but after the towers chess gave him what everyone has been looking for: a subculture entirely normal and predictable, a round of places to go to, a clean, clear series of wins and losses.

The impulse—to lose yourself in a dependable routine when your world is in many ways fractured and upturned—is common. You could choose eating or sleeping or polemicizing about Islam, or you could choose to learn how to play chess. There are said to be three centers of chess excellence in the city: the private schools, like Artists & Anglers; the Russians in Brighton Beach; and everywhere the Koreans. We saw mostly the upper-crust chess players, and I can't say that they—that we—were an entirely attractive bunch. There was that wise-guy sense of being at the center of the universe, here tied to a cheap kind of expertise. The sensitivity in the eyes of French children is tied to their oppression: The world presents difficulties and problems, ineradicable and near impossible to beat. The French child plays chess every day with an implacable opponent, the School; New York kids play chess when they are playing chess, and the rest of the time they play a game called Your Life, where any move is legal and all gambits earn applause. There is something limiting and civilizing about chess. It opens up into a world of lore and pleasure, it closes down into a business of memorizing openings, and it is decorated by nerdy seven-year-olds working chess computers and looking puzzled. I hope it is only a phase for Luke, but I think it is a good phase.

I am invested in his chess playing. Fiercely competitive myself, I must physically hold back my desire for him to win, my moment's disappointment when he doesn't. He manages it much better than I do. It's been a good experience for both of us, and when he brought home his first trophy—second place! second, but still an accomplishment, three games out of four won—it was a fine moment for all of us. I like his chess teacher, an Eastern European who wears a tie and a wool suit in every circumstance and weather and hisses out his instructions and plans. I have always been terrible at chess, too impatient and too restless and too blind to the future right around the corner. Luke has whatever the skill or knack is for being good at the game: seeing ahead, planning for the future. When I try to play with him, it becomes obvious that I'm not good enough.

But I also see that being good at chess depends not on a wide-ranging but on a close-observing intelligence. I had imagined the chess prodigy as someone who could see far into the strategic future, all the right moves, but that turned out not to be it. The kids who are really good at chess—much better than Luke—see *less,* in a sense, than normal kids, but they see what they need to see: not some vast series of possible moves but the immediate and short-term encirclements, the four-turns-ahead effect of one move, which will lead to the forced series of moves that might end with a mate. The trick is to see not twelve moves ahead but four forced moves ahead. *I go here, he has to go there, and then I go here, and he has to go here. . . .* It is short-term thinking with a dagger in hand.

I suppose that as they get better, the sequence of forced moves gets longer, but the essential point, I sense, is always tactical, not strategic: From the overwhelming universe of possible moves, you choose one line and follow it. Half the game is sizing up your opponent to see whether he already knows the line or will fall for it, like a seducer sizing up a maiden: Has she heard *this* song before? The innocent moment before the game, when the children shake hands and we beam on them and they pretend to wish their opponents good luck, is, I realize now, the killer moment, the moment when they take each other's measure, reading all the thousand small and nameless clues that faces and fingers provide, and decide: *Yeah, I got him. This he won't have seen before.*

Last Sunday we went to one of the tournaments—the tough one. Luke came back. "I won," he said. He had launched his favorite attack with his bishop and queen, a line that, if you haven't seen it before, is devastating and can even produce a four-move mate. Even if you have seen it before but don't remember precisely the right sequence of defense, it can ruin you; I bear the scars. If you are prepared for it, though, it is trivially easy to defend and leaves the attacker vulnerable, his queen out there exposed like a playmate. Luke next played a slow girl who was taking everything down in proper notation. I settled him in his chair, and, after a long game, he lost. "Girls with notebooks are risky," he said, truer words never having been spoken.

I conscientiously say, "Don't do it if you don't want to," and offer lots of outdoors alternatives, but he always chooses chess. The chess teachers occasionally remind themselves to Generalize About the Benefits of the Game. They say that it is a preparation for life. But in fact, it is a preparation for life only because it involves a comforting illusion. Life is like chess only because in life, too, you seize on a short-term tactic, stick to it, and call it wisdom, until it stops working and you have to learn another.

The two people—the only two people—I know who are not scrambled and shaken by what has happened are Kirk Varnedoe and our neighbor Sally. Both are acutely aware of absurdity and therefore all but imperturbable. Kirk faces the absurdity of illness, while Sally takes as her subject the absurdity of life. They are aligned in this awareness, and aligned as well in the odd, subdued stream of courage their knowledge provides.

Kirk is dying, and this colors his view. Fools that we are, at the end of that happy summer, on a Monday night we went to celebrate his fifth year of being cancer-free, a fine dinner with Volnay and talk about life and art. That very Friday—*that very Friday;* how crazy we were to tempt the demons—he called, his voice shaky.

"How are you?" I tried to boom, expecting, as I'd heard so often in twenty years, his happy, confident booming back.

"Not so well, it seems," he said, calmly but quietly, fear just audible as a tremor beneath the pauses between words. He explained that they had found a shadow on his chest, something that hadn't been there before. We went to the hospital along with Elyn, his wife, and the thoracic surgeon showed us the X-ray and said, "Look, I think it's probably cancer, colon cancer that's spread from the original site, and since it's lining the pneuma, I can't get it out. I'll go in and look, but I suspect that's what it is. I'm sorry."

"This is devastating news," Kirk said simply. They had gone in, and sure enough, that's what it was, colon cancer in the lung, incurable and inoperable. "But treatable," Kirk said positively. "They say it's treatable. Like a great tree with a root system that's been in my body all this time and is now suddenly coming into leaf." A strong image, his own.

We were supposed to have lunch on September 11, but we didn't; they canceled his chemo. But it is Kirk who, looking death right in the face, is filled with confident indignation. "How can they pull this crap?" he says, meaning the cold exploitation of fear. "I'm supposed to put myself in a state of permanent panic and accede to anything these bastards say? Where's the confident spirit? Where's the *American* spirit—you know, Ed Harris in *Apollo 13*." He does a quick impression: " 'Let's . . . work . . . the . . . problem, let's not make things worse by running around in hysterics.' *All* these guys do is work the hysteria." There is an injury, he insists, real but limited, and an imagery, which, placed on a perpetual loop, can never be escaped. "The thing to do is not to give way to fear in a way that reduces the possibilities of life."

Of course he knows, and I do, too, that he has internalized the historical circumstances to the personal fact. Calculating odds, working the problem, is all that stands between him and despair. "Those were my two lungs up there," he says grimly, and I know what he means, and that his two lungs will not stand long, either.

He is unrattled, though, and has been from the first day. "Don't tell me about God saving America, because God saving somebody was what those guys in the planes were all about," he said in the interview we did when, after he got the news, he decided to leave the museum and go to Princeton to get a couple of years of coherent intellectual work done. He has the courage and the heedlessness of someone who can speak without fear because he is not afraid of *saying things;* saying the wrong thing is the least of his fears. We went, the six of us, to see the Richard Serra pieces in Chelsea, and the children ran through them, and he admired them, and we took common pleasure in the tangible, the necessary, the real—in things that kids can run around and art historians can debate. "I refute it thus," Dr. Johnson said, kicking his stone in empirical defiance of Bishop Berkeley's idealism. We refute it—the horror—thus, by kicking a big torqued ellipsis around in our heads, and with our eyes, and then going to lunch to debate it.

People who look mortality in the face every day have kinds of wisdom that may be acquired, even by those of us who try never to look it in the face until we have to.

Sally, on the other hand, seems unrattled because it is hard to rattle her about anything. She has a different spiritual gift, less noble, perhaps, than that of a wise man facing death, but just as real: She has the steady optimism that comes of a pervasive, cheerful cynicism about life and human motive. When the panicky conversations about leaving and moving and running away begin, Sally simply sits at the dinner table, never eating—perpetually, metaphysically dieting, she never does, we used to send the children upstairs with waffles only to find that it made her squirm—just looking on, puzzled. The look on her face when people talk this talk isn't disagreement, and it is certainly not denial; it's a kind of amusement, a wit that is the elegance of realism. For Kirk, future certainty has become absurd; for Sally, future certainty is *obviously* absurd, so why pretend that it isn't? You're *not* leaving New York; it's too much work. You're not joining the army, because you can't. You're not *actually* going to do anything. So what do hysteria and fear get you except the indulgence of hysteria and fear? The dying and the sardonic, comedians and cancer patients, have the gift of four-move thinking: Bad things will happen that you can't imagine, but some good things will surprise you, too. You don't know what's going to happen. Could be worse—it often is. Could be better—it often is, too. Don't think ahead of the game. Compulsively imagining what *might* happen, instead of observing what does, is an insult to reality, and it takes your mental pieces right off the board.

But Luke has become a Yankees fan, too, and, further sign of the strange times, I have not done anything to stop him. People like the Yankees now in a way they didn't only a year ago, and though people like to say it has to do with the players, I am beginning to suspect that the real reason for this affection has more to do with the queer doubleness of New York's symbols right now, and a general inversion of sympathies, than with the Yankees themselves.

What the new love for the Yankees really meant, in fact, only began to become clear for me when Luke started rooting for them. It was just after they had gone down two games to the Oakland A's in the "division championship," a new concept to me after six years away. I will confess that, even then, well into the New Era, I was not much inclined to root for the Yankees. Not even terrorism, I thought, could make me pull for George Steinbrenner *(If you let them make you root for the Yankees, then they've won)*.

I hate the Yankees, even after so many years here, for the reasons that decent people have always hated the Yankees—not because they win (nobody hates the Celtics or my beloved Canadiens) but for their smugness while they do it. Since my return to New York, I had been assured by my friends that these new four-time-champion Yankees were improved, decent Yankees, a better kind of Yankees than the old ones, full of class and poise and team spirit and good manners, a kind of reformed or Protestant Yankees—what a diplomat might even call "moderate Yankees." I knew better; there are no moderate Yankees. There was still enough old Yankees stuff clinging to them—they still played Sinatra singing the only vulgar record that great man ever made, and Steinbrenner, though often invisible, like Dick Cheney, was still there—to keep me from liking them better than decent people ever had. Hating the Yankees had never been forbidden to someone who loved New York; just the opposite, really. Yankees loving was one more optional activity, like clubbing or insider trading. It was available, not compulsory.

Luke, though, fell hard. Chess and the Yankees became his two obsessions, and what touched and intrigued me was that he fell hard exactly when and exactly because they were *losing*. I had always made an exception among Yankees fans for local kids who became fans without, so to speak, knowing any better—who became fans because this was what they believed a home team looked like. Not having the Expos or Royals or Phillies or some real home team to root for—a real home team loses every year, except once—I understood that they had to make do with what was around. (I assumed they hadn't chosen to root for the Mets out of some mistake or wrong turn or subway confusion, borough solidarity by other means.)

We idly watched those first couple of Oakland games together and saw them go down, and Luke asked, "Is it finished?" "No," I said, "it isn't finished—they still have a chance, but they don't have much of a chance. They're as good as finished. They're done." "Oh," he said, and then, more quietly, "I'm sorry they've lost." He was just discovering baseball and, of course, just discovering loss. For years I told Luke a bedtime story about baseball—a story about a six-year-old pitcher for the old Giants—but I don't think he entirely connects the rather rule-bound sport he sees on television with the game we used to tell stories about. We went out with Jacob to see a game this summer—a Mets game—and they had a good time, but I think they mostly had a good hot-dog-and-Dixie-cup time, with the ball game around as mere atmosphere, snacks being to baseball games for seven-year-old boys what sex is to movies for sixteen-year-old boys: the real activity for which the ostensible activity is just the wraparound excuse.

Then, together, we watched the Yankees come back, out there in California—a neat pitching performance, and then Jeter's Play, the fabulous backhanded flip for the key out. Luke rooted like crazy, and I found myself rooting, too. I saw that in the midst of so much emotional confusion at home and at school—mostly inarticulate and veiled but evident all the same—what he was seeing was not one more Yankees October but something better and more personal: the underdog coming back against the odds, the defeated and the depressed getting back up. The Yankees were like the firemen; when all hope was lost, they came through. You're *never* finished. It's not over till it's over, and even when the grown-ups says it's over, it isn't, not really. We can always come back. Losing is for unbelievers.

This was not entirely wrong, of course—resilience is one of the lessons we want kids to take from sports—but I also saw that it was misleading, even a little dangerous. We *don't* get up off the mat, not always; the firemen, limitlessly courageous, were also limitedly effective. Yet rooting for the Yankees is, for Luke—and, I'm told, for lots of other New York kids who have developed a similar affection in recent weeks—one more way of turning a frightening, half-understood moment into a reassuring one. With the doggedness of youth, they have made up a positive story of their own out of whatever they could find lying around—firemen and rescue workers and Derek Jeter—and have chosen to trust in that.

Luke came home the other day and excitedly proposed that we build, in the empty space at the World Trade Center, a new statue: a colossal statue of a Fireman saluting the Lady in the Harbor, a Statue of Bravery to join the Statue of Liberty. I told him it sounded like a fine idea.

This confusion of powerful and powerless (or at least of what we perceive as one or the other) became a general rock-solid proposition for me right around the time the Yankees were beating the Mariners. At a cocktail party, I mouthed off about how shocked I was to find, in my walks around the city, that while working New Yorkers were full of hope—basically feeling that they could take anything as long as they were still around to take it—the elite was panicky, hoarding Cipro and heading out of town. A property tycoon (another Canadian émigré, in fact) who happened to overhear me said pretty gently that he would like to take me on a walk around midtown, and the next day we went.

It was a cold, crisp fall day, and as we looked at all the great glass skyscrapers of Park Avenue—the Seagram Building and Lever House and the Citicorp Center—he unraveled for me the complicated secrets of their financing and construction: how this one depended on a federal bond, and this one on a legendary thirteen-year lease with a balloon payment, and this one on the unreal (and unprofitable) munificence of a single liquor baron and his daughter, and why each of these formulae, which were the real story behind the glass and steel, could not be duplicated right now.

A wind blew, and he wrapped his scarf tighter around his throat. In his eyes, above his fine Aquascutum raincoat and Charvet tie, as he stared up at the glass towers, there was not arrogance but a pleading, worried neediness. A kind of lost love. "I'd build if I could," he said longingly. "I'd love to build. Just show me how to do it." I mimicked his stare, craning my neck, and suddenly, the glass towers, which for all my life, and theirs, had looked phallic and complacent, now looked vulnerable—as though, coy and nymphlike, they wanted to cover themselves and had been robbed of arms with which to do it.

"I'd build if I could," he repeated.

I asked him, sadly, if New York was doomed, and he cheered right up. "Oh, no," he said, his voice again full of quick, gravelly expertise, "not at all." The key long-term demographic fact about the city, he said, lay in the practice of delayed marriage. As long as people were having their first children at thirty-four rather than twenty-four, the city would thrive even in the face of fire and fear and anthrax.

"This is because," he went on, "you can ask thirty-year-olds with children to move to New Jersey, but you can't ask a single thirty-year-old to move out there before he or she has found a mate. He or she would basically rather die. I mean it; a twenty-five-year-old without a mate and with no children would rather face anthrax and terrorists and smallpox than leave the city and take his chance to get laid in the suburbs. He'll go somewhere else and find another job . . . and meanwhile, he's eating in restaurants and buying co-ops, and they're young and fearless, so they're moving into dangerous neighborhoods." He shrugged. "That's the great secret, the key demographic of New York. Kids at twenty-five, cities die; kids at thirty-five, cities thrive. It's just that simple." Everything good that had happened to restore the city, it seemed, rested on that small demographic, that ten-year delay. People in their twenties would rather risk being killed by anthrax or bombs than give up searching for a mate while practice-mating along the way.

This is the rock on which New York has built twenty years of prosperity, and on which it must still build. Sex is not only in the city; from a real estate tycoon's point of view, it *is* the city, all the city's hope. As long as people seek out mates for fifteen years instead of fifteen months, they will need New York.

"So you're an optimist," I said. "So in the long run, New York is fine?"

"No, I'm not an optimist. I'm a— You know that thing of Keynes, how, in the long run, we're all dead? Well, here in New York, in the short run, we're all dead, and we have been for years. But in the long run, we're all fine somehow. Though don't ask me how, or when, or why. And that's always been true, decade after decade. I don't see how we're going to get out of this. But in the long run, we're all fine as long as we're having sex, if you know what I mean. As long as people look for sex for ten years before they start having children, the city will manage. If that changes, we've seen the last tower in our time. But I don't think it will." *Don't worry,* he was saying, *you just have to trust me.*

We went on into the Mariners series, on frigid fall nights not made for baseball. For Luke and his friends, the Yankees were the Mets—no, the Yankees were the Brooklyn Dodgers, the Yankees were the Senators of *Damn Yankees,* the Yankees were my Expos. Where, for almost seventy-five years, to be a Yankee fan was to identify with power, now, suddenly, it was to identify with powerlessness—or rather, seeming powerlessness suddenly empowered: They were down, but they were not out. It was exactly the same feeling I had when I looked up at the skyscrapers and imagined them cowering.

This transformation in perception—the powerful into the powerless, the powerless into the powerful—has great resonance here because New York, pretty much alone among great cities, has always been a two-speed city, one city of power, one city of soul, and all of us racing back and forth between them. That New York has always had two baseball clubs, one clearly marked underdog and one just as clearly marked overdog, is part of that division. The Yankees and the Giants, then the Yankees and the Dodgers, then the Yankees and the Mets—even when the Mets were an overdog back in the eighties, they still made like an underdog. New York is not a Goliath that has become a David; it is a city that combines David and Goliath, and that doubleness is one of the things that draws us to New York. We come here not just or even primarily because we are drawn to power—King of the Hill, Top of the Heap, as they sing at Yankee Stadium—but also because we are intrigued by powerlessness. We come to the city of the overdog in order to have the thrill of feeling like an underdog. Yankee hating, in this way, is an expression of a certain kind of New York loving, a certain kind of New York pride—it is a way of declaring yourself apart from power. When the towers fell and the city wept, many of us thought, in an instant, that it would be the second, David city that we would need to support and cherish.

Now it seems that it was the power city, the symbolic power city, that was wounded and needed to be nursed. It is not so much that the Yankees have become lovable as that the Yankees have become the Mets, just as the Empire State Building has become the Washington Square Mews: an endangered urban artifact that we cherish and protect. The midtown skyscrapers look like naked women, and the Yankees look like hometown boys.

Last Sunday, Luke played in a chess tournament, won only two games (out of four; he usually nails three), and still got a trophy, a big deal with gilt. I was puzzled—it usually takes three games for him to win a trophy—but what the hell. He looked puzzled, too, and put it down to having had to play with black in his last game (it's harder, apparently, because white goes first).

We walked the five blocks home, Luke clutching the enormous trophy in his hand, at first humming and then pausing. I turned it over in my head as we walked, coming eventually to a sense that there must have been a mistake, and decided that we ought to turn back and find out. He was silent, thinking hard. We walked another block, and I decided I was going to turn him back by the time we got to Ninetieth Street.

But it didn't take that long. At the corner of Ninety-second, he stopped. "Let's go back and talk to them. *I'll* do the talking." We marched back, and he said to the organizer, simply, "I think there may have been a mistake." It turned out that there had been a scoring mistake, and the trophy belonged rightly to another, slightly younger child. We got the boy's number and walked his prize over to his apartment building, which, fortunately, wasn't far away, just up on Ninety-sixth.

When the boy opened his door, Luke said, "I think this is yours," and took the other, smaller trophy in exchange. Then they played together for hours. The younger boy had a chess computer that he practiced on, and, sweetly, with a tribal sense of obligation, he insisted on loaning it to Luke for a couple of weeks in exchange for the trophy. It was a beautiful thing, and at dinner that night I made a toast to Luke, saying that for me, of all the trophies he would ever win, the best would always be the trophy he took back.

But we discussed it again the next day, and I asked him, quietly enough, what he thought the Moral of the Incident was—honesty is the best policy, we always feel better when we play fair, etc. He said, ironically but honestly, "To win three games." And I realized that he was being just as honest at that moment as he had been when he'd taken back the trophy.

Virtue is not its own reward; virtue is its own punishment. You have to give back the trophy and get a smaller one. Doing the right thing has real costs, and you do it, essentially, not because of the way it feels inside at that moment—at that moment you want the trophy—but because of the way it will feel inside later, when your friends find out. That was what he had been considering as we walked those blocks. Conscience is not the still, small voice in the soul; it is the name we give to the anticipated opinion of our friends, and the pleasure of having the fruits of the unfair advantage isn't worth the shame of having an unfair advantage. Desire takes place in the trophy room; conscience happens on the street. I now know that it takes about ten minutes, and three New York City blocks, to make itself felt in the mind of a bright, good-natured, competitive seven-year-old.

I recalled that poem by Philip Larkin, the one that begins "None of the books have time / To say how being selfless feels, / They make it sound a superior way / Of getting what you want" and then goes on to say that selflessness is really like wearing a badly fitted suit on a damp morning, or something equally British and uncomfortable. Luke has won a lot—the respect of the tournament masters, the friendship of a nice kid, and a computer chess game, for two weeks, anyway. He has also learned that moral decisions are a form of tactics: seeing four forced moves ahead in the game of life. But he lost the trophy, and he really wanted it. Now he will have to go out and get it honestly.

A few days later, after we saw the Yankees wallop the Mariners in the fifth game, I had to explain to Luke, who was celebrating, that this was not the end—that though the Bronx Bombers ("Why are they called the Bronx *Bombers*?," suddenly anxious. "It's good. Trust me," I replied) had won the Championship Series, they would now have to move on to the *World* Series, the really big one.

He paused and took a deep, dramatic, heaving breath. "Tell me true things," he said, which is what he says when he really wants the truth from his father—on oath, no teasing. "Tell me true things," deep breath again, then, in a strangled voice, "Have the New York Yankees ever won the World Series?"

He was in real doubt, and I recognized in his voice exactly the same tone he uses to ask me if he can stay up until ten o'clock to watch *Dexter's Laboratory*. He knows he's asking too much of life but, oh well, what's life worth if you don't ask?

I paused. This seemed like as big a moment as we could ever have. I was in possession of crucial knowledge about a subject he had come to consider close to his heart, and I was almost afraid of giving it away too casually, without sufficient buildup or a sense of momentousness. It seemed like the sort of thing you at least sat down to say. ("You see, Luke, the team you've chosen to support—well, they're a very *special* team, in a way. Most teams, it's normal for them to lose. A lot. But your team . . .") Yet to tell him flatly that the Yankees always won was to make him an accessory to power, and what I found beautiful about his attachment was that it was rooted in a feeling of doubt, of powerlessness, of soulfulness. He had been a Yankees rooter for two weeks, five games, at the worst time in the city's history, and to reassure him that he had actually made a good bet on a big-market team would undermine the meaning of his allegiance. It seemed somehow that the better, emotionally apt, appropriate answer was "No, they never have. But you know—they just might this year."

But that was a lie, easily discovered, so I said, "Ask the kids around school if the Yankees have ever won a World Series." He did, and when he came home, he said cautiously, "Well, they say they won last year." That seemed about as far back as the collective first-grade memory went. I was pleased. It was good news, but not too much good news—a way of attaching a young New Yorker to hope without going all the way back to omnipotence. Someday I will tell him about twenty-six, twenty-seven Series victories, but not just now. I want him to root for something that might not always work out. It seems healthier than rooting for a sure thing, just as giving back a trophy teaches more than keeping one.

At night, with the Series coming on, I can sometimes actually see the Statue of Bravery looming, slightly ridiculous but noble, on the Lower Manhattan skyline—leering hungrily at the big humorless French woman across the harbor, as the property tycoon would want him to, securing the future of the city by his iron lust.

Thanksgiving goes well: It is good to have the crowd around the table and the children, laughing. Decent heritage turkey, which I brined. The old group, for one more year . . . The Yankees lost at the very end, but Luke seem unperturbed by it. Hey, they did darn well. He still doesn't get it, thank God, is not yet really a querulous, demanding rooter, a true Yankees fan.

The next day we go with the Kogan family to Rockefeller Center and Bergdorf Goodman. There is a lonely Santa at Bergdorf's, a real

Bergdorf's Santa, elegantly dressed, with an little live dog at his feet, all alone. The children reluctantly volunteer to sit on his lap, Luke reluctantly because he is getting a bit old for it, and Olivia because she lives in fear of grown-ups in costumes. (We encountered the Easter Bunny in the park earlier this year, a guy in a bright pink suit handing out promotional candy, and Olivia's screams could be heard from one end of the Great Lawn to the other. She still talks about it, the way Odysseus must have talked about that encounter with the Cyclops.) But they sat and asked for stuff, and then we had a picture taken—the children on Santa's lap, smiling that cheesy, forced, alarmed public smile one sees on the faces of Chinese Communist officials at the Annual Party Congress.

Then we went skating at Rockefeller Center, thinking it would be nearly empty, which it wasn't, just the opposite, mobbed. We waited in line, put on our skates—proud Canadians, bringing our own—and then whizzed around, holding the children's hands, each of us grown-ups sneaking off for a quick one-time-only dash around the rink before rejoining our stately family chain.

After the skating was over, as the Zamboni came out, we saw a single couple left on the rink, a youngish man and younger woman. Suddenly, he fell to his right knee, and he handed her a little box, and we watched as her shoulders collapsed in tears. A single moment of caution—what the hell is *this*?—and then we all realized what had happened: He had proposed, and she had accepted. He hugged her and they skated off hand in hand, she still wiping tears away from her face, he looking embarrassed and empowered.

The applause, which began as a ripple and then spread into waves of thunder, was something larger than kind and something more than sentimental; it was a cheer for continuity, and for cheap gestures, and for life.

But, over hot chocolate in the café, as we analyzed the moment, Martha was indignant. "Of course!" she cried. "What was she supposed to do? What if she *didn't want to marry him*? She was going to give him back the ring right in the middle of Rockefeller Center? It wasn't a romantic gesture. It was erotic coercion." It was, I thought, at least a good chess move, tactical and designed to throw your opponent—or, in this case, your conquest—so off balance that you get what you want.

Expensive public declarations of eternal loyalty are the best short-term erotic tactic, as generations of lovers have learned. What it leaves you with—a lifetime of debt and uncertain obligation—is worth the feeling of triumph and the promise of sex as you skate off the rink to music and applause. The wisdom of betrothal is like the wisdom of comedy, which is not very different from the wisdom of medicine or parenting: there is no true long run, no final result that will make sense of everything, only an endless sequence of short runs placed end to end. You have the pleasure of short-term satisfaction even if, in love, anyway, you almost always have to give back the trophy when the tournament is over. (You *always* have to give back the trophy in the true long term, the Keynes long term.)

I love you forever really means *Just trust me for now,* which is all it ever means, and we just hope to keep renewing the "now," year after year. I looked at the now-engaged faces, to see how old they were and if the city could trust them to remain here to have their children, as the property tycoon would want. But I couldn't tell.

The lover on skates, appealing to eternity, was actually two moves—one hidden ring, one romantic gesture—ahead of his beloved, which is as far ahead as you can reasonably hope to be these days. What we had applauded (en masse, in Rockefeller Center) was just one more short-term tactic disguised as a long-term plan, like all the other good New York moves in chess, sex, ethics, property development, and family trust.

Bumping into Mr. Ravioli

My daughter, Olivia, who just turned three, has an imaginary friend whose name is Charlie Ravioli. Olivia is growing up in Manhattan, so Charlie Ravioli has a lot of local traits: He lives in an apartment "on Madison and Lexington," he dines on grilled chicken, fruit, and water, and, having reached the age of seven and a half, he feels, or is thought, "old." But the most peculiarly local thing about Olivia's imaginary playmate is this: He is always too busy to play with her. She holds her toy cell phone up to her ear, and we hear her talk into it: "Ravioli? It's Olivia . . . It's Olivia. Come and play? Okay. Call me. Bye." Then she snaps it shut and shakes her head. "I always get his machine," she says. Or she will say, "I spoke to Ravioli today." "Did you have fun?" my wife and I ask. "No. He was busy working. On a television" (leaving it up in the air whether he repairs electronic devices or has his own talk show).

On a good day, she "bumps into" her invisible friend and they go to a coffee shop. "I bumped into Charlie Ravioli," she announces at dinner (after a day when, of course, she stayed home, played, had a nap, had lunch, paid a visit to the Central Park Zoo, and then had another nap). "We had coffee, but then he had to run." She sighs sometimes at her inability to make their schedules mesh, but she accepts it as inevitable, just the way life is. "I bumped into Charlie Ravioli today," she says. "He was working." Then she adds brightly, "But we hopped into a taxi." What happened then? we ask. "We grabbed lunch," she says.

It seemed obvious that Ravioli was a romantic figure of the big exotic life that went on outside her little limited life of parks and playgrounds—drawn, in particular, from a nearly perfect, mynah-bird-like imitation of the words she hears her mother use when she talks about *her* day with *her* friends. ("How was your day?" Sighing: "Oh, you know. I tried to make a date with Meg, but I couldn't find her, so I left a message on her machine. Then I bumped into Emily after that meeting I had in Soho, and we had coffee and then she had to run, but by then Meg had reached me on my cell and we arranged . . .") I was concerned, though, that Charlie Ravioli might also be the sign of some "trauma," some loneliness in Olivia's life reflected in imaginary form. "It seems odd to have an imaginary playmate who's always too busy to play with you," Martha, my wife, said to me. "Shouldn't your imaginary playmate be someone you tell secrets to and, I don't know, sing songs with? It shouldn't be someone who's always *hopping* into taxis."

We thought at first that her older brother, Luke, might be the original of Charlie Ravioli. (For one thing, he is also seven and a half, though we were fairly sure that this age was merely Olivia's marker for As Old as Man Can Be.) He *is* too busy to play with her much anymore. He has become a true New York child, with the schedule of a Cabinet secretary: chess club on Monday, T-ball on Tuesday, tournament on Saturday, play dates and after-school conferences to fill in the gaps. Already, their conversation tracks their chromosomes.

"Luke, how was your day?" Olivia asks him at three-thirty after he has come from school, as they sit eating cookies and cocoa.

"Okay, I guess," he says indifferently.

"What did you have for lunch?" she persists.

"Uh—I don't remember. A sandwich, I guess."

"Luke, what did the teacher say about your birthday poem?"

"Nothing. It was okay, I guess."

Longer pause. She waits patiently. Finally, pointedly: "Luke. How was *my* day?"

But Olivia, though she counts days, does not yet really *have* days. She has *a* day, and into this day she has introduced the figure of Charlie Ravioli—in order, it dawned on us, to insist that she does have days, because she is too harried to share them, that she does have an independent social life, by virtue of being too busy to have one.

Yet Charlie Ravioli was becoming so constant and oddly discouraging a companion—"He canceled lunch. Again," Olivia would say—that we thought we ought to look into it. One of my sisters is a developmental psychologist who specializes in close scientific studies of what goes on inside the heads of one- and two- and three-year-olds. Though she grew up in the nervy East, she lives in California now, where she grows basil in her garden and jars her own organic marmalades. I e-mailed this sister for help with the Ravioli issue—how concerned should we be?—and she sent me back an e-mail, along with an attachment, and, after several failed cell-phone connections, we at last spoke on a landline.

It turned out that there is a recent book on this very subject by the psychologist Marjorie Taylor, called *Imaginary Companions and the Children Who Create Them*, and my sister had just written a review of it. She insisted that Charlie Ravioli was nothing to be worried about. Olivia was right on target, in fact. Most under-sevens (63 percent, to be scientific) have an invisible friend, and children create their imaginary playmates not out of trauma but out of a serene sense of the possibilities of fiction—sometimes as figures of pure fantasy; sometimes, as Olivia had done, as observations of grown-up manners assembled in tranquillity and given a name. I learned about the invisible companions Taylor studied: Baintor, who is invisible because he lives in the light; Station Pheta, who hunts sea anemones on the beach. Charlie Ravioli seemed pavement-bound by comparison.

"An imaginary playmate isn't any kind of trauma marker," my sister said. "It's just the opposite: It's a sign that the child is now confident enough to begin to understand how to organize her experience into stories." The significant thing about imaginary friends, she went on, is that the kids know they're fictional. In an instant message on AOL, she summed it up: "The children with invisible friends often interrupted the interviewer to remind her, with a certain note of concern for her sanity, that these characters were, after all, just pretend."

I also learned that some children, as they get older, turn out to possess what child psychologists call a "paracosm." A paracosm is a society thought up by a child—an invented universe with a distinctive language, geography, and history. (The Brontës invented a couple of paracosms when they were children.) Not all children who have an imaginary friend invent a paracosm, but the two might, I think, be related. Like a lonely ambassador from Alpha Centauri in a fifties sci-fi movie who, misunderstood by paranoid Earth scientists, cannot bring the lifesaving news from his planet, perhaps the invisible friend also gets an indifferent or hostile response, and then we never find out about the beautiful paracosm he comes from.

"Don't worry about it," my sister said in a late-night phone call. "Knowing something's made up while thinking that it matters is what all fiction insists on. She's putting a name on a series of manners."

"But he seems so real to her," I objected.

"Of course he is. I mean, who's more real to you, Becky Sharp or Gandalf or the guy down the hall? Giving a manner a name makes it real."

I paused. "I grasp that it's normal for her to have an imaginary friend," I said, "but have you ever heard of an imaginary friend who's too busy to play with you?"

She thought about it. "No," she said. "I'm sure that doesn't occur anywhere in the research literature. That sounds *completely* New York." And then she hung up.

The real question, I saw, was not "Why this friend?" but "Why this fiction?" Why, as Olivia had seen so clearly, are grown-ups in New York so busy, and so obsessed with the language of busyness that it dominates their conversation? Why are New Yorkers always bumping into Charlie Ravioli and grabbing lunch, instead of sitting down with him and exchanging intimacies, as friends should, as people do in Paris and Rome? Why is busyness the stuff our children make their invisible friends from, as country children make theirs from light and sand?

This seems like an odd question. New Yorkers are busy for obvious reasons: They have husbands and wives and careers and children, they have the Gauguin show to see and their personal trainers and accountants to visit. But the more I think about this, the more I think it is—well, a lot of Ravioli. We are instructed to believe that we are busier because we have to work harder to be more productive, but everybody knows that busyness and productivity have a dubious, arm's-length relationship. Most of our struggle in New York, in fact, is to be less busy in order to do more work.

Constant, exhausting, no-time-to-meet-your-friends Charlie Ravioli–style busyness arrived as an affliction in modern life long after the other parts of bourgeois city manners did. Business long predates busyness. In the seventeenth and eighteenth centuries, when bourgeois people were building the institutions of bourgeois life, they seem never to have complained that they were too busy—or, if they did, they left no record of it. Samuel Pepys, who had a navy to refloat and a burned London to rebuild, often uses the word "busy" but never complains of busyness. For him, the word "busy" is a synonym for "happy," not for "stressed." Not once in his diary does Pepys cancel lunch or struggle to fit someone in for coffee at four-thirty. Pepys works, makes love, and goes to bed, but he does not bump into and he does not have to run. Ben Franklin, a half century later, boasts of his industriousness, but he, too, never complains about being busy, and always has time to publish a newspaper or come up with a maxim or swim the ocean or invent the lightning rod.

Until sometime in the middle of the nineteenth century, in fact, the normal affliction of the bourgeois was not busyness at all but its apparent opposite: boredom. It has even been argued that the grid of streets and cafés and small engagements in the nineteenth-century city—the whole of social life—was designed self-consciously as an escape from that numbing boredom. (Working people weren't bored, of course, but they were engaged in labor, not work. They were too busy to be busy.) Baudelaire, basically, was so bored that he had to get drunk and run out onto the boulevard in the hope of bumping into somebody.

Turn to the last third of the nineteenth century and the beginning of the twentieth, though, and suddenly everybody is busy, and everybody is complaining about it. Pepys, master of His Majesty's Navy, may never have complained of busyness, but Virginia Woolf, mistress of motionless lull, is continually complaining about how she spends her days racing across London from square to square, just like—well, like Charlie Ravioli. Ronald Firbank is wrung out by his social obligations; Marcel Proust is constantly rescheduling rendezvous and apologizing for being overstretched. Henry James, with nothing particular to do save live, complains of being too busy all the time. He could not shake the world of obligation, he said, and he wrote a strange and beautiful story, "The Great Good Place," which begins with an exhausting flood of correspondence, telegrams, and manuscripts that drive the protagonist nearly mad.

What changed? That James story helps supply the key. It was trains and telegrams. The railroads ended isolation and packed the metropolis with people whose work was defined by a complicated network of social obligations. Pepys's network in 1669 London was, despite his official position, relatively small compared even with that of a minor aesthete like Firbank, two centuries later. Pepys had more time to make love because he had fewer friends to answer.

If the train crowded our streets, the telegram crowded our minds. It introduced something into the world that remains with us today: a whole new class of communications that are defined as incomplete in advance of their delivery. A letter, though it may enjoin a response, is meant to be complete in itself. Neither the apostle Paul nor Horace Walpole ever ends an epistle with "Give me a call and let's discuss." By contrast, it is in the nature of the telegram to be a skeletal version of another thing—a communication that opens more than it closes. The nineteenth-century telegram came with those busy-threatening words "Letter follows."

Every device that has evolved from the telegram shares the same character. E-mails end with a suggestion for a phone call ("Anyway, let's meet and/or talk soon"), faxes with a request for an e-mail, answering-machine messages with a request for a fax. All are devices of perpetually suspended communication. My wife recalls a moment last fall when she got a telephone message from a friend asking her to check her e-mail apropos a phone call she needed to make vis-à-vis a fax they had both received asking for more information about a bed they were thinking of buying from Ireland online and having sent to America by Federal Express—a grand slam of incomplete communication.

In most of the Western world outside New York, the press of trains and of telegraphic communication was alleviated by those other two great transformers: the car and the television. While the train and the telegram (and their love children, subways and commuter trains and e-mail) pushed people together, the car and the television pulled people apart—taking them out to the suburbs and sitting them down in front of a solo spectacle. New York, though, almost uniquely, got hit by a double dose of the first two technologies and a very limited dose of the second two. Car life—car obsessions, car-defined habits—is more absent here than almost anywhere else in the country, while television, though obviously present, is less fatally prevalent here. New York is still a subject of television, and we compare *Sex and the City* to sex and the city; they are not yet quite the same. Here two grids of busyness remain dominant: the nineteenth- and early-twentieth-century grid of bump and run, and the late-twentieth- and early-twenty-first-century postmodern grid of virtual call and echo. Busyness is felt so intently here because we are both crowded and overloaded. We exit the apartment into a still-dense nineteenth-century grid of street corners and restaurants full of people, and come home to the late-twentieth-century grid of faxes and e-mails and overwhelming incompleteness.

We walk across the park on a Sunday morning and bump into our friend the baker and our old acquaintance from graduate school (what the hell is she doing now?) and someone we have been avoiding for three weeks. They all invite us for brunch, and we would love to, but we are too . . . busy. We bump into Charlie Ravioli and grab a coffee with him—and come home to find three e-mails and a message on our cell phone from him, wondering where we are. The crowding of our space has been reinforced by a crowding of our time, and the only way to protect ourselves is to build structures of perpetual deferral: I'll see you next week, let's talk soon. We build rhetorical baffles around our lives to keep the crowding out, only to find that we have let nobody we love in.

Like Charlie Ravioli, we hop into taxis and leave messages on answering machines to avoid our acquaintances, and find that we keep missing our friends. I have one intimate who lives just across the park from me, whom I e-mail often, and whom I am fortunate to see two or three times a year. We are always . . . busy. He has become my Charlie Ravioli, my invisible friend. I am sure that he misses me—just as Charlie Ravioli, I realized, must tell his other friends that he is sorry he does not see Olivia more often.

Once I sensed the nature of his predicament, I began to feel more sympathetic toward Charlie Ravioli. I got to know him better, too. We learned more about what Ravioli did in the brief breathing spaces in his busy life when he could sit down with Olivia and dish. "Ravioli read your book," Olivia announced, for instance, one night at dinner. "He didn't like it much." We also found out that Ravioli had joined a gym, that he was going to the beach in the summer, but he was too busy, and that he was working on a "show." ("It isn't a very good show," she added candidly.) Charlie Ravioli, in other words, was just another New Yorker: fit, opinionated, and trying to break into show business.

I think we would have learned to live happily with Charlie Ravioli had it not been for the appearance of Laurie. She threw us badly. At dinner, Olivia had been mentioning a new personage almost as often as she mentioned Ravioli. "I talked to Laurie today," she would begin. "She says Ravioli is busy." Or she would be closeted with her play phone. "Who are you talking to, darling?" I would ask. "Laurie," she would say. "We're talking about Ravioli." We surmised that Laurie was, so to speak, the Linda Tripp of the Ravioli operation—the person you spoke to for consolation when the big creep was ignoring you.

But a little while later, a more ominous side of Laurie's role began to appear. "Laurie, tell Ravioli I'm calling," I heard Olivia say. I pressed her about who, exactly, Laurie was. Olivia shook her head. "She works for Ravioli," she said.

And then it came to us, with sickening clarity: Laurie was not the patient friend who consoled you for Charlie's absence. Laurie was the bright-toned person who answered Ravioli's phone and told you that unfortunately, Mr. Ravioli was in a meeting. "Laurie says Ravioli is too busy to play," Olivia announced sadly one morning. Things seemed to be deteriorating; now Ravioli was too busy even to say he was too busy.

I got back on the phone with my sister. "Have you ever heard of an imaginary friend with an assistant?" I asked.

She paused. "Imaginary friends don't have assistants," she said. "That's not only not in the literature. That's just . . . I mean—in California they don't have assistants."

"You think we should look into it?"

"I think you should move," she said flatly.

Martha was of the same mind. "An imaginary playmate shouldn't have an assistant," she said miserably. "An imaginary playmate shouldn't have an agent. An imaginary playmate shouldn't have a publicist or a personal trainer or a caterer—an imaginary playmate shouldn't have . . . *people*. An imaginary playmate should just *play*. With the child who imagined it." She started leaving on my pillow real estate brochures picturing quaint houses in New Jersey and Connecticut, unhaunted by busy invisible friends and their entourages.

Not long after the appearance of Laurie, though, something remarkable happened. Olivia would begin to tell us tales of her frustrations with Charlie Ravioli, and, after telling us again that he was too busy to play, she would tell us what she had done instead. Astounding and paracosmic tall tales poured out of her: She had been to a chess tournament and brought home a trophy; she had gone to a circus and told jokes. Searching for Charlie Ravioli, she had "saved all the animals in the zoo"; heading home in a taxi after a quick coffee with Ravioli, she took over the steering wheel and "got all the moneys." From the stalemate of daily life emerged the fantasy of victory. She had dreamed of a normal life with a few close friends and had to settle for worldwide fame and the front page of the tabloids. The existence of an imaginary friend had liberated her into a paracosm, but it was a curiously New York paracosm—it was the unobtainable world outside her window. Charlie Ravioli, prince of busyness, was not an end but a means: a way out onto the street in her head, a declaration of potential independence.

Busyness is our art form, our civic ritual, our way of being us. Many friends have said to me that they love New York now in a way they never did before, and their love, I've noticed, takes for its object all the things that used to exasperate them—the curious combination of freedom, self-made fences, and paralyzing preoccupation that the city provides. Now when Martha and I ask each other, "How did you spend the day?" instead of listing her incidents, she says merely, "Oh, you know . . . just . . . bumping into Charlie Ravioli," meaning, just bouncing from obligation to electronic entreaty, just spotting a friend and snatching a sandwich, just being busy, just living in New York. If everything we've learned in the past year could be summed up in a phrase, it's that we want to go on bumping into Charlie Ravioli for as long as we can.

Olivia still hopes to have him to herself someday. As I work late at night in the "study" (an old hallway, an Aalto screen), I keep near the "nursery" (an ancient pantry, a glass-brick wall), I can hear her shift into pre-sleep, still muttering to herself. She is still trying to reach her closest friend. "Ravioli? Ravioli?" she moans as she turns over into her pillow and clutches her blanket, and then she whispers, almost to herself, "Tell him call me. Tell him call me when he comes home."

The Cooking Game

I enjoy the company of cooks. I admire them because they are hard workers, and because they make delicious things. But, more than that, I like to contemplate the way they have to think in order to make the things they make. They are the last artists among us who still live in the daily presence of patronage. In the two centuries since the Romantic revolution, the arts have, one by one, been Byronized, set free from the necessity of pleasing an audience—a process that began with the poets and painters and took in the architects and novelists and has swept up, most recently, the rock musicians and shoe designers. All have taught themselves that they are there to instruct and puzzle an audience, not to please it.

But although cooks are a source of romance, they are not themselves Romantic. They practice their art the way all art was practiced until the nineteenth century, as a job done to order for rich people who treat you as something between the court jester and the butler. Cooks can be temperamental—cooks are *supposed* to be temperamental—but temperament is the Byronism of the dependent; children, courtesans, and cooks all have it. What cooks have in place of freedom is what all artists had back before they were released from the condition of flunkydom: a weary, careful dignity, a secretive sense of craft, and the comforting knowledge of belonging to a guild.

I also enjoy the company of cooks because I have always wanted to be one. A surprising number of writers I know, apart from the bitter ones who dream about being publishers, share this fantasy. Words and food are bound together in some inexplicable way, a peculiar communion that lends grace and mystery to what otherwise would seem to be a simple exchange of gluttony for publicity.

Overt collaborations between writers and cooks, however, are rare, and I was therefore happy and surprised last March when two cooks whose company I enjoy a lot asked if I would, so to speak, write them a meal. The two cooks were Dan Barber, of Blue Hill, in Greenwich Village, and Peter Hoffman, of Savoy, in Soho. It was Peter who called me first and asked if I would be interested in organizing a *jeu de cuisine,* a cooking game. The game, he said, had been invented by Robert Courtine, who, under the name of La Reynière, was the gastronomic columnist of *Le Monde* for many years. (He had been a full-fledged collaborator with Vichy during the war; afterward, he became a reactionary of the table and flourished.) In the early seventies, when nouvelle cuisine was just appearing, Courtine chose a list of ingredients from the Paris markets and then had five cooks prepare a menu from them. Peter told me that five young New York chefs had agreed to cook for a week from a list of ingredients of my choosing from the farmers' market in Union Square. The cooks would use the foods I chose in whatever way they wanted, with whatever else they wanted to add. (It wouldn't be a competition, he said, in the tone in which extremely competitive people say those words.) I agreed, of course, although I later explained to him and Dan Barber that they would have to be responsible for my education: I had to confess that I had never visited the green market. They seemed unsurprised by this information; whatever they were coming to me for, it wasn't expertise.

I have known Peter since 1990, when he opened Savoy, a lovely, neighborly restaurant, with a golden-lit Arts and Crafts–style room, all blond wood and copper mesh and candlelight and welcome, eclectic food. Dan Barber was a more recent friend. A year ago, I wandered into Blue Hill, which he oversees with his fellow chef Mike Anthony, expecting the kind of well-meaning meal you get from a young guy who has cooked for a couple of years in France; and instead, I ate as good a meal as any I have had outside the three-star places in Paris. Describing food is difficult, not because we can't capture in words things that are sensual—we do fine with painting and pubic hair—but because memorable description depends on startling metaphors, and startling metaphors depend on a willingness to be startled. Nobody did much with landscape, either, until it suddenly became respectable to compare a Swiss mountain to the whole of human destiny. We don't allow that freedom when it comes to what's on our plates. If someone wrote, for instance, that Dan Barber's foie gras with ground coffee beans is at once as inevitable as a tide and as astonishing as a wave, the reader's first response would be to think, quite rightly, that it is not at all. (And yet it is.) People used to feel this way about metaphors for sex—the English still do. They have just gotten over Evelyn Waugh writing "I was made free of her narrow loins." But we all still resist "I was made free of his thick loin chops."

Dan is not merely an aspirant to intellect but a real-live émigré from academe. In 1991 he had been waiting to go to China on a Fulbright in political science when his grant program was canceled, and he set off instead to a job at a bakery. "Dan has this whole right-brain, left-brain thing going, which is rare for one of us," another cook said. There was something almost Salingeresque about him. He grew up on the Upper East Side—a Dalton lifer, kindergarten through high school; he cooked for his father after his mother died—and the way he generally looks and talks (acerbic, observant, self-critical), added to the natural diffidence of chefs, puts one in mind of the way Zooey Glass would have, had he chosen cooking over acting.

The three other chefs were to be Philippe Bertineau, of Payard Pâtisserie & Bistro, on the Upper East Side; Sara Jenkins, of Patio Dining, in the East Village; and Romy Dorotan, of Cendrillon, in Soho—one French cook, three Americans, and a Filipino. All of them did most of the shopping for their kitchens at the farmers' market in Union Square, and all of them were, directly or indirectly, sons and daughters of Alice Waters, the Jeanne d'Arc of Chez Panisse, in Berkeley, who brought to America the doctrine of the seasonal, the organic, and the sincere. The doctrine includes the belief that all shopping, if humanly possible, should be done at a farmers' market, that small producers are better than large, and that the cook should decide only after seeing what's in the market what he or she wants to cook that night.

When I got home and told my family that I had been specially selected as the point man for a demonstration of the virtues of the seasonal and the natural, of farmers' goods and nature's bounty, they were unimpressed.

"Will it be like *Iron Chef*?" my son, Luke, asked. He has become a great fan of the bizarre Japanese cooking competition that is broadcast on the Food Network every Friday night. On this program, two grim-faced chefs have an hour in which to cook a four-, five-, or even six-course meal, built around a single ingredient chosen by the host—a strange, melodramatic figure in black, who spits out Japanese. The special ingredient rises from beneath the floor, like the Phantom of the Opera's organ, in dark expressionist lighting.

"You'll be the guy in the black leather pants," Luke said, and barked "Tuna!" in a mock Japanese accent.

"No, I won't," I said. "This is not going to be a competition. Just an exhibition. Like the Dodo's race in *Alice's Adventures in Wonderland*. All must have prizes."

After years of Paris markets, with their abundance and bad faith—the Marché Biologique, the organic market on the Boulevard Raspail, sells a lot of terrific produce, but I have always doubted that pineapples are actually being grown organically on the Île-de-France—I confess that I found the pickings at the Union Square green market on a spring morning a little scrappy. The rules of the market insist that only a narrow band of local farmers can participate, and this limits your choices, especially between seasons.

"There's a lot of ramps and some good rhubarb" was the kind of cheering but not exactly inspiring summation you would hear on an April morning. "And some nice storage potatoes and some, uh, storage apples." (I didn't even know what ramps were, though I quickly learned: They are small wild leeks, which have suddenly become fashionable. Why this should be is hard to say, the appeal of a wild leek not being so great that it makes you regret that leeks were ever tamed.) In truth, the chefs, too, found the market disappointing on most mornings, and that, I realized, was exactly what appealed to them. Instead of ranging through the market like cooks in a television commercial—

squeezing an apple, smelling a ramp, feeling up a chicken—they tended to go where they knew they wanted to go, seeing at a glance if what they were looking for was there, and then quietly taking as much of it as they could get. They didn't taste much, because experience with the vendor and the look of the item told them what it would taste like. Expertise, I was reminded, isn't seeing all there is. Expertise is knowing what you're looking for.

And knowing what you're looking at. Peter could station himself in front of a fruit and give you twenty minutes on its pedigree and possibilities, like an Icelander telling you her family history. Once we stopped in front of a crate of strawberries at the stall of Franca Tantillo, one of the more vivid farmers at the market. "These are the only good strawberries," Peter said. "Franca and the people at Fantasy Fruit are the only two people who are growing those strawberries right now. They're day-neutral, which means they completely ignore the usual Circadian cycle. They continue to flower even though the day is getting shorter." I tasted a couple. They were nothing like the familiar American Driscoll's strawberries—bright red outsides and hard white mealy insides. Instead, they were sublime tiny berries with the fragrance of a French *fraise des bois,* perfumed and intensely sweet.

On another visit, we stopped at a table of desultory-looking green leaves, the kind of things you cut off the ends of leeks before you put them in a soup. It was a cold and rainy morning, and there didn't look like much that was worth taking the subway for.

"These are scapes," Peter said. "And to understand what they are, you gotta understand the truth about garlic. There are two major groupings of garlic: hard neck and soft neck." We were examining the hard neck. It looked like garlic with a leek stalk. "Hard-neck garlic grows a flower stalk that pulls energy away from the bulb. So you have to cut the flower off each plant, which takes forever, and only a handful of farmers are willing to do it—they cut off the flower stalks and we call them garlic scapes. Real hard-neck garlic came from Central Asia, and it requires a cold winter to get that juicy, full, pungent garlickness. We have a very Central Asian–, Afghanistan-garlic-type winter here." I tasted a scape. It had a sharp and intense garlic flavor and a green, leafy undertone.

"You know, we have to put up with certain frustrations," Peter went on as we tramped through the market. "But that's part of the whole expression. What produces great taste? One thing. *Stress.* French winemakers are always pushing the limit of viability. You can't really grow grapes in Champagne because it's too damn cold, and you can't really grow grapes in Châteauneuf-du-Pape because there's no soil there, but you force the vines to adapt to the environment and search for nutrients, and where the season is short enough and you have to crop close enough, you get terrific flavor. What drives great taste in the field is stress."

"Thanks, Peter," Dan said dryly. "I'm going to tell that to everybody in the kitchen tonight."

One morning as Dan and Peter and I walked around the market, I complained about how little meat was on offer. "Well, for the best veal, you have to meet Amy, this woman upstate," Dan said. "You know, most veal is white, and it's sort of awful and immoral how they raise it, because they want white meat. But she has a dairy farm, and instead of getting rid of the male calves, she just, well, she brings them up like her own children." Dan's eyes glowed. "They're grass-fed, and she lets them run as free as you or I. It's a hard sell for a restaurant, because it's a reddish meat and customers expect white, but it's absolutely delicious, and she's a completely admirable person. I mean, she's amazing, the way she treats them. She really brings them up like her own children."

"She brings them up like her own children until they're nine months old and she slaughters them," Peter said equably.

I soon became a convert to the limited palette and small victories of the green market. I started coming home with a satchel filled with New York City produce: scrappy, hard-necked, stressed-out.

"We're going to have greens with scapes and ramps," I announced.

"Can't we just have chicken fingers?" Luke asked.

"Scapes and greens and ramps: It sounds like a Ted Hughes poem," my wife said dubiously.

. . .

Over a few dinners and many post-market breakfasts, I came to know the chefs involved in the game, and thought that I had begun to glimpse something about their curious mix of entrepreneurial savvy, high principle, sensual engineering, and mordant despair. There was, for instance, a story Dan Barber loved to tell about the moment he thought he had identified the *Times* food critic William Grimes incognito in his restaurant.

"So by this point, I know, I mean *I know,* that this is Grimes. I mean, it's obvious, he's coming in night after night, he's trying different bits of the menu, very professional—it's obvious that the guy is a food critic, and I see him and I sort of recognize him." A visit from Grimes determines a restaurant's mood, because a Grimes review will determine its future. Dan Barber paused, and there was a quick, is-this-okay-in-front-of-a-civilian? glance between him and the other chefs before he went on. "We even put it out over the credit-card line. That's this informal system a couple of chefs have where they fax the fake credit-card names of the *Times* critic to all the other restaurants." He shrugged. "So the very next day, Grimes actually calls from the *Times* and asks for a wine list. Now, this guy, let's call him Mr. Hudsucker, had taken a menu with him—but not a wine list! So, I mean, now we're getting obvious." He went on, "That Friday, a 'Diner's Journal' article comes out that lists all the dishes Mr. Hudsucker ate at the bar! So, okay, the next week H. M. Hudsucker makes another reservation, and we flip over backward for him, creating all these tasting menus, and the servers going through hula hoops. You have to be careful about that stuff, of course, because it's like the Enigma secret—you want to use it, but you don't want it to be obvious you've broken the code. Anyway, finally, someone comes into the kitchen and I say, 'That's Grimes!' and he says, 'No, it isn't. I know Grimes, and that's not Grimes.' And I say, 'That's not Grimes? Then who the hell is that?' Later, a waiter went over without my knowing it and said, 'You seem so, uh, *passionate* about food, Mr. Hudsucker, are you in the business?' And he said, 'What business?' And the server said the food business. And Mr. Hudsucker said, 'The food business? I'm in the insurance business. I just like it here.'

"And the really terrible part of the story is that he came back and we didn't do anything for him—not because we're malicious. It's just, just that at this point we're sort of disillusioned with H. M. Hudsucker, no fault of his own. And he walked out upset. It's ironic because . . . *he was the ideal diner!* He ate like a food critic without being one! The ideal guest."

Cooks, I learned, indulge the gaping outsider—I want to run away with the circus!—without even trying to explain to him what they know too well, that the tricks are easy; the hard part is preventing the clowns from committing suicide and the lion trainer from getting in bed with the ringmaster's wife. They're glad that people like the circus, but they understand that the circus is not the show; the circus is the ring around the show.

Though cooks worry about food and carp about critics, they obsess about their staffs. (I once saw Dan Barber struck dumb—speechless and incapable of movement—by the news, conveyed to him at the morning market by one of uptown's snazzier French chefs, that he had just hired away Dan's first-rate general manager.) This is partly because they have to, or there will be no one there to serve, but also because, just as good baseball managers know that an awful lot of what looks like pitching is really fielding, restaurant owners know that a lot of what tastes like good food is really good service. "The thing is, what's a good taste is a feeling, not just a sensation," Peter Hoffman said once. "So if you're feeling welcomed and warm, right then the food tastes better—the whole feeling is better, and you're not going to start prying apart your sensations, unless you're a writer. You just know you're having a good time, and you tell the next person, 'The food's wonderful there.' Once we had a girl seating people, and some friend of the house came in and she said, 'Just a minute, please.' *Just a minute, please.* Not rude or anything—but, for that person, everything we've been working to build up about Savoy is *gone* in that moment."

The craft secret, I realized, was that the craft was not the secret. There are lots of good cooks. The quality of the cooking in a good restaurant really depends on the daily preparation of a context, a hundred small sensations that precede any one bite and transcend it. The understanding that the food was not the thing from which all else came but the thing to which all else led was shared by all the harried and overworked cooks in the *jeu*. (The chefs who owned restaurants felt it most keenly, of course, but even those who worked for other people knew that the quality of the cooking depended on choices that were made before the cooking even started. No cook will ever talk about "a great recipe.") Philippe Bertineau is the perfect Frenchman—he was the original sous-chef at Daniel—and the American cooks looked on him as their Horowitz, their technical genius. He has the worried, harassed, ironic eyebrows that French cooks always seem to have. He grew up on a farm in the Poitou-Charentes region, and was perplexed by the American cooks' belief that their doctrine was a doctrine rather than a revealed truth. "On the farm where I grew up, everything came from the farm," he told me. "Where else could it come from? I can't *believe* how impatient Americans are. They want to start"—he shrugged and made a mournful "O" with his mouth—"oh, mixing trout and cumin seed after they've worked in the kitchen for a day, before they know how to fillet a turbot."

Sara Jenkins, it turned out, was the daughter of an American foreign correspondent and grew up in Spain and Lebanon and on a farm in Tuscany, and she practiced Tuscan farm cooking with an exceptional sincerity and purity of spirit. She believed in the doctrine with the conviction of someone who has given up "sophistication" in order to believe. She was a true Daughter of Alice, with the wide-eyed, militant innocence of the Salvation Army girl in *Guys and Dolls*. "I think *anything* can be delicious if it's really fresh and seasonal," she told me once over coffee. "I've always had problems with frog, for instance, until I went to Cambodia one summer. And, I mean, you may *think* you don't like frog, but what you don't like is frozen frog. These Cambodian frogs had been caught and skinned only minutes before, and it was . . . Once you've had fresh frog, you have a completely different feeling about what frog can be."

Romy Dorotan, the Filipino cook of Cendrillon, had been working part-time at a restaurant in Philadelphia while he got a degree in economics at Temple in the seventies. One day the cook quit, and he had to take over. He managed, he explained, because he had read a lot of books by the gloomy British sensualist Elizabeth David. "She really showed me the way," he said. "I would read a bit of Elizabeth David every day, and her writing gave me the courage to cook." It turned out that it was Romy who had been the Courtine reader.

I was drawn to Dan Barber, though, because, alone among the cooks, he had what every doctrine ought to inspire, and that is doubts, and not just doubts but Doubts. At the time we were going to the market together, *Food & Wine* named him and Mike Anthony two of the best new chefs in America, and they posed on the cover in their whites. But he still wasn't sure he wanted to spend the rest of his life cooking. He is in the position of a trombone virtuoso who never exactly intended to be a trombone player. "I mean, do I really want to spend my life doing this?" he said one morning. "It's incredibly hard to have a happy family life if you're a cook. I've heard about people who have, but I've never met any. And the money—I mean, we make money, but you could make more money by investing it in a C.D." Chefs, like writers, are wrung out by the work. "It's insane, insane, insane, *insane,*" one said cheerfully. "All cooking is monotonous," another said. "No matter how varied you think your technique is, you always end up taking something flabby and making it crunchy on the outside, tender on the inside. Food is always crispy out and tender in, over and over and over again."

Dan even had doubts about the doctrine. One spring morning as we were walking through the market, we saw some hydroponic tomatoes. The other cooks walked right past them. "Now, this is a problem for me," he said, stopping in front of the red pile. "You see, I mean, here it is a nice day, it's a hot day, and someone is going to come in and ask for a tomato salad, and a steak, and I'm going to have to be the virtuous guy who tells him, 'No, you can't have it.' I mean, is that a slightly weird role for me to be playing? The tomatoes are good, this local guy is growing them, and I have to be too goddamn virtuous to serve them because they aren't dirt-grown in August? It worries me a lot, so I'm always trying to make compromises. I mean—Alice, forgive me, but I don't know if I always want to be that pure. Tonight we'll do a cold tomato soup with coriander—and we'll press that on the tomato-hungry public."

Peter walked over to the tomato stand. "The way I see it," he said, "it's part of the pleasure of the seasons—waiting. I want to be satiated with tomatoes when tomato time comes. I want to wait."

"Yeah, but the stockbroker or whatever doesn't want to wait."

The conversation turned to a new restaurant that had just opened, three stories high and full of restaurant theater (specially designed uniforms, that kind of thing).

"I love that stuff," Dan said brightly.

Peter stopped. "You're . . . kidding, right?"

"No, I'm not. I love that stuff." He shrugged. "I guess I'm not reverent enough."

It would be easy to be irreverent about what might be called the snob appeal behind the doctrine. All status, including the status of what we eat, depends on invidious comparison. At the turn of the last century, when only the wealthy could obtain out-of-season ingredients—strawberries in December, oranges in August—hothouse fruit had the prestige that organic fruit has now. When anyone at any time can go to the Food Emporium and shop for cherries and raspberries, glory attaches to someone who has the leisure to go to a market and shop for ramps and rhubarb.

But then all values in real life get expressed as manners; the mistake is to think that values are *only* manners. Everything is a show; what matters, as the bishop said to the mermaid, is what you're showing. "Seasonality," whatever snobbishness it may express, also expresses a desire to connect, to a region, a place, a locality. (The larger, ecological point of the doctrine, that agribusiness is bad for civilization, is, of course, independent of the aesthetics of taste, but that point, in turn, could be met by the counterpoint that agribusiness of one kind or another is, on a desperately overpopulated planet, necessary for the survival of civilization at all. And this conversation can turn round and round over a dinner table until you are hungry again.)

. . .

After a two-month marination in the farmers' market, I had come to my own conclusions about what in the market was affectation and what real gain. Some things that you could find outside the market—oranges and lemons and pineapples and onions, red and yellow, and eggplant, and the tougher cuts of beef and pork, even raspberries and cherries and fresh herbs—were perfectly okay in their supermarket form. Other things, though—strawberries, potatoes, asparagus, fresh peas, green beans, poultry—had come to seem to me so inferior in their mass-produced versions that they ought to be made to do a perp walk from the produce bin to the compactor.

The list I finally decided on for the menus was composed of pale or delicate things: veal, trout, day-neutral strawberries, green garlic and its scapes, mustard greens, small sour cherries, snap peas shelled. The veal would be Amy's child-raised veal and the trout from Max Creek farms at the market. (Of all the things I have loved to eat, trout seems to me the one that has almost disappeared from the world of tastes; farmed salmon is pleasant if uniform, but most farmed trout doesn't even taste like fish.) I threw in sorrel because I love it, and also because I have seldom seen it used except in a sauce for salmon. Since there was no starch, I allowed each cook to fill in as he or she wanted to.

The week after I chose the ingredients, we went from place to place, to see what each cook had made of the writer's list. As it turned out, each one created something far more individual than you could have imagined from the list of ingredients I'd e-mailed. At this point, of course, I should give out recipes, or at least pass around a platter of hors d'oeuvres. But I will do the best impression I can of Robert Courtine's sonorous style of assessment and boldly unleash a raft of exotic metaphor. So let it be said that Philippe Bertineau's version of the menu was a visit to a region of France: The innards of the veal, sweetbreads and kidneys, were crisped above the crunchy snap peas; on one side, a little blush of color, the sour cherries were recused from dessert and turned into a chutney. Although Bertineau cooks high, his references are to regional cooking: All French food aspires to the condition of country cooking; all haute cuisine pines for the farm where it began. His trout was stuffed with the mustard greens, so that the sweetness of the fish was set off by the startling spice of the greens, and he snipped the sorrel with scissors and used it in a chiffonade, rather than the expected imitation of sorrel sauce.

Sara Jenkins turned the same list into a July day in Tuscany. Her veal got minced up, yet not dumbed down, into a ragù, and she mixed her mustard greens with fresh ricotta over rigatoni. A poached or sautéed trout was, I think, too finicky for her country heart, and so she served smoked trout as a starter, on bread. It was an American's Tuscany, perhaps, but all flax and terraced fields nonetheless. Romy Dorotan seemed to turn everything toward the East, with sudden juxtapositions of cool courtyards and hot sunlight (the farm-raised veal was curried; the sweet trout heated with cayenne; the baby fennel chilled with watermelon ice), and yet the more time you spent with his menu, the more its European and Davidian origins emerged. Though the ambitious juxtapositions of flavor were Eastern, the idea of bringing those juxtapositions forward, rather than leaving them lurking in the shadows of tradition, was entirely French.

With the two chefs I knew best, not just their origins but their entire characters were evident. Peter Hoffman, whose commitment to the idea of the menu was most intense, made the most intensely committed menu. It was, if anything, too intense, too varied: He marinated the brook trout, for instance, so that it became a kind of superior, briny herring, and then married it with the mustard greens. We liked his dessert best of anything: a sour-cherry-and-day-neutral-strawberry compote, simple and sweet and acid, with buttermilk ice cream. Even Dan Barber's doctrinal doubts, I would insist, could be tasted in the menu he prepared with Mike Anthony. They shelled the snap peas and turned them into a sublime sweet-pea puree with yogurt and fresh herbs. It was a cultivated dish masquerading as a rustic one, from the market, certainly, but not entirely of the market. Their veal was slow-roasted in the Parisian manner, with the mustard greens and garlic reduced to a single resonant tang.

Like I say, I should give out recipes. But, failing that, I can hand out an insight. It was not a game. The metaphor of the *jeu,* at least, was all wrong. Cooks have no time for games. They do what they have to do. I had not created a game for them to play. I had created one more stress in a life of stresses, and they had turned it into a taste.

. . .

When the week of the menu was done, I had the cooks over for Sunday brunch. They looked at one another's menus: Part of the pathos of their work, I realized, was that they were too busy to eat out much. Dan couldn't make it. A Con Ed power failure had hit his restaurant on Saturday morning, and he and Mike had spent the whole day distributing their produce to other people's fridges, then had to spend all Sunday collecting it.

The cooks asked how it had been for *me,* and the only metaphor I could come up with was a homely one. I said that it had been like listening to each of them talk; and then, as they ate and argued, something else became clear to me. Searching for an occult connection between cooking and writing, I had missed the most obvious one. They are both dependencies of conversation. What unites cooks and writers is that their work flows from the river of human talk around a table. People cook to bring something to the table; people write to keep something that was said there. I enjoy the company of cooks, I realized, because I love the occasions they create for conversation.

Everyone agreed to try the game again in the fall, and, over bagels and lox, Peter said that he and his wife, Susan, had decided to remodel Savoy—to take out the beautiful candlelit room and put in a bar and new decor, with framed black-and-white photographs, to make it more accessible to the Armani shoppers who now fill Soho. Their idea had always been to make a first-class neighborhood restaurant; now that the neighborhood had changed, they'd have to change, too. Cooks, it struck me, are even more immediately vulnerable to life's difficulties than writers are, and life, though it looks tender on the outside, is very crunchy on the inside, which may be why we prefer it with food.

Third Thanksgiving: Bitterosities

Olivia tells us that Kweeda has died, and we mourn her as we might mourn ourselves. Everyone has sobered up now—or our circle has, anyway; the intoxicated are downtown, making love and taking coke, not up here in the parent belt, where grown-ups make dates for sex as their children make dates to play.

Only Charlie Ravioli, prince of the city, seemed immune from the sobriety as he raced around town, bumping into Olivia. But now even he has begun to learn through suffering, as epic characters must, I suppose, even epic characters that begin as imaginary friends.

He had been married, and then . . . well, it happened this way. A few days before Thanksgiving, Olivia mentioned that Ravioli had gotten married. Gotten married! we said. Who to? Or to whom? To a girl named Kweeda, Olivia announced. (I am guessing at the spelling, obviously, thinking it likelier that a guy like Ravioli would marry an African princess, Kweeda, than Queeda, mere Balkan nobility.) They went to a place called Cornfields on their honeymoon, which Martha and I imagined as one of those golf-and-baked-ham Wasp resorts in Virginia or Tennessee that you used to see advertised in *Gourmet* ("Come to Cornfields for the Finest in Traditional Dining . . .").

But then something happened. Olivia was at her usual speaking station, the little café table where she has lunch with Martha while I work, hidden behind a screen. She forgets that I am there and then launches into dreamy flights of invention; she informs Martha that she was with Luke when he told jokes before the Purim crowd. "My brother had a microphone, and I had a microphone."

But today there is a new seriousness. "Mommy," she says as she eats her tuna sandwich, "I'm sorry to tell you that Kweeda has died."

"She's died!" Martha says, genuinely shocked. "What did she die of?"

"She died of a disease called Bitterosity."

"Bitterosity!" Martha exclaims.

Olivia nods grimly. Bitterosity had taken down Kweeda; it could happen to anyone. She had moved to New York, I guessed, and gotten it there, as we all do, or will, if we're not careful. What might Bitterosity *be*? Bitterness born of betrayal and disappointment, jealousy and resentment—half of life here involves safeguarding yourself from the plague of Bitterosity. It *is* a plague: You see the buboes of Bitterosity swelling on your body, the flush of Bitterosity rising on your face, and soon the cheerful young woman who arrived with a black leotard and desire to dance, or the young man with a manuscript in his suitcase and an ache in his heart, becomes another grumbling embittered crank, a querulous angry radio-talk-show caller, an anonymous poster, a failed writer complaining about his publisher and the stupidity of the critics and the public, or just another person contributing bad reviews of inoffensive restaurants to Zagat. Bitterosity has you in its grip, and, like poor Kweeda, you die from it. (Actually, I can count at least four people I know who have already died of Bitterosity, though not all of them quite know it. They are vampires of Bitterosity, living on in the strange Manhattan gloaming of its afterlife.)

One cure for incipient Bitterosity is company. People write as if anxiety and fear are the same thing, or interchangeable things. Every day in the city we are learning that they're not. Anxiety is provocative, a stimulant that makes you act out; fear is silencing, a paralytic, and it makes you burrow in. Movement and activity can eliminate or reduce anxiety, but fear can be cured only by retreat, or alleviated by sudden bursts of hope, or comforted by the company of friends.

The most magical company-creating thing I've seen in the past year is a machine—a machine that listens to the world, reads its mind, and tells you exactly what's up in there. The machine, a Jimmy Neutron assemblage of display monitors and loudspeakers and copper wire, is the brainchild of a Bell Labs statistician named Mark Hansen and a sound designer and artist named Ben Rubin. Mark is a scientist and engineer who looks like one, and Ben is one of those downtown people who are somehow half Laurie Anderson and half Mr. Wizard. For most of the past year, you could find their machine in a loft on the Bowery; you could just drop in, if you knew it was there. It was made partly as a work of conceptual-computer art, partly as a real attempt to take the world's temperature at any given moment, actually to hear the unconscious of the übersoul.

I went to see the machine during a jittery moment. I found its block of Chinese restaurants and restaurant supply houses and walked up a flight of steep wooden stairs. The machine, or "Listening Post," as it is called, works in a way that would be hard for an anxiety-ridden computer-illiterate type to understand, but the basic idea, as I understand it, is this: Hansen and Rubin have written a program that allows them to probe into all the unrestricted Internet chat rooms in the English-speaking world and dredge up thousands upon thousands of random sentences even as they are being typed. The program is an "octopus." The casual remarks, desperate pleas, and lecherous queries that are sucked out of the stream of world chatter are then relayed in various ways on the two hundred or so small screens and ten loudspeakers that make up the machine's public face. The found words and sentence fragments can be strung out at random on the display monitors or made to race across the screens in constant streams, like a Times Square zipper, giving the thing a Jenny Holzer–like gnomic and oracular quality. Better yet, a speech synthesizer can read aloud from the found chatter—either intoning words and sentences one by one in a sepulchral BBC announcer's voice or chanting and singing them in fugue-like overlay. The craziness and weirdness that are harder to find now on New York streets are still there sunk down deep. Joe Gould is the patron saint of the Listening Post; his oral history of our time is in there.

Quite often the sequences of words and sentences are meaningless, but sometimes they take on striking shapes. Today, for instance, the machine produced a kind of found poem on the theme of "orange" and duct tape: "WARNING: CODE ORANGE where'd my ORANGE go? And plastic sheeting! duct tape and plastic people tape ducks now President PlasticWrap Who's got DUCK TAPE!? buy stock in duct tape duct tape and lingerie."

From fear to affirmation, or at least to sex, in nine lines. I walked back to the subway feeling comforted. I half expected one of the screens to announce the death of Kweeda, one of the voices murmuring to mourn her passing, until I recalled that only Olivia knows of it, and she is still too young for a computer.

Martha's antidote for the strange disease called Bitterosity is movement. She wants us to do things: for me to learn to drive at last, and to sail, as I've long wanted to, for us to move to Connecticut or New Jersey, where there are houses with gardens and you know one season from the next when you wake up and look outside, not when you check the front page of the paper to see what the weather is.

She has a need to believe in freedom and mobility. Not that, if the shoe drops, we will somehow escape Manhattan, fleeing the fire like the last Trojans, in a sailboat, gliding out past the Statue of Liberty, or, for that matter, in a station wagon. One only has to try to get across the George Washington Bridge to realize how ridiculously cut off all of Manhattan would be in any real kind of crisis. (In Manhattan, we used to think, we are ruined, and now we think we are doomed, when we are probably neither.)

But the emotional symbolism of potential escape is worth something, and so she is urging me to learn to do things, rather than to watch things. She has enrolled Luke and me in a sailing course all the way down in Annapolis, while she and Olivia go away to her mother's for the holidays. I am aware, have been made aware, as I have crisscrossed the country on planes for the past two years—becoming that bizarre early-millennium figure, the author on a book tour, who will be as incredible a figure to our children as the author on a Chautauqua lecture tour, like Howells and Twain and all the lesser figures, is to us—just how weird a place New York is, how unlike the country it claims to superintend. In some ways, the manners and habits of New York are as remote from the rest of the country as Venice is from Italy. Not just remote geographically, or because the city's head still turns toward Europe tropically. Remote in the basic patterns of the basic activities of civilization, movement and eating and laundry. New York is a walkers' city in a country of cars; New York is a compressed city in a country of malls; New York is a city where you take your dirty clothes to the local dry cleaner and walk three blocks to do it. We rely on foot and train, and an occasional recreational bike ride, while America is, first and last and above all, a country of cars and washing machines.

I do not discount the love of cars just because I can't drive one. When we are on holiday by the ocean, the appeal of the car to America becomes apparent. It is not only speed; it is a vehicle of intimacy. Conversation takes on a different hue. People need to share secrets in boxes, and cars are confessional-shaped. Lacking that, New Yorkers have the sauna in the health club, where grown men groan, wordlessly but meaningfully, sweating the Bitterosity out of their bodies. Perhaps if I could learn to sail, I would have the thrill of expertise without the necessity of driving, be able to move a vehicle from place to place without having to park.

Luke's solution to the problem of Bitterosity is intense engagement in the game of Yu-Gi-Oh! This is a bizarre Japanese card game that has swept through the third grade of Artists & Anglers like a brushfire through a dry forest in August. The parts I see are decks and decks, hundreds of cards to collect, each of which bears the (surprisingly well-drawn) picture of a figure from a Sword & Sorcery fantasy, a wizard or ghost or monster or elf or hero or ghoul. They have elaborate names, all translated from the Japanese into just slightly unidiomatic English, like images printed out of register in old comic books: Manga Ryu-Ran and Blue-Eyes White Dragon (rather than the Blue-Eyed Dragon); Maneater Bug and Relinquished; Black Illusion Ritual and Dark (rather than Black) Magician; Graceful Dice and Launcher

Spider. There is an elaborate backstory as well, about a small Japanese boy called Yugi, who somehow reawakened Egyptian deities, apparently long resident in Japan, who, in a neat bit of Escher-like self-reference, taught him the card game that represents their cosmic struggles.

The game, when you play it, has mind-numbingly elaborate rules, but you never seem to play it. The goal is to collect the cards and *plan* to play it someday. Weeks go by when all the boys talk about is what's in their decks—not who's won and lost, but what they have collected in their steady trips to the grungy little newsstands where the cards are sold (their money for new cards earned through bed making or begged through homework doing).

When they do at last play, it is like watching very small boys do their taxes: Two decks of cards confront each other, as in our old games of War, and each player slaps down a card. Then the small boys, with set frowns and knitted brows, read the front of the cards, trying to deduce what the result should be: "I think it's like the Blue-Eyed Dragon presented with, like, no hex, present on the board, is worth eight thousand points . . . no, it should be six thousand points, because I haven't presented my Dragon Enhancer yet. . . ." On and on, a purely literary, or at least literate, tedium that one would have thought doomed by video games, and yet the children seem drawn back into the cards by their very boringness. Happiness is absorption, and though by screens they are merely excited, by the cards they are absorbed.

I was reminded of this myself this year, when I found my own version of bliss while absorbed in the role of school safety patrol, wandering the neighborhood as a local pro tempore sentinel, a happy member of the new homeland-security culture. Sudden Flatfoot, I would have been called, had I been turned into a Yu-Gi-Oh! card. At Artists & Anglers, there is a long-standing requirement that every parent go out on safety patrol at least once a year. The obligation, like the patrol, dates from the seventies, when muggers hid in the subway station and thieves around the corner, when the park was dangerous, nightfall brought its risks, and kids really did get mugged occasionally on their way home.

These days the likeliest crime, I suppose, is some overstoked stockbroker stopping a seventh-grader to try to steal his attention-deficit medication. But the tradition persists, partly because it always has, partly because we are superstitious that if we stop it, the muggings will come back. (That's what a cultural tradition is, a pointless habit everyone is too scared to stop, like venerating Johnny Hallyday in France.)

I went to the school at three-thirty on the assigned day and was given my regalia: an eye-shatteringly orange safety vest and a walkie-talkie that made reassuring static noises when you pressed the talk button, and with which I was to stay in touch with home base at Artists & Anglers in case of an emergency, the shape, structure, and possible location of which were all left comfortably undefined. Then I was given my security perimeter: a three-block beat up and down Eighty-eighth Street (where Martha and I first lived in our nine-by-eleven basement room for three years), down to Eighty-seventh Street, and back. I was supposed to have a partner, one of the more determinedly artistic mothers, but she somehow hadn't shown. I had to go solo. I didn't mind. It made me more of the real *Lethal Weapon* thing—a cop with a beat, a grievance, and a lost partner.

It was the first *purely* happy time I'd know in years. Round and round the blocks, seeing the kids going home, saying with truly obnoxious officiousness (and to Luke's extreme embarrassment, when he saw me), "Okay, kids—let's move on! Okay, kids—let's get home. Everybody home now." I had become the voice of the Listening Post, calm and Olympian. Shooing them toward their homes, clad in the brief authority of an orange vest and a walkie-talkie.

The kids gave me steady, opaque, disbelieving looks. My achievement was the opposite of Holden Caulfield's ambition. Not to be the catcher, keeping the kids from the edge of the field, but rather the pusher on the pavement, urging them on back home.

I loved walking my beat, with the cocky, flat-footed insouciance of Charlie Chaplin in *Easy Street*, swirling my (mental) billy club while adjusting my (imaginary) Mack Sennett–style bobbie hat. Last summer we visited Rome and stood outside the Trevi Fountain, and we watched in awe as a specially designated group of cheery but forceful Italian policemen appeared every half hour or so to clear all the American college kids out of the fountain, where they were bathing their sore feet and splashing their overheated foreheads. The cops were nice about it, but they were cops: Their job was to protect the integrity of the fountain from American feet, and no kidding. "Dad," Luke said, "that's the job for you. You'd be a perfect fountain policeman." It was true: He'd spotted my love of pointless officiousness, of being right and well armed and indignant with absolutely nothing at stake. Being a fountain policeman is, I suppose, a "thankless" Sisyphean job—you clear out the kids from Dartmouth only to be overrun an hour later by Buckeyes. (But then what job is not Sisyphean, pushing the same stone up the same hill over and over again? The policeman walks the same street beat; the essayist, finishing one humane-liberal essay, watches it disappear and begins another. All of us spend all day pushing our stone to the top of the hill and find it back at the bottom when we show up the next morning. Sisyphus's real punishment was that he still had to hold down a normal job even after he was dead.)

I learned a lot on my beat, about why cops are the way they are, whether fountain police or homicide detectives or security patrolmen. The closer you looked at the blocks you were walking, over and over and over again, the more each block revealed itself—and the more suspicious, even paranoid, you became about what the signs of the block *really* meant, what was really going on there. You become conscious of the intricate variety of stores and storefronts. Density reveals itself as a particular pattern of parts: this odd little auction house, and this garage entrance beside it, and the two rival rental-car offices anchored by the garage, and the tailors down the stairs into this basement, and the Chinese restaurant that no one ever seems to enter or order from two doors away. On one street, a thousand small efforts at making a living, none seeming obviously to thrive; all, in fact, to a single policeman's passing eye, as empty and soulful as a Hopper afternoon interior, and yet it works. Somehow it thrives. (What Hopper was showing, it occurred to me, was not the desolation but the energy of American life: This is what a capitalist city looks like most of the time, half asleep and waiting.)

And then you became conscious of the play of people on the street. Why are these same people hanging out here, minute after minute and hour after hour . . . Why is this young messenger still standing in front of the auction house? Could be nothing . . . but go around the block once more. Hmmn, he's still there. Why? Waiting for a friend or a fix or a . . . That tone cops have—that steady wariness, even if you ask them for something simple and innocent, directions or advice—is the product of their experience. There really are sinister jigsaw-puzzle patterns out there, and you may be one of the pieces. That is why cops, so to speak, examine your edges even as they answer your entreaties.

I also understand now the other great policeman trait: why cops are both mildly paranoid and desperate for donuts. Craving carbohydrates is a natural consequence of police work: It's cold, you're paying attention to six things at once, and there's nothing that sounds so comforting as a shot of caffeine and a bit of pastry. The need for donuts is a product of the physical work of being outside in the cold coupled with the mental work of trying to find a pattern where there may be none, but where, if there is one, it could be sinister enough to cause a crime, get somebody hurt.

So as I made my rounds, I began to eye, wistfully, a busy Starbucks on the corner of Eighty-seventh Street, full of laughing people knocking back hot drinks. The craving began to work on me so strongly that, after a solid, virtuous hour of safety patrol, I decided to stop for a quick, excusable, union-sanctioned break. (The union would have blessed it had they known about it, and had I belonged to one.) I ducked into the Starbucks—leaving my poor private school charges, I suppose, for a moment completely naked to the Hobbesian elements—and got in line. Just a quick triple-grande cappuccino and a biscotti, I swore, and I would be back outside keeping the peace.

I got in line. The guy in front of me, a white guy in a suit with a loosened tie, was ordering one of those baroque-flavored and sweetened seasonal drinks that Starbucks sells: an eggnog latte or a gingerbread latte, that kind of thing. More incidental sweetness. There was some kind of confusion on the part of the girl behind the register—was it tall or grande or caf or decaf?—and he sighed hard and said, "What is *wrong* with you?" He had a nasty, bad New York tone.

"Hey," I said, about as sternly as I have ever said anything. "Let's keep it polite here." He swiveled and saw me standing there, an obnoxious shrimp, and was about to start letting me have it. But I held up my walkie-talkie and hit the button, surprising him with a blast of static. Then I stood there, impassive. He took me in : my orange vest and electronic communications gear, my look of official purpose. Perhaps the fuzz—*obviously* the fuzz, though whether bona fide Starbucks security or sinister private contractor, he was as yet uncertain.

He took one nano-step back, unsure. I scowled and hit him with another burst of static. Then I spoke into the radio. "It's all right," I said to no one in particular, "this situation secure."

It sounded like just what Starbucks security might report to Seattle. Then I looked at him again, hard. The hiss and cough of the milk steamers continued in the background. He shrugged and stepped to the back counter where you pick up your drink. I hit the back of his jacket, hard, with one last long-distance burst of meaningless electric noise. I felt utterly vindicated, in love with the booming security professions, at home in the new epoch, a lover of my time: administering homeland safety, proud and paranoid among the paper cups.

When I told the family about it over dinner—how I had curbed hate crime at Starbucks and brought justice to the baristas—I thought they would be pleased: their First Line of Defense, their very own First Responder, tested and ready.

They looked at me long and pityingly. "The really sad thing, children," said my wife, "is that he means it. If he can't be with the fountain police, your father would like to be some kind of cappuccino commando, making sure that milk steamers don't get used nefariously."

"But all the kids got home safe, at least," I said.

"They always do," Luke pointed out.

"See?" I said, and I thought I had a point.

Security, security, its rites and rituals. To dramatize our insecurities, to hold Bitterosity a moment at the arm's edge, we do . . . well, many things. The Listening Post hears us redefining even the miraculous. A few months ago we all spent a lot of time watching a man stand on a pole in Bryant Park. Then he jumped off. It happened not far from the office, and several of us would go over during lunch or after work to watch him. David Blaine, the magician who did the standing and the jumping, is a local boy from Brooklyn, and in years past he has tried such self-improving stunts as having himself imprisoned in a block of ice in Times Square for three days and being buried alive in a closed coffin on West Sixty-eighth Street for a week. This time, in Bryant Park, he stood for almost thirty-five hours in baggy clothes on a small platform atop a ninety-foot pole.

The strange thing is that this magician wasn't doing anything magical. He was just *standing* there. For P.R. purposes, I guess, Blaine invoked the tony pedigree of certain earlier columnists: the saintly stylites, out there in the Byzantine desert at the dawn of the last Dark Age. But what he was doing in fact belongs to a very different local tradition of doing nothing in midair. They called it flagpole sitting back in the twenties, when it was all the rage in this part of town, and it, too, had its heroes: Alvin "Shipwreck" Kelly, who perched at the top of a sky-high pole above the old Madison Square Garden for twenty-two days and six hours, and fifteen-year-old Avon Foreman, who, over on Broadway, reportedly established the "juvenile flagpole-sitting record"—ten days, ten hours, and ten minutes. (I went back to the office and looked it up.)

Back then, though, flagpole sitting was never confused with magic. Magic was what Harry Houdini was doing down the street at the Hippodrome—an office building and parking garage now—struggling in and out of straitjackets, slipping in and out of handcuffs, escaping from locked safes underwater. Magic was work. Magic was activity. Flagpole sitting was simply endurance, its only prerequisite an endless capacity for standing there.

That's not magic, that's just a stunt, I thought as I watched him. But each age calls magic whatever stunt it needs to marvel at, and each age gets the magic it deserves. David Blaine, standing up there, was actually as good a magical metaphor for the moment as Houdini, fighting his way out of the straitjacket of immigrant identity toward prosperity, was for his, or David Copperfield, causing whole monuments to disappear while having dubious assignations with supermodels, was for the Gilded Age, now in twilight. (He made the Statue of Liberty vanish—a stunt no one even wants to *think* about now.) David Blaine is the magician as stoic, the magician as the nonmagical bystander, drawing on the ancient Egyptian gods of extremely tedious normality, the magician as the guy from the outer boroughs who just stands there and puts up with it.

A Steinbergian drawing of New York in these years would show eight million people, each person standing on a pole above an abyss of anxiety—not looking down, never looking down, looking only from side to side, warily. Yet with so many people perched together, New York life in this hair-raising time looks just like—well, just like New York life, only somehow heightened. We are scared, and we stand there. The leaders of the country seem to have abandoned the first and oldest principles of leadership—don't panic the troops and always lead from the front—which have long held good for everything from leading armies to victory to leading your kids to the Port-A-John at halftime. The new model is frighten everybody you can and dive into a secure bunker. *The bad guys are out for the Statue of Liberty, they're out for the Brooklyn Bridge, they're on the number 6 train, and they're probably down the hall in 6-F—but don't ask us what you can do about it, and don't expect us to join you while you wait. You're on your own.*

On the last night of Blaine's performance, I was working late and so went back to watch the magician jump down. One felt almost grateful for his gracelessness: After a clumsy back flop onto cardboard boxes, he emerged, not pumping his fist, triumphant, but huddled in a blanket, his voice shaking. "I'm all right," he said; but his body language seemed to say, *It's scary up there, it's scary down here, and it's scary when you're in midair.* It is a curious thing to be grateful for a frightened daredevil. That is the Great Blaine's queer period appeal: After each stunt he seems to say, in effect, not "I transcended!" but "Hey, fuggetaboutit—I was freezing, I almost lost my mind, I thought I was going to die, this was a lot harder than I thought it was going to be." But he also says, "I'm still here," and we call it magic.

. . .

Kirk uses his mind every day to discipline his fear, not because his fear is not real—it is, absolutely—but because to give in to it would be to die before death comes. I go with him to the chemotherapy, where he sits with two catheters in his veins, one putting in saline solution, the other the hyper-powerful chemo, which I imagine as something like Drano, which, horribly, it probably is; and he talks and talks: about the lectures he will give next year, about the Metrozoids, the flag football team he is coaching for Luke, about the state of the world. He throws the *Daily News* across the chemotherapy suite, infuriated by the cultivation of fear. We discuss Christmas, approaching for the children.

Luke wants a Yu-Gi-Oh! structure deck, some kind of Japanese super-game that gives you the, I don't know what, ghosts and magicians and Egyptian pharaohs large enough to win tournaments. But it costs fifty dollars, and we agonize about whether to get him this—a deck of cards, after all. Kirk nods wearily. Normally, he is all for toughening and inspiring the children, but not now, not exactly. "Buy him the structure deck," he says. "It's fifty dollars, not fifty thousand."

Fear is the great solvent, the great freezing agent, the great chill. It leads us toward superstition and into the bus. Lately, I like to ride the buses, the ordinary city buses, those vaguely purposeless-looking, bulbous-faced, blue-and-bone M2s and 3s and 4s and 5s that chug up and down the avenues and along the cross streets, wheezing and whining, all day and night.

For twenty-odd years in New York, I never took the bus at all. Even if I had been on a bus, I don't think I would recall it. Bus blindness is a standard New York illness; of all the regularities of life here, the bus is the least celebrated, the least inclined to tug at the heart or be made into a symbol of our condition. The taxi has its checkered lore, the subway its legend, and the Town Car a certain Michael Douglas in *Wall Street* icon quality; but if there is a memorable bus scene in literature, or an unforgettable moment in a movie that takes place on a New York City bus, I have not found it. It isn't that buses are intrinsically inimical to symbolism: The London bus has a poetry as rich as the Tube's—there is Mary Poppins, there is Mrs. Dalloway. In Paris, Pascal rides the bus, Zazie dreams of riding the Métro, and that is, evenly, that. In L.A., Keanu Reeves rides the bus, round and round in desperate Dennis Hopper–driven circles. But as a symbolic repository, the New York City bus does not exist. The only significant symbolic figure that the New York bus has had is Ralph Kramden, and what he symbolizes about the bus is that being stuck in one is one more form of comic frustration and disappointment; the bus is exactly the kind of institution that would have Ralph Kramden as its significant symbolic figure.

If you had asked me why I avoided the bus, I suppose I would have said that the bus was for old people, or that taking the bus was one step short of not living in New York at all, and that if you stayed on the bus long enough, it would take you right out of town. Riding the bus, I thought, was one of those activities, like going to Radio City, that was in New York but not really of it. My mother-in-law rode the bus when she came to New York to visit, and that, to me, said whom the bus was made for: elegant older women who didn't mind traveling forty-five minutes every morning to visit their grandchildren.

And then I didn't ride the bus because when we first arrived here I loved the subway so. The subway was anxiety-filled. Compared with the vivid, evil, lurid subway, the bus seemed a drab bourgeois necessity—Shirley Booth to the subway's Tallulah Bankhead. In the late seventies and early eighties, the subway was both grander and stranger than a newcomer can imagine now. The graffiti, for one thing, was both more sordid inside—all those "tags"—and more beautiful outside. When the wild-style cars came roaring into a station, they were as exciting and shimmering as Frank Stella birds. The air-conditioning was a lot spottier, too, and sometimes the windows were open, driving the stale and fetid air around in an illusion of cooling. When the air-conditioning worked, it was worse. You walked from steambath to refrigerator, as if changing continents, and your perspiration seemed to freeze within your shirt, a phenomenon previously known only to Antarctic explorers.

Feral thugs and killer nerds rode the subway together, looking warily at one another. And yet there was something sublime about it.

Although it was incidentally frightening, it was also systematically reassuring: It shouldn't have worked; it had stopped working; and yet it worked—vandalized, brutalized, a canvas and a pissoir, it reliably took you wherever you wanted to go. It was a rumbling, sleepless, snorting animal presence underfoot, more a god to be appeased and admired than a thing that had been mastered by its owners. If the stations seemed, as people said, Dantesque, that was not simply because the subway was belowground, and a punishment, but also because it offered an architectural order that seemed free from any interfering human hand, running by itself in its own grim circles. It was religious in the narrow sense as well: Terror and transportation were joined together, and fear propelled you to a higher plane. (The taxis, an alternative if you had the money, were also alarming then—a silent or determined driver in a T-shirt, resting on a mat of beads and demanding, fifty blocks before your destination, which side of the street you wanted, without being at all sublime.)

The bus also has its order, old-fashioned and patriarchal, maintained by an irritable chief. The driver has control over his world and delights in the exercise of arbitrary authority, like a French bureaucrat. On the bus, if your MetroCard turns out to be short fifty cents, the driver will look at you with distaste, tell you to find change from fellow passengers (surprisingly, to a subway rider, people dig into their purses cheerfully), and if this doesn't work, he will wearily wave you on back. You are included, fool though you are, and this grace is often bestowed even as the driver ignores the pounded fists and half-audible pleas for admission of the last few people who, running for the bus, arrived a second too late. The driver's control of the back door is just as imperious. A zone of acceptable access, a five- or six-foot expanse exists around the bus stop, known only to the driver, who opens and closes the door as he senses the zone appearing and receding.

When I first started riding the bus, I mentioned it to people sheepishly, almost apologetically, as one might mention having had a new dental plate put in, or the advantages of low-fat yogurt—not downright shameful, perhaps, but still mildly embarrassing. But to my surprise, almost everyone I talked to (women, I think, in particular) turned out to feel the same way I do about the bus. "The bus lets you feel that you're in control, or that someone's in control," one woman said to me, and another friend said flatly, "You can see what's coming." The bus feels safe. Of course, there is no reason for the bus to feel safe. (A friend from Jerusalem got on the bus with understandable watchfulness.) Yet we have decided to create in the city a kind of imaginary geography of fear and safety that will somehow make us safer from It—the next attack, the Other Shoe, the Dreadful Thing that we all await.

I have thought about it a lot (there's time to think on the bus) and have come to the conclusion that while anxiety seeks the company of excitement, fear seeks the illusion of certainty. Anxiety is the ordinary New York emotion. It is a form of energy, and it clings, like ivy to a garden wall, to whatever is around to cling to, whether nationalism or the Knicks or Lizzie Grubman, as readers of the *New York Post* recognize. At the height of the bubble, anxiety was all around us: the anxiety of keeping up, of not falling behind, of holding one's place.

Fear, well earned or not, is a different thing. People who live with the higher kinds of fear—the sick, the soldier—go on living mostly by making structures of delusional domesticity. They try to create an illusion of safety, and of home. At Waterloo, soldiers welcomed the little signs of farm-keeping evident around them; in the dugouts of the Somme, every rat-ridden alley had a designation and every rat itself a pet name. The last time New Yorkers were genuinely afraid, as opposed to merely anxious, was during the great crime wave of the sixties and mid-seventies, and they responded in the same way: by constructing an elaborate, learn-it-by-heart geography of safe and unsafe enclaves, a map of safe rooms. The knowledge that your map of safe rooms could not truly protect you from what you feared then, any more than riding the bus can save you from it now, did not alter the need to have a map. People say that twentysomethings have sex out of fear—that terror sex—but twentysomethings have sex out of sex, and the adjective of the decade is always attached to it. In the eighties, they had safe sex, and in the nineties boom sex, and they will have sex among the ruins, if it comes to that.

What we have out of fear is not sex, or any other anxiety-energized activity, but stillness. It's said that people in the city are nicer now, or more cooperative, and I suppose this is true. But it is true for reasons that are not themselves entirely nice. The motivation of this niceness is less rectitude and reform than just plain old-fashioned fright. There are no atheists in foxholes, but there are no religious arguments in foxholes, either. The fear we feel isn't as immediate or as real as the fear soldiers feel. But our response is the same. These structures of delusional domesticity are the mainstay of many lives in New York now. The bus, a permanently running dinner party among friends, a fiction of family for a dollar fifty, a Starbucks on wheels, is the rolling image of the thing we dream of now as much as we wanted the broadband pipe to wash away our sins three years ago, and that is the safe room. For the first time, the bus has something strange enough to symbolize.

But then fear and the delusions that go with it are everywhere. After Thanksgiving, my friend the great property developer invited me to dinner, and there I met men who were planning a war. In his huge apartment on Fifth Avenue he had them all, the wise men and gurus of the neo-con initiative. The guru spoke on the Arabs: "They either want to be at the table or on the menu," he said dismissively. Seeing the worry on my face, F.A., who a year ago had been wise about the concentric circles of culture, reassured me. "This is no big deal," he said. "It's two weeks, three weeks, at most."

It occurs to me, walking home, that they are seeking their own delusional domesticity; a familiar place, and a very weird safe room. Invasion, occupation, radical reform—all of this belongs not to a new agenda but to an old and, in its way, comforting one, where states hit other states over the head with billy clubs and drag them to the slammer. To think of terrorism as a police problem, rather than a military one, is not to minimize it in a comforting way; it is to confront the real fear in its true, even more terrible dimensions. Since terrorism starts off as the weapon of war's losers, another victory in war will not make terrorists disappear. It will only make them multiply. The true thing we have to fear—the "non-state actor," the atomic bomb smuggled into Times Square—is more real as a problem for the overmatched police right here than one that can be solved by the overweening military somewhere over there.

I didn't say any of this, of course, but listened, made a small squeak of doubt, was silenced, and then went home.

And the children—are they frightened, too? It is hard to know. There are moments when they seem warped, in some way, by what has happened. Luke is certainly fearful in ways that I don't think I was at his age. Is it him or the time? He quizzes us about the possibilities of catastrophe—what would happen if a tornado hit, an earthquake, a tsunami. But his class did a "theme" project on the Empire State Building, and they don't seem to make any particular connection between height and height, tall building and tall building. They are fearful but not phobic.

On the train in Canada, we are playing Twenty Questions. Olivia says, "Something that is a thing and isn't a thing." We ponder it, used to the metaphysics of Twenty Questions as four-year-olds play it. "The Twin Towers," she says happily, and we shudder—but she doesn't. I think often of that movie *Hope and Glory,* children of the Blitz, completely nonchalant.

Luke and I went down to Annapolis this summer to learn to sail. I had dreamed of sailing for so long, so intensely, that it was sad to learn that I would never be any good at it. I couldn't keep straight which direction to turn the wheel—couldn't tell left from right, or port from starboard, whatever they call it. The other students in our boat came from deep in America: They were bass fishermen and recreational boaters, sportsmen who drove up in their SUVs. They wanted to know how much speed you could get up in a sailboat and whether you could hope to sneak up on the salmon in the early morning. (Not much. Yes, certainly.)

The truth was that, never having learned to drive, I could not now substitute sailing. The necessary reflexes, the coordination of starting and stopping and turning and pointing and docking, wouldn't imprint on my nervous system no matter how I tried. There was too much else in there already, and the bits that could have learned were burnt out, neural chains long ago discarded, like Armani suits from the late seventies. My neural networks are in place now; I am their prisoner, like Jacob Marley of his little bills, enchained by my own neurons, on paths I will never leave.

It wasn't much better for Luke, even though he is young enough to be making new chains. The sailing teachers, with some combination of safety consciousness and sadism, emphasized the consequence of capsizing a boat, and they turned the boat over in shallow water and had all the kids breathe underneath it. I made encouraging noises when Luke went to do it, *it's nothing,* but I knew it threw him—and why not? Who wants to cower beneath a capsized boat? Then they showed a safety film: boats exploding, turning over, running into docks, red flame and white smoke. By the time we got back to the motel for a barbecue meal, Luke was alarmed. So was I. He crawled into my bed that night, and the next day, seeing his shoulders droop in the hundred-degree heat, and feeling my own frustration with left and right, I looked at him, and he looked at me; let's get out of here. We rented a taxi, got the train in Baltimore, and went home, playing Five Crowns, a new card game, all the way.

When we were back outside Penn Station, I could almost see him breathing easier again, could feel my own breathing ease. I thought: *I am fit for playing cards on intercity trains, walking the school street beat, doomed to foot-propelled movement, or at least to being a perpetual passenger as other people master speed, a bus and taxi rider, a New Yorker.* I bought some fresh tuna and grilled it in the cast-iron pan with the window open, and then we put on our shorts and walked over to First Avenue to Sedutto for a sundae, throwing a tennis ball from baseball glove to baseball glove as we walked and talked, playing our own game, a couple of cockneys, home for good.

. . .

The children become more finished every month, less like an image and more like themselves. Luke is more like his mother, graceful, Scandinavian-looking, with narrow almond eyes—good-humored, fair-minded, easily distracted, and a bit dreamy; Olivia is like one of my Sephardic aunts, sharp-jawed and -chinned, quick, soulful and a *fresser.* He accepts the city, she adores it. She even speaks, for all her four-year-old phonology, like a New Yorker, words tripping over one another, with a mouth full of Spoonerisms: her hometown, New York, becomes New Nork, or often Yew Nork. She doesn't quite care.

Coming home from the summer after Labor Day, we all went out for pizza, to an open-air place on Second Avenue. Luke, I could sense, was sorry the summer was over, but Olivia was breathing in the joy of another New York fall. One could feel the autumn alteration on the streets: the people in shorts walking one step quicker than they did only two weeks before, the fresh breeze just hinted at in the air blowing into town.

A man went by, a drunk, and called out the loud empty cry of New York rage: "F—— you, a—hole," he hollered, to no one in particular that I could see.

Olivia, having no idea what the words meant, still recognized the familiar cry of her familiar jungle, another sound you always hear back where I come from. Her eyes lit up.

"Daddy," she said, knowing I would share the feeling, almost sighing with the pleasure, "Daddy, aren't you glad to be back in Yew Nork?"

The Listening Post keeps on listening. After Christmas they moved it to the Whitney Museum as an "installation." I took Luke at the height of another terror alert, and together we sat in the dark on a bench and watched and listened as the fragments of other people's dream lives went by, spoke up, made themselves appear and then disappear again.

It was a week of unseasonal snow, and the city was suddenly bright white, a peaceful and reassuring sight, but strange. The machine revealed a world of men and women standing on poles, looking down—but gesturing to one another, too, I now saw, cupping their hands over their mouths and calling out: "I am here. Where are you?" The speech synthesizer was really a kind of mental X-ray machine; all that each of these people was doing was writing, merely writing, and the ghostlike voice that enunciated their words was making loud something that was in reality soft and inward, buried deep.

Some of the sequences were larksome and even obscene, and I worried that Luke would get the wrong impression. Other sequences had a more Joycean flow. Finnegans Terror Alert: "Duct tape and plastic for the White House duct tape, and water in the bathtub, eheh hmmm, i got to wear my orange shoes again i like orange and yellow and pink and red its all a plot by saranwrap and duct tape mcm. . . we always shave duct tape. . . always."

When the machine was set to take in whole sentences, I found, unsurprisingly, that the music of the world's mind was less monstrous than mundane. At the height of the terror alert, some remarks were crass ("if a womans breasts look like two oranges stuffed in a tubesock ill tell em"), others explanatory ("the plastic bags are to cover the windows incase of chemical or bio warfare"), still others darkly ironic ("damn if only the wtc used duct tape on the windows we wouldn't be in this mess"). Some people were eager for instruction ("they are saying the alert level is 'High' . . . is that orange, red, or purple??"), others eager to instruct ("I looked, duct tape and plastic sheeting don't have a product expiration date"). A few were truly panicky ("Does anyone know how to get duct tape glue off a dog??").

No one, not even the machine or its makers, knew where any of this is coming from. The man with duct tape on his dog may be an anxious New Zealander or he may be the president of the United States. Even in moments of crisis, though, the music of the world's mind is remarkably constant: There is a steady bass line of lust ("I am naked, I like my naked butt"), a middle range of appetite ("I like smoked salmon"), and a high tremolo of keening anxiety.

The world, it seems, is ruled by sex and worry; mankind's two passions are to be safe and satisfied, at once upright and getting laid. Even when most of us are trembling on orange alert, someone somewhere is trembling at the thought of sharing a chat room with a Swedish teenager unencumbered by shame or parents. When it started snowing again outside, the machine was snowing, too, as all that snow passed through all those millions of minds. Some people were indignant ("NE people are a bunch of pansies! Here in North Western Montana, we've been getting snow like that forever. You environmental pukes screwed up the East and now want to do the same out here. I think we need to put a pack of wolves in central park"), while others used the occasion to focus on the news that really counts ("I don't know, I would probably throw his butt out in the snow and take 60% of what he was worth. If you can't be honest and tell your spouse that you want out, then you deserve to have half of your possessions removed. You don't deserve to be murdered, but I suppose that is a risk you take when you make a fool out of your spouse").

By the time I went back alone the following day, even the snow had passed out of the machine, along with all that orange, and the world was back to its usual muddle of fear ("When people refer to Israelis as Zionists . . .") and appetite ("I am looking for a girl who wants . . .") The false colors of the world are orange and yellow and red, the bright artificial colors of fear, the overstressed scarlet flush of the onset of Bitterosity. Leaving the Whitney for the slushy street outside, I felt that the inside of all of our heads had, for a moment at least, returned, like the city itself, to the world's true colors, gray and green.

Under One Roof

The great department stores of New York now lie on the avenues like luxury liners becalmed in a lagoon, big ships in shallow water. All around them, the dhows and junks and speedboats of the new national retailing, Staples and Victoria's Secret and Banana Republic and the Gap, honk at them and insult their sisters and get in their way. (And the newcomers hunt in pairs, so that no Duane Reade appears without a Starbucks nearby, no Staples without a Victoria's Secret minding its rear, as though the urge to tickle your husband and the urge to buy discounted stationery goods, the urge to caffeine and the urge to Coricidin were twinned deep in the desire system of the brain.) Saks and Bergdorf's and Bloomingdale's, immense and slow, look down at them and try to continue on a stately course, but the water is ebbing from around their keels.

Our sense of this, our mental image of it, is real and grounded in what we read—just this summer, Lord & Taylor, whose New York store is the southernmost ship of the Fifth Avenue fleet, and which is owned by the May company, lost nearly four thousand employees and thirty-two sister stores and was sent back to dry dock to be remade, nothing left but its signature. "Lackluster upon lackluster" is how a Piper Jaffray analyst describes the department-store sector. The professional retail trade papers worry about the disappearance of the department store exactly as the theater people worry about Broadway. But the decline is also intuitive and grounded in what we feel about the city. As recently as the early nineties, when Bloomies almost fell and women wept, department stores still mattered; they mattered as talk shows mattered then, as cable news matters now. One day we feel that something is big, and the next day we know that it is not. Without even looking at a receipt, we know somehow that the romance of the department store is fading, and we wonder what life will be like when it is gone.

Some of the department stores in town are in good shape—chiefly those that have been narrowly redefined as upscale clothing stores with small secondary lines in furniture and cosmetics. The seventh floor of Bergdorf Goodman hums, the eighth floor of Saks sings, and there are few places that seem more entirely of Manhattan than Fred's at Barneys on a Saturday at noon. But we miss the big stores, because they defined a world, little duchies of commerce, with their faith in literal display: not the cunning and Duchampian show windows of a Simon Doonan but the things themselves shown as the things themselves, these shirts, these ties—the wooden escalators and crowded elevators, and the ghosts of elevator operators wearing small hats and announcing, "Notions." (There is a beautiful, forgotten song in the old Johnny Mercer show *Top Banana,* sung in the elevator of a department store, listing the contents of the floors as though they were poem enough: "Third floor rat-traps and radios, cheesecloth, cupcakes and cameos / Fourth floor peanuts and piccolos / leftover ushers from Loews.")

Lord & Taylor still gives one a sense of the department store as it once was, a last lingering resonance of the old dispensation. It is not a very distant world. The first floor of the store, at Thirty-eighth and Fifth, is laid out sweetly and expectantly, all mirrors and cosmetics; the salespeople in the Clinique department look serious in their white coats, as though actually about to attempt something cliniqual. There are no divisions, no urgency, no one spraying perfume—it is a ground floor seemingly arranged by the hand of God for displaying goods. There are striped men's ties placed like salmon fillets and men's shirts hanging like partridge. There are hats. The store plays the national anthem at ten o'clock every morning. On the sixth floor, the restaurateur Larry Forgione has opened a new café, complete with wine by the glass and a sweeping panoramic view of sturdy ladies' coats. The chowder is tasty, the wine decent. But there is something about Forgione himself—someone who has become a brand without ever quite having been a name—that extends the sense of a time warp, another era of hope. The old Lord & Taylor implies a rhythm of time, of women's time, in particular, a pace not slowed but purposeful and expansive: It takes a morning and lunch, or tea and an afternoon, to make a survey of the place, shopping as a setting out rather than a dropping in.

At last, up on the tenth floor, in the men's department, one can find an awe-inspiring demonstration of the sheer numbing stasis that capitalism can achieve—for it is insensitivity to the immediate pressure of the market that separates big-ticket capitalism from the rug bazaar and the vegetable stall. Capital slows down the market and places it within the shell of The Firm, firm in every sense, so that things can linger after their appeal to the market has passed. The brand names are Jack Victor and Grant Thomas, name brands that are neither really names nor really brands, and seem to set off the commercial logic of brand-naming in a twilight zone of pure performance: No one wants to wear Jack Victor slacks, but there they are, hanging in poignant rows, their creases abjectly offered. It is a kind of installation piece: the department store as an abstract exercise in naming and branding and display, without commercial urgency and, mostly, without customers.

To understand the department store's decline, you have to go back to the department store's founding, according to Richard S. Tedlow, a professor at the Harvard Business School who has written a lot on retailing. "The department store began in an era of a hub-and-spoke transportation system for cities, before the automobile," Tedlow says. "In Chicago, for instance, the large downtown department store, Marshall Field's, became in and of itself The Brand. And for a store like that in, say, 1870 or 1880, the competition was basically mom-and-pop shops. Department stores were a new mode of retailing. They became destinations—they became places where you shopped not solely for procurement but for entertainment."

At the same time, Tedlow explains, the nature of the transaction changed. Before that, shopping was still done by barter, with each party expecting to be cheated. Department stores had fixed prices. The phrase "Satisfaction guaranteed or your money back" was radical, introducing a new kind of merchandising. As Tedlow says, "The department stores were one of America's first commercial institutions of trust. They worked to take your mind off price."

For over half a century, in New York particularly, department stores presided over everything from Thanksgiving Day parades and patriotic lectures to Cubist exhibitions. John Wanamaker was one of the greatest merchants in America, and his store at Astor Place and Broadway, which had an entrance hall and an art gallery and was said to have more windows than the Empire State Building, was the model and master of the department store as a civic-seeming institution.

Historians of retail will tell you that it was Wanamaker, more than anyone else, who transformed the department store from a place where women bought stuff to a place where they simply and necessarily went, the way people had once wandered into and out of church. With the usual acceleration of New York retailing, the zone of the stores moved uptown with astonishing speed: The cast-iron Ladies' Mile of department stores, between Eighth and Twenty-third streets and between Broadway and Sixth Avenue, reigned for a generation before it was replaced by Fifth Avenue farther uptown. But the continuity of purpose, and even of names, was there.

Tedlow dates the beginning of the decline to the period just after World War II, when what seemed at first to be a great gift to the growth of the department store—the mall—first appeared, in places like Minneapolis and Kansas City. The spatial arrangement of the department store within the mall, he thinks, helped spell its doom. "Malls depended on being anchored by two department stores, one at either end," he says. "What's in between those two stores? Small stuff at first. But eventually, there's a Gap, a Limited, a Banana Republic. By going out to the malls and anchoring them, these department stores created traffic for a great many specialty stores that otherwise would have had a hard time creating any demand—essentially because they couldn't afford the advertising, which is a necessary cost of doing business in a department store. The boutique businesses could attack the department store from the safety of the shadow of the department store. What has replaced the department store is the mall itself, which now plays the role of amusement place and social center."

Another revolution in retailing began with sharp competition in price, making Wal-Mart by far the biggest retailer in the country. Then came the heavily advertised national boutique brand, bringing a Victoria's Secret and a Gap to every mall. The department stores fought back by attempting to re-create the mall environment of boutiques within each store. But, by bringing in the boutique, by building the idea of the brand, they created an appetite for true brands. A Bloomingdale's filled with boutiques is not so much a brand of its own as a street filled with boutiques—which, sooner or later, it comes to resemble.

In other cities, the department store died from undernourishment, from white flight and the death of the inner city. The great Philadelphia Wanamaker's sickened and shrank until it lost, at last, everything but its eagle; it stays on as a minor satrapy of the May empire, ironically rebranded as a Lord & Taylor. In New York, though the physical infrastructure was changing all the time (by the sixties Wanamaker's was merely a memory attached to a mixed-use block), the cultural infrastructure held on. For a period that some now think was a historical bubble, the old patterns of retailing persisted, partly because zoning codes made it hard for the large discount stores to get in, and partly because it was difficult to break down New York shopping habits. When the new retailers arrived, they did on the streets what they had done in the mall. The precincts of New York retailing, Fifth Avenue, Broadway, and Soho, became, as many people noted, mall-like themselves, with a predictable range of national boutiques and a predictable effect on the department stores, which continued to "make" the neighborhoods and continued to lose market share. (You have to look at Ninth Avenue from Fifty-seventh to Thirty-fourth, or Lexington from Sixty-eighth on up to Ninety-sixth, in order to see what the old environment was like, distinctive and one-off, puppy stores on the first floor, dance studios above, and stores that specialized in Sea-Monkeys neighboring stores that specialized in reggae recordings or kosher pastry.)

Closing a circle begun a century before, the cast-iron palaces of the old Ladies' Mile became home to Bed Bath & Beyonds and Old Navys and giant Barnes & Nobles. The new retailing had arrived, until at last, just a few years ago, a Kmart showed up on Astor Place, occupying space, with an irony harder than iron, in the original Wanamaker's. It is a grim place to visit, with its fluorescent glare, its vast area marked but undivided, as though made for surveillance, its anti-theatrical insistences: The stuff is here, and the stuff is as cheap as we can make it, or so these orchestrations suggest. The choice is now between Kmart and Prada, and the institutions that joined them together are finished. We've gone from shopping through trust to a culture of discounting and edge, and edge is the one thing that seems to baffle the department store.

The trouble with the classic business-school account of the decline of the department store is that some version of it has always been true—or has been for at least fifty years, which in retailing is the same as always. "When I was at Harvard Business School in 1949, just after the war, my professor showed us clearly why the department store was dead, and was shocked when I said I wanted to work in one," Marvin Traub says, frostily if genially. It is the second week of August, and the dining room of the Regency at seven-forty-five is filled with the great merchants of New York. They wear Italian suits, tropical-weight wool, but wool all the same, and gleams of sweat appear as they walk from limo to booth, and become gleams of virtue. All of them stop to genuflect to Traub, the godfather of the New York department store. In the 1950s, he started work in the bargain basement of a discount department store on Lexington Avenue and turned it into Bloomies, and even now, a dozen years since he left, his legend compels retailers to bow to the older man with the single red thread of the Légion d'Honneur in his buttonhole.

Traub thinks that there is no problem of the department store that a good merchant can't solve. He uses the word "merchant" in an old-fashioned way, as distinct from "businessman" or "salesman"—"and he's a fine merchant, too," he will say of some protégé now enmeshed in the upper reaches of a giant retail firm, and he means, clearly, not merchant as in "merchandise" but merchant in an almost medieval sense, as one might say "monk" or "summoner" or "pardoner," an ancient calling, not a job. A businessman is someone who knows how to make money, where he doesn't care, and a salesman is someone who knows how to sell, what hardly matters, but a merchant is someone with a gift for where and what—the specifics and particulars are the whole of his craft. He is himself a shopper of the higher kind, a man who knows how to order his shop. (It is a significant distinction: Wanamaker himself always said that he was a merchant, not a capitalist.)

"The department store is a function of its leaders," Traub says. "All the great department stores had great merchants at their head: Stanley Marcus at Neiman Marcus, Adam Gimbel at Saks Fifth Avenue. Each one had a vision and an understanding of the connection between the department store and the shopper, and that connection is emotional and even theatrical.

"The first thing that happened to damage the department store was that the role of the buyers was diminished. In the fifties and sixties, to be a buyer at Bloomingdale's or Saks was a highly prestigious and highly important job. Buyers felt passionately about their work, and they knew their clientele intimately. They knew their sizes and insecurities, and they could sense instantly what to buy from a vendor."

The buyers, many of them women, were an elite group; Doris Salinger, J.D.'s sister, was a buyer of designer clothing at Bloomingdale's. "Nowadays, of course, no ambitious person would stay as a buyer for any length of time," Traub says. "It would be regarded, understandably, as merely a stop on the way to an executive position. The buying is all done at the corporate level, and so the connection between the customer and the product is damaged. They order from the central headquarters with, say, twenty to thirty percent for the individual store. The department store depends on trust and belief, and if you knock down the reasons for belief, you damage it."

But at the heart of Traub's complaint, and his diagnosis, is the now quaint-sounding problem of short-termism. Stock price dictates value, and quarterly profits determine stock price, so, where the department store's construction of trust and emotional connection depends on having areas of the store that are profit centers, and areas that lead you to the profit centers, the short-termer dreams only of profit centers. "What is a department store?" Traub asks rhetorically. "It's simple: It's a place where you can get everything under one roof. Books and *fraises des bois*, dishwashers and Prada bags, everything under one roof. That was the excitement of the department store." Little by little, he explains, the things that were not profitable have been shed, and these are precisely the things that conspired to create trust and confidence and an attachment.

"When we flew *fraises des bois* to the Bloomingdale's gourmet shops, it created greater traffic and excitement," Traub says. "And in the long run, it's those associations, that sense of event, that help to make a great store. If you're under pressure to create profits throughout the store, then it diminishes opportunities for unique and special things that may not be profitable. Bloomingdale's did not make money flying in the *fraises des bois*, but it appealed to our customers.

"What would you do for a romantic department store today? It wouldn't be the aspirational store we had at Bloomingdale's. Today, for instance, people want computers and electronics and online services, and we need to bring them in. A store that would take in the Web and the Internet would also sell everything. Everything would be under one roof again."

Everything under one roof. The great question in the theory of retailing, one learns as one reads the texts and talks to the mavens, is not "Why buy it?," a question that belongs, if anywhere, to the theory of life, but "Why buy it here?" All merchants try to answer this question by creating a sense of fate. Why buy it anywhere else? Most luxury merchants create this attachment by appealing to the customer's sense of insecurity. (Buy it here and you will be envied and admired.) The discount store does it by appealing to your intelligence. (Buy it here and you will be shrewder than your neighbor.) The department store does it, or did it, uniquely, by appealing to the customer's sense of trust, to a long cycle of safety. Everything can be found, and everything can be returned. You shop at Bergdorf's not because it is cool—no one will know—but because it is yours.

All life in a mercantile society, one sometimes feels, is dedicated to the disguises of wanting. The sin of capitalism, perhaps, is to make wants feel like needs, to give to simple silly stuff the urgency of near-physical necessity: I must have it. The grace of capitalism is to make wants feel like hopes, so that material objects and stuff can feel like the possibility of something heroic and civic. The urge of the great department stores was to hide acquisition as sociability, to disguise acquisitiveness as membership, so that one entered them not as one entered a store—with one eye on the beseeching salesgirl, one hand on the knob of the door, just looking—but as one entered a library or a club: striding in with pleasure. The department store was the cathedral of that material aspiration, and its diminishment leaves us with one less place to go and hope in.

Times Regained

This year marks the hundredth anniversary of the decision to take an hourglass-shaped traffic funnel between Forty-second Street and Forty-seventh Street on Broadway, which had been called Longacre Square, and rename it after *The New York Times,* which had just built its office there. This was less an honor than a consolation prize. The other, then bigger and brighter newspaper, the *New York Herald,* had claimed the other, then brighter and better square, eight blocks south, which still bears its ghostly name. Nine years later, in 1913, the *Times* scurried off to a prim side street and a Gothic Revival bishop's palace, where it has been lifting its skirts and shyly peeking around the corner at its old home ever since.

No other part of New York has had such a melodramatic, mood-ring sensitivity to the changes in the city's history, with an image for every decade. There was the turn-of-the-century Times Square, with its roof gardens and showgirls; the raffish twenties Times Square of Ziegfeld and Youmans tunes; the thirties Times Square of *42nd Street,* all chorus lines and moxie; the forties, V-J *On the Town* Times Square, full of sailors kissing girls; the wizened black-and-white fifties Times Square of *Sweet Smell of Success,* steaming hot dogs, and grungy beats; and then the sixties and the seventies Times Square of *Midnight Cowboy* and *Taxi Driver,* where everything fell apart and hell wafted up through the manhole covers. No other place in town has been quite so high and quite so low. Within a single half decade, it had Harpo Marx in the Marx Brothers' valedictory movie, *Love Happy,* leaping ecstatically from sign to sign and riding away on the flying Mobilgas Pegasus, and, down below, the unforgettable image of James Dean, hunched in his black overcoat, bearing the weight of a generation on his shoulders.

Now we have the new Times Square, as fresh as a neon daisy, with a giant Gap and a Niketown and an Applebee's and an ESPN Zone and television announcers visible through tinted windows, all family retailing and national brands. In some ways, the square has never looked better, with the diagonal sloping lines of the Reuters Building, the curving Deco zipper, even the giant mock dinosaur in the Toys "R" Us. There are people who miss the old Times Square, its picturesque squalor and violence and misery and exploitation. Those who pointed at the old Times Square as an instance of everything that capitalism can do wrong now point to the new Times Square as an instance of everything that capitalism can do worse. Where once Times Square was hot, it is now cold, where once varied, now uniform, where once alive, now dead.

Whatever has been gained, something really is missing in the new Times Square. The forces that created it, and the mixed emotions that most of us have in its presence, are the subject of James Traub's *The Devil's Playground*, which is both an engaged civics lesson and a work of social history. The book begins with an ironic moment—Traub takes his eleven-year-old son to the new Forty-second Street to see the old *42nd Street*—and then spirals back into history, moving decade by decade over the past century.

Traub, who is the son of Marvin Traub, has a gift for filtering social history through a previously invisible individual agent. As always, the vast forces of mass culture turn out to be the idiosyncratic choices of a few key, mostly hidden players. The character of the signs in Times Square, for instance, was mostly the invention of O. J. Gude, the Sign King of Times Square. Gude, a true aesthete with a significant art collection, was the first to sense that the peculiar shape of Times Square—a triangle with sign-friendly "flats" at the base and the apex—made it the perfect place for big electric national-brand signs, or "spectaculars," as they were called, even before World War I. In 1917, when Gude put up a two-hundred-foot-long spectacular, on the west side of Broadway between Forty-third and Forty-fourth, featuring twelve gleaming "spearmen" who went through spasmodic calisthenics, it was as big an event in American pop culture, in its way, as the opening of *The Jazz Singer* ten years later. Gude also had the bright idea of joining the Municipal Art Society, the leading opponent of big signs, and later helped shape the zoning ordinances that essentially eliminated big electric signs anywhere in midtown except in Times Square.

Times Square is famous for what used to be called its "denizens"—Damon Runyon, George S. Kaufman, Clifford Odets, A. J. Liebling—and Traub writes brief lives of a lot of them. But the history of the place isn't really a history of its illuminati; it's a history of its illuminations. Though social forces and neon signs flow out of individuals, they don't flow back into individuals so transparently. George S. Kaufman, to take one instance, was exclusively a creature of the theater; if, like the galleries in Soho in the 1990s, the Broadway theater had in the thirties picked up and moved to Chelsea, Kaufman would have followed it blindly and never would have been seen on Forty-second Street again. Even Runyon has about as much to do with the history of Times Square as P. G. Wodehouse does with the history of Mayfair: His subject is language, not place, and in all of Runyon's stories, it would be hard to find a single set-piece description of Times Square, a single bulb on a single sign. Individual artists help make cities, but cities don't make their artists in quite so neatly reciprocal a way. Dr. Johnson's "London" is a poem; "The London of Dr. Johnson" is a tour-bus ride.

One must not give a false gloss to the decay of Times Square; it was really bad. The neighborhood declined to a point where, by the mid-seventies, the Times Square precincts placed first and second in New York in total felonies. (Harlem had a third as many.) These were crimes of violence, too: A rape or an armed robbery or a murder took place nearly every day and every night. Stevie Wonder's great 1973 song "Living for the City" has a spoken-word interlude in which the poor black kid from the South arrives on West Forty-second Street and in about five minutes is lured into the drug business. This was a song, but it was not a lie.

Traub's account of the area's transformation is lit from behind by another, still longer and larger one—Lynne B. Sagalyn's masterly *Times Square Roulette: Remaking the City Icon.* Sagalyn teaches real estate at the University of Pennsylvania, and her book, the fruit of over a decade of scholarly labor, is as mind-bendingly detailed an account of the relations of property and culture as one can find outside Galsworthy or Trollope. It's full of eye-opening material, if one can keep one's eyes open long enough to find it. Sagalyn's book is written, perhaps of necessity, in a prose so dense with city acronyms and cross-referential footnotes that it can defeat even the most earnest attention. Nonetheless, its material is the material of the city's existence. Reading it is like reading an advanced-biology textbook and then discovering that its sole subject is your own body.

Traub and Sagalyn agree in dispelling a myth and moving toward a history, and the myth irritates them both—Traub's usual tone of intelligent skepticism sometimes boils over here into exasperation. The myth they want to dispel is that the cleanup of Times Square in the nineties was an expression of Mayor Giuliani's campaign against crime and vice, and of his companion tendency to accept a sterilized environment if they could be removed, and that his key corporate partner in this was the mighty Disney, which led the remaking of West Forty-second Street as a theme park instead of an authentic urban street. As Traub and Sagalyn show, this is nearly the reverse of the truth. It was Mayor Koch who shaped the new Times Square, if anyone did, while the important private profit-makers and players were almost all purely local: the Old Oligarchs, the handful of rich and mostly Jewish real estate families—the Rudins, Dursts, Roses, Resnicks, Fishers, Speyers, and Tishmans, as Sagalyn crisply enumerates them. Mayor Giuliani, basically, was there to cut the ribbon, and Disney to briefly lend its name.

The story follows, on a larger scale than usual, the familiar form of New York development, whose stages are as predictable as those of a professional wrestling match: first the Sacrificial Plan; next the Semi-

Ridiculous Rhetorical Statement; then the Staged Intervention of the Professionals; and at last the Sorry Thing Itself. The Sacrificial Plan is the architectural plan or model put forward upon the announcement of the project, usually featuring some staggeringly obvious and controversial device—a jagged roof or a startling pediment—that even the architect knows will never be built, and whose purpose is not to attract investors so much as to get people used to the general idea that something is going to be built there. (Sometimes the Sacrificial Plan is known by all to be sacrificial, and sometimes, as in "The Lottery," known to everyone but the sacrifice.) The Semi-Ridiculous Rhetorical Statement usually accompanies, though it can precede, the Sacrificial Plan, and is intended to show that the plan is not as brutal and cynical as it looks but has been designed in accordance with the architectural mode of the moment. ("The three brass lambs that stand on the spires of Sheep's Meadow Tower reflect the historical context of the site . . ." was the way it was done a decade ago; now it's more likely to be "In its hybrid facade, half mirror, half wool, Sheep's Meadow Tower captures the contradictions and deconstructs the flow of . . .") The Staged Intervention marks the moment when common sense and common purpose, in the form of the Old Oligarchs and their architects—who would be in charge in the first place—return to rescue the project from itself. The Sorry Thing Itself you've seen. (At Ground Zero, Daniel Libeskind supplied the Sacrificial Plan, and now he is pursuing all of the Semi-Ridiculous rhetoric in the forlorn hope that when the professionals stage their intervention, he will be the professional called on.)

The only difference in the Times Square project was that because of its size, it all happened twice. (Actually, there were two dimensions to the remaking of Times Square—the West Forty-second Street projects, and the reclaiming of the square itself—but each depended on the other, and, though administratively distinct, they were practically joined.) The first Sacrificial Plan appeared in the late seventies and was called "the City at Forty-second Street." Presented by the developer Fred Papert, with the support of the Ford Foundation and with proposed backing from Paul Reichmann, of Olympia & York, it envisioned a climate-controlled indoor-mall Forty-second Street, with a

500,000-square-foot "educational, entertainment, and exhibit center," and a 2.1-million-square-foot merchandise mart for the garment trade, all strung together with aerial walkways and, lovely period touch, equipped with a monorail. Mayor Koch wasn't happy about the plan: "We've got to make sure that they have seltzer"—that it's echt New York—"instead of orange juice," he said. But mostly he worried because someone else would be squeezing the oranges.

Still, the plan did what such plans are meant to do: establish the principle, civic-minded rather than commercial, that something had to be done here, and the larger principle that whatever was done should be done on a large scale—the old, outdoor theater-and-arcade Forty-second Street could be turned into "a consumer-oriented exposition center with people moving across 42nd Street by means of pedestrian bridges," as one early draft of the rhetoric put it. As the initiative passed from the developers to the Koch administration, a further principle was established. The transformation could be made only by large-scale condemnation of what was already there, and the city and state together proposed a new way to link up private and public: The developers would get the right to build on condition that they paid directly for public improvements. The price of your tower on top was a cleaner subway station below.

Still more significant, and what should have been seen as a portent in the first Sacrificial Plan, was the felt need to pull away from the street completely. This was not simply snobbery but self-preservation; Forty-second Street wasn't dying but raving. The porno shops on West Forty-second Street weren't there because the middle class had fled. They were there because the middle class was there. The people who bought from the porn industry were the office workers who walked by the stores on the way to and from work, and the tourists who wanted to take back a little something not for the kids. The XXX video rooms and bookstores and grind-house theaters were going concerns, paying an average of $32,000 a year in rent; peep shows could gross $5 million a year. Though the retailers were obviously entangled with the Mafia, the buildings were owned by respectable real estate families—for the most part, the same families who had owned the theaters since the thirties, the Brandts and the Shuberts. Times Square was Brechtville: a perfect demonstration of the principle that the market, left to itself, will produce an economy of crime as happily as an economy of virtue.

This—the crucial underlying reality in the Forty-second Street redevelopment—meant that the city, in order to get the legal right to claim and condemn property to pass it over, had to be pointing toward some enormous, unquestioned commercial goal, larger or at least more concrete than the real goal, which was essentially ethical and "cultural." For once the usual New York formula had to be turned right around: A question of virtue had to be disguised as a necessity of commerce. On Forty-second Street, a group of perfectly successful private businessmen in the dirty movie-theater business were being pushed aside in favor of a set of private businessmen in the tall-building business, and the legal argument for favoring the businessmen in the tall-building business was they had promised if you let them build a really tall building, they would fix up the subway station.

This produced the Second Sacrificial Plan, of 1983: Philip Johnson and John Burgee's immense four towers straddling either side of Times Square on Forty-second, each with a slightly different pedimented top. The Semi-Ridiculous Rhetorical Statement invoked for this plan was that the pedimented tops "contextualized" the big buildings because they recalled the roofline of the old Astor Hotel, a victim of development twenty years before. They were by far the biggest and bulkiest buildings that had ever been proposed for midtown; Sagalyn gasps at the sheer zoning outrage of it. They had to be that big to establish their right to be at all. The Brandt family, which owned many of the theaters, sued and lost. "The Durst family interests put their name on five lawsuits," Sagalyn reports, "but the rumors of their financial backing of many more are legion." (The Dursts owned various individual lots along the street, which they intended to put together for their own giant building.) After ten years, they lost, too. Forty-seven suits were launched, and the plan withstood them all. The Johnson models, fortresses designed to withstand a siege of litigation, had triumphed. But nobody really wanted to build the buildings.

. . .

In the interim between the First Sacrificial Plan and the Second, however, something had changed in the ideology of architecture. A new orthodoxy had come into power, with an unapologetic emphasis on formal "delirium" and the chaotic surface of the city. In Rem Koolhaas's epoch-marking manifesto *Delirious New York* (1978), the buzz, confusion, danger, and weirdness of New York were no longer things to worry about. In fact, they were pretty much all we had to boast of. To an increasing bias in favor of small-scale streetscapes and "organic" growth was added a neon zip of pop glamour. The new ideology was Jane Jacobs dressed in latex and leather.

By what turned out to be a happy accident, this previously academic, pop-perverse set of ideas had influenced minds at the Municipal Art Society—the very group that had fought against the idea of signs and signage in Times Square at the turn of the century. In 1985, after the appearance of the Johnson plan, the Municipal Art Society, under the impeccable direction of the white-shoed Hugh Hardy, took on as its cause the preservation of the "bowl of light" in Times Square and "the glitz of its commercial billboards and electronic signs." After being digested in various acronymic gullets, this campaign produced not only new zoning text (sections ZR81-832 and ZR81-85, as Sagalyn duly notes) but, as an enforcement mechanism, an entirely new unit of measurement: the luts, or "Light Unit Times Square." (Each sign had to produce a minimum luts reading; the lighting designer Paul Marantz gave it its name.)

And so the Municipal Art Society became the major apostle of a continuing chaotic commercial environment in Times Square, while the big developers had to make the old Beaux Arts case for classical order, lucidity, and space—for "trees and clean streets . . . museums and sidewalk cafés," in the plaintive words of the developer David Solomon. Eventually, in the early-nineties decline, Prudential, which had been holding on to the development on West Forty-second Street, was forced to sell its rights at a discount—to the Durst family, which had been leading the litigation against the plan all along but which, as everyone could have predicted, was there at the finale to develop and build, including 4 Times Square, the big building where these words are being written.

None of this, however, could have created the new Times Square had it not been for other, unforeseeable changes. The first and most important was the still poorly explained decline in violent crime. (Traub tours the Eighth Avenue end of Forty-second with one of the district's privately financed security officers, who points out that there is still plenty of prostitution and drug trafficking but very few muggings or assaults; even chain snatching and petty theft are now rare.) This decline allowed for the emergence of the real hyperdrive of the new square, the arrival of what every parent knows is the engine of American commerce: branded, television-based merchandise directed at "families" (that is, directed at getting children to torture their parents until they buy it). The critical demographic fact, as a few have pointed out, is the late onset of childbearing, delayed here until the habit of New York is set and the disposable income to spend on children is larger. When Damon Runyon was writing, the presence of Little Miss Marker in the square was the material for a story. Now Little Miss Marker runs the place.

Of all the ironies of the Times Square redevelopment, the biggest is this: that the political right is, on the whole, happy with what has happened, and points to Times Square as an instance of how private enterprise can cure things that social engineering had previously destroyed, while the left points to Times Square as an instance of how market forces sterilize and drive out social forces of community and authenticity. But surely the ghosts of the old progressives in Union Square should be proudest of what has happened. It was, after all, the free market that produced the old Times Square: The porno stores were there because they made money as part of a thriving market system. Times Square, and Forty-second Street, was saved by government decisions made largely on civic grounds. Nothing would have caused more merriment on the conservative talk shows than the *luts* regulations—imagine some bureaucrat telling you how bright your sign should be!—but it is those lights that light the desks of the guys at the offices of Clear Channel on Forty-second Street and bring the crowds that make them safe. Civic-mindedness once again saved capitalism from itself.

And yet you don't need to have nostalgia for squalor and cruelty to feel that some vital chunk of New York experience has been replaced by something different and less. Traub ends with the deconstructionist Mark Taylor, who trots out various depressions about the Society of Spectacle to explain the transformation, all of which are marvelously unilluminating. Times Square may be spectacular—that is what its signmakers have called their own signs for a century—but in the theoretical sense, it's not a spectacle at all. It's not filled by media images that supplant the experience of real things. It's a tangible, physical, fully realized public square where real people stare at things made by other people. The absence of spectacle, in that sense—the escape from the domination of isolated television viewing—is what still draws people on New Year's Eve, in the face of their own government's attempts to scare them away. (Dick Clark, of course, is a simulacrum, but he was born that way.)

Traub toys with the idea that the real problem lies in the replacement of an authentic "popular" culture, of arcades and Runyonesque song pluggers, with a "mass" culture, of national brands and eager shoppers. But it's hard to see any principled way in which the twenty-foot-tall animatronic dinosaur at the new Toys "R" Us howls at the orders of mass culture, while O. J. Gude's dancing spearmen were purely Pop. The distinction between popular culture and mass culture is to our time what the distinction between true folk art and false folk art was to the age of Ruskin and Morris; we want passionately to define the difference, because we know in our hearts that it doesn't exist. Even fairy tales turn out to be half manufactured by a commercial enterprise, half risen from the folkish ground. The idea that there is a good folkish culture that comes up from the streets and revivifies the arts and a bad mass culture imposed from above is an illusion, and anyone who has studied any piece of the history knows it.

All the same, there is something spooky about the contemporary Times Square. It wanders through you; you don't wander through it.

One of the things that make for vitality in any city, and above all in New York, is the trinity of big buildings, bright lights, and weird stores. The big buildings and bright lights are there in the new Times Square, but the weird stores are not. By weird stores one means not simply small stores, mom-and-pop operations, but stores in which a peculiar and even obsessive entrepreneur caters to a peculiar and even an obsessive taste. (Art galleries and modestly ambitious restaurants are weird stores by definition. It's why they still feel very New York.) If the big buildings and the bright signs reflect the city's vitality and density, weird stores refract it; they imply that the city is so varied that someone can make a mundane living from one tiny obsessive thing. Poolrooms and boxing clubs were visible instances of weird stores in the old Times Square; another, slightly less visible, was the thriving world of the independent film business, negative cutters and camera-rental firms.

There is hardly a single weird store left on Broadway from Forty-second Street to Forty-sixth Street—hardly a single place in which a peculiar passion seems to have committed itself to a peculiar product. You have now, one more irony, to bend east, toward respectable Fifth Avenue, toward the diamond merchants and the Brazilian restaurants and the kosher cafeterias that still fill the side streets, to re-create something that feels a little like the old Times Square. (Wonderful Forty-fifth Street! with the Judaica candlesticks and the Japanese-film rental and the two-story shops selling cheap clothes and stereos, lit up bright.) Social historians like to talk about the Tragedy of the Commons, meaning the way that everybody loses when everybody over-grazes the village green, though it is in no individual's interest to stop. In New York, we suffer from a Tragedy of the Uncommons: Weird things make the city worth living in, but though each individual wants them, no one individual wants to pay to keep them going. Times Square, as so often in the past, is responding, in typically heightened form, to the general state of the city: The loss of retail variety troubles us everywhere, as a new trinity of monotony—Starbucks, Duane Reade, and the Washington Mutual Bank—appears to dominate every block. We just feel it more on Broadway.

Do we overdraw Times Square history, make it more epic than it ought to be? Piccadilly and Soho, in London, and Place de Clichy, in Paris, are similar places, have known similar kinds of decline and similar kinds of pickup, but without gathering quite the same emotion. We make Times Square do more work than it ought to. Other great cities have public spaces and pleasure spaces, clearly marked, and with less confusion between them. When Diana died, it was Kensington Palace, not Piccadilly, that got the flowers, and in Paris it is the Champs-Élysées, not Place de Clichy, that gets the military parade on the fourteenth of July. Which returns us, with a certain sense of awe, to the spell still cast by the original sin of the 1811 grid plan. We make our accidental pleasure plazas do the work of the public squares we don't have. This is asking a lot of a sign, or even of a bunch of bright ones lighting up the night.

The Running Fathers

The Running Fathers are sorry that they ever started, but they cannot seem to stop. Two and three and sometimes four times a week they put on their Walkman loaded with the Stones or Sting—it is really a Discman now, but the old name seems to suit the thing better, implying forward motion and a wandering impulse rather than a disc merely revolving, too quickly, round and round—and they run around the reservoir in Central Park for as long as their feet and lungs allow.

They recognize one another's presence as they lap the cinder track, and nod as they pass, between breaths and gasps. They wear sober gray tracksuits and plain black pullovers, gray sneakers and wool hats. They run reasonably well, considering how long it has been and how cold the air can be. They understand that they are distinct from the True Runners, with their skintight Lycra pants, their stopwatches and high-stepped knees, and their studied, educated panting. But they are distinct, too, from the Good-Natured Joggers, who wear old sweaters and torn gray sweatpants, and who huff and puff cheerfully, remnants of another, macramé universe.

They are sorry that they ever started, for they never meant to be here. Once, not so long ago, they would mock the men who went running around the reservoir. Back when they began life in New York, the runners at the reservoir seemed like symbols of a life of narrow needs and self-absorption, as vacant and mechanical as the toy animals turning slowly around the Delacorte clock at the entrance to the zoo. "Young executive types," they called them, the word "yuppie" having not yet even been invented.

"This is a *path*!" one of them recalls shouting to the runners as they went by, "not a track!" They thought they were defending the idea of the park as a refuge, a meditative place for retreat and retrenchment. Now the difference seems harder to define, the distinction between a track that leads you around and a path that leads you forward harder to believe in.

Why, then, are they running; why are they out here in the morning and at dusk? They could go to the gym, of course, and run there, or bike there, or step there, or do something there. But somehow the gym has lost its charm, its magic, its promise of renewal. For years to go to a gym was pure pleasure—a feeling of infinity, "The 59th Street Bridge Song" made flesh, twenty again—but it has changed, and, in its changing, a feeling of expulsion has attached to it.

Is there something about approaching death that makes them run? Not that death feels imminent or even nearby; it is simply real. The Running Fathers envy those who knew it all along, who were running from the first, who got existential despair early on, Larkin-like, and then had only to settle in to make things pleasant while they waited, like condemned men decorating a cell. You start to run, perhaps, when you discover that something is gaining on you, when you discover not just that death is real, but that it is banal, too, that the end of life is merely like—there should be a higher or tonier metaphor, but there isn't—a canceled television series. First surprise at the sudden ending (were the ratings really that low, the heart really that fragile?), then shock, then a wistful hanging on, and then vague memories, afternoon syndication, and then nothing, only nostalgia and perhaps a website.

Even to be remembered after you are gone is always to be remembered wrong. A biography is to a life exactly as the movie-feature remake of an old television series is to the television series: a sequence of agreeably open-ended adventures, suddenly terminated with a rush to tie up a few loose ends in a last episode, is turned into something suspiciously well shaped, with an arc and a story and a backstory and a clear hierarchy of "choices" and motives. Charlie's Angels are given parents and old lovers, childhood traumas and life choices; Mannix is made over into a man with a past and, more important, a destiny, just as the dead subject of a biography is made a character in a story, with a character's neat consistency and regulated growth. The shape is imposed, and the essential appeal and pleasure of all lived experience, as it is the pleasure of all old television series—that it had no real plot, no pleasure outside the sequence of open-ended episodes with the same repeated characters, the same promise of more like it next week at the same time—is gone, vanished. And so they run, even though they are beginning to hear rumors that running does no good.

The Motionless Mothers are in tune with their time. They have stopped running; they have stopped going to step class; they have almost stopped moving. And yet they bloom. Every morning they do their twelve yoga poses, rooted to a mat, saluting the sun and downing the dog, hardly stirring, just rocking back and forth in the lotus position, and then once a week they go to a cool, pure room and for twenty minutes do their SuperSlow. They sit in the silent, cold room of the SuperSlow trainer—you cannot call it a gym; it lacks music, and all conviviality has been banished—and, eyes shut, breathing in short decisive pants, ten seconds up and ten seconds down, they lift great weights with their legs and arms and backs and torsos, hundreds of pounds for twenty uninterrupted minutes. They close their eyes and pant as they do it, the way they learned to do in childbirth. They have found a way to beat the odds, the genes, time itself: to be absolutely still and lift great weights very slowly.

The Motionless Mothers can lift two and three hundred pounds and see the results in the shower and bedroom. They now have the bodies of Puerto Rican flyweight boxers, narrow waists and long taut biceps and elongated thigh muscles. They are wise. They have grasped intuitively that we live in a slower time, that this epoch is not a running epoch. The glittering and the gleaming, the brilliant of all kinds, have ceded their place to the self-knowing and short-winded, to the stubborn and simple and still. We have passed from the Age of the Gilded Hare into the Age of the Armored Tortoise. Slow and steady wins the race, because the hare is broke, or in prison, or hiding in fear in his hutch. Even the truly rabbity must pretend now to have been turtles all along.

Within the new dispensation, the Motionless Mothers flourish motionlessly. Their backs are straight, their breath strong, their muscles eerily long and taut. They are, every inch of them, body and soul, in every sense, *defined*. Their husbands, merely running, are as vaguely defined as an acronym left over from the Cold War—SEATO, or MIRV—whose history no one can quite remember. What *do* they mean, exactly?

There *is* something saintly about the SuperSlow trainer, the Running Fathers think when they go at last to see him—a gentle, powerful youth who hides his physique, delicately, within loose T-shirt and jeans, and who has a shy smile and a diffident manner. And yet the trainer has, as well, the shining patient persuasiveness of the convert, of the man who has seen and who knows. The old hollering, the old-style trainer's "You can do it," or "Give me three more!," are anathema to him. Instead, he stands beside the machine and whispers, instructs his student through the three or four repetitions that are all that is needed. He smiles gently, seeking nothing, never raising his voice. The weight goes up, comes back down to the pile, and then goes back up, ten counts up, ten counts down.

"Okay. When you're ready. Just *sneak* out of there—crawl out, inch by inch. Hold it—now, slooow negative, coming back. Feel for the tap, don't look for it, feel for it, and then just sneaky-slow back out of there . . ."

The strange thing is that the two-hundred-plus-pound weight, which feels immovable on first contact, *moves*. It nudges forward and then, through a swell of mixed pain and effort, really moves, and slips back down, and then moves again. Four times, no more; a minute and a half, no longer.

The theory is impeccable, or at least persuasive. Muscles learn only from failure, like French schoolchildren, and they can be made to fail only by repeated stress slowly applied. The stress, if it is applied longer, cannot then really be stress. The mark of real stress is that the body cannot bear it long or often. The man in the gym rushing through his sets, the push-up artist doing his thousand push-ups—

they are cruising in a comfort zone of their own creation, an imaginative illusion of their own conceit. They are making sweat, not muscle.

"I'm going to stop you at a minute or half or failure," the trainer whispers, "whichever comes first. We're hoping for failure, of course." His hushed voice is the voice of the old game-show announcers whispering the password into the microphone behind the isolation booth, so the contestants cannot hear it. "Just inch out of there, sneaky-slow starting out—don't explode, don't throw it, just ease out, and hold it, and then slooowly back."

There are six machines, no more, and the program really *is* over in twenty minutes, in a blaze of breath and pain. It takes place in the cold room, with windows overlooking the cold avenue. But the speed with which the workout ends is not presented as a gift on the other end of the pain—it is a limitation, a sign of the stupidity of the body. "If you destroy a muscle sufficiently, it has no choice except to make more muscle for the task. If you challenge it to its accustomed limits, which is what most people call exercise, it is just satisfied with itself." The runner can see that muscle, complacent as a young painter of the 1980s, not really trying. "The beautiful thing is that if you stress it and then give it time to recover, when it recovers, it will recover stronger than before. If you did it more often, it would have less time to recover from the stress, so you'd be doing *less* strength building, not more."

What about running? the Running Fathers ask anxiously, don't you need aerobics to improve your lungs, couldn't the two things be complementary? The trainer is patient, humorous, kind, but absolute; running is not inadequate exercise—it is just not really exercise at all. It is recreation.

"We-ell," he explains, with the good-humored patience of the true convert, "why is it that they ask you your weight before you input your time on one of those stationary bikes? Okay: It's because they need to know how many calories you're going to burn *just by sitting there,* just naturally, without doing anything. Let's say that's you burn a hundred calories just while you're standing still or sleeping or thinking. Well, thirty minutes of running will burn about a hundred calories more—so if, let's say, you have an iced tea right after because of the thirst you've created by the 'exercise'"—he beams with amusement as his voice brackets the word—"then you're back more deeply in debt than you were before! You're actually *gaining* calories. The same thing is true about running outdoors. I don't think it can harm you too much, but most of what we see"—he sounds like a doctor giving bad news kindly—"I mean, if it feels good and adds something to your life, by all means, keep running! But all you're doing is stressing your heart rather than training your muscles. Not every runner dies of an early heart attack. But I'm afraid that it's no accident that some of them do, and none of them . . ." His voice trails off.

And the pain? "I have, well, I have this thing someone said to me once." The young trainer blushes, frightened of seeming too aphoristic, wanting to share his wisdoms but not wanting to seem to show off. "It, well, it works for me in a strong way. It's just this—" He pauses and swallows and then recites earnestly: " 'Flee the pain and the pain will seek you; seek the pain and the pain will flee you.' "

And the weird thing is that it *does* work, sort of. It is not that the pain really runs away; it is that if, at the moment when your knees are screaming, you simply turn *into* the scream, turn toward the pain and concentrate on it, seize it with your mind so that it engulfs you, then the pain becomes somehow a subject rather than an object—a thing outside yourself, gaining on you, but never quite catching up.

Yet beneath the gentle voice and patient rational explanation of the SuperSlow trainer, one senses a hard Protestant rigor: Exercise is exercise, medicinal rather than recreational and absolute rather than open. The old gyms, the Running Fathers realize, were Catholic and Mediterranean in their spirit, a form of genial folk magic tied to a ritual practice. Everyone went, no one truly improved. Exercise from the seventies through the nineties, for a certain class of New Yorkers, was what communion and confession were for Italian peasants—not means but ends, not paths to heaven but the Godhead itself. If you "worked out," you did not need to succeed at it—in fact, no one *did* succeed at it, really, no one seemed much thinner or stronger or (aside from a few gay men and professional athletes) truly altered. Considering the total number of hours spent in the gym, one would have expected a city of Samsons, a metropolis of Babe Didriksons. Instead, people went on dieting, and the gym existed as the church does in a Sicilian village, as a gathering place, an intermediate institution, where fitness, like grace, would eventually descend on your head just from being there—and if it didn't, what of it, death was a long way off, and the body, like the Mediterranean God, was forgetful, largely forgiving. They were not running on a track or a path but in a village square, a piazza where people took a morning run in place of morning espresso.

The new slow exercise is a form of Protestantism, and has the Protestant knack of combining a grim view of the meaninglessness of activity with a faith in the necessity of action. Grace is hard to come by, and you may never achieve it. Predestination, in the form of genes, applies nearly everywhere, to every wish and muscle. Yet you do it anyway, because good work, however painful, is your only hope, however faint.

Beyond the trainer's charming and diffident help, the Running Father senses a grim core to the SuperSlow philosophy, a dark Geneva of the heart behind the smiling and helpful Unitarian facade. The Founder of the new slow exercise lives in Florida and performs his rites in some cool large strip mall. Every month or so, he writes a screed, never longer than a few pages, that is distributed, silently but significantly, at the front desk of the workout room.

The Founder has contempt—not gentle condescension but furious, barely contained contempt—for runners and running, aerobics and aerobics classes, disdain for all the manners of the old exercise regimen, which pretended to have a point and were merely recreation. Even the words infuriate him; the concept of aerobics and aerobic exercise he treats with the cold hatred that Luther gave to the invocation of saints or to the selling of indulgences. "Aerobic activities are dangerous! Running is extremely high force activity," he writes. "You cannot 'train your wind.' The lungs can always perform their job quite actively. Maximal oxygen uptake is 95.9 percent genetically determined. It is the muscles that actually perform work, and only the muscles can be trained. The 'wind' and 'lungs' and 'aerobics' have nothing to do with it. The enthusiastic aerobic dancer or jogger will pay the price for all that 'healthy activity.' If everyone in the U.S. immediately stopped performing the activities they pursued as 'exercise' the collective health of the nation would improve dramatically," he concludes, nailing his theses, not quite ninety-nine but counting, to the door of every false gym in the country.

All that matters to the body (and, so the hidden corollary runs, to the soul, as well) is resistance. That is what the body is made to learn from, and all that it is made to learn from. "When you are dead, will your muscles still have resistance? Yes." Death is the perfect exercise condition; and for a moment he sees the dead being exercised by their personal trainers. The Founder in Florida minces no words, makes no concessions to niceness. He warns repeatedly against something called Val Salva's maneuver, which sounds like an erotic act performed on Kim Novak or Angie Dickinson by a lounge singer from the Rat Pack era, but is in fact the act of holding your breath while working your muscles. ("Elderly people are commonly found dead of a stroke on the commode," he writes mordantly, "as a result of the increase in BP as they Val Salva.") Overweight? "The real problem with modern obesity is food abundance," he writes flatly. Eat less.

Above all, the Founder underlines the difference between exercise and recreation. "Elevated heart rate is not an indicator of exercise intensity, or value. It is quite possible to experience an elevated pulse, labored breathing, and profuse sweating without achieving valuable exercise. Intense emotional experiences commonly cause these symptoms without a shred of exercise benefit. . . . The 'experts' say that gentle low-intensity activities use the aerobic pathway to a greater degree than they use the anaerobic pathway. We agree with this statement completely and feel that it should be taken to its logical conclusion: The most 'aerobic' activity that a human being can engage in," he concludes, "is sleeping."

The dream of the perfect tortoise seems to have penetrated even to the children. The boys lend their fathers their iPods and MP3s to go running with, ashamed of the old Discman, and their contents are stunning in their catholicity, their embracing universality. There are hundreds of melodies, countless songs, everything from Aerosmith to Al Yankovic. The new songs are wonderful but very much like the old songs: Donovan could have sung "Yellow," the MC5 "American Idiot."

"Who do you like more, Green Day or Coldplay?" the father says, looking at the range of songs on the two-hundred-song list, thinking, *He must have favorites.*

The boy shrugs. "They're both good. It's like asking who you like more, the Beatles or the Stones." And the father is stunned, both by the serene wisdom of the answer and by its ease with history; the Beatles' music is thirty years old, no, forty years old—any knowledge he would have had at that age, of music in the 1920s or '30s, dearly won, teased out of old Ella Fitzgerald records.

But the boy must be chasing *something*. In the past, to choose a band was to not choose some other band. Kids really hated things—stupidly, of course, since their hates extended to the very best things there were. (They hated sensitive singer-songwriters, and then these turned out to be Joni Mitchell, evergreen and blue.)

"Isn't there anybody who you really hate? Britney Spears? Or what's-her-name, Avril Lavigne?" Avril Lavigne had been very big a year before, the Gidget of grunge, and, he senses, is no longer.

But the boy shrugs. "She's okay, I guess. Some of her songs are okay, I guess. I just don't listen to the ones that aren't." The iPod is a protective shell; by including everything, it eliminates the rooting interest—reduces albums brutally to playlists, eliminates choices as surely as the CD eliminated sides. You don't have to choose; you don't have to be enraged; you just glide right past the bad songs. Their attitude isn't a form of cool, and is a million miles from irony, more a form of sobered-up acceptance. The children live in comfort and understand fear, and they prepare their iPods for a dark age, like a medieval monk stocking his library with the classical essentials just before the vandals come. Even their idea of exercise is like their idea of music: a little of this, a little of that. They wear their Heelys, shoes with wheels that pop out from their soles, enabling them to walk and then run and then stutter-step and then suddenly and smoothly glide down the sidewalk in imperturbable cool, rolling right away, so that walking and running and stepping are all one fluid thing. They come to the edge of the reservoir and watch their fathers run, and smile benevolently, practicing their gliding on the edge of the grass. "Running is, like, so over, Dad," the boy says when his father appears at last, and he glides away to school.

Speed is over," the Motionless Mothers say, mocking the trend writers but meaning it, too. "You should slow down. Give it up."

Books now appear every month in praise of slowness, volumes raining down. The new books inventory all the new *kinds* of self-improving slowness: They appear in praise of slow music, slow food, slow exercise, and slowed-down living, *Slow Food* and *Bonjour Laziness* and *How to Be Idle* and *In Praise of Slowness*. Tantric sex and seven-hour lamb are the pleasures of the moment, signs of virtue restored and sanity renewed. If you do everything more slowly—cook, make love, work out—your muscles will be larger, your food tastier, your children saner. You will, in short, *have won the race*. The tortoise is not merely wiser than the hare; he is actually faster, if the race course is long enough. Astonishingly, the authors seem unaware that they, too, are hamsters trapped on a wheel set by publishers, condemned to their contrarianism. (The rhetoric of slowness in the books is belied by the speediness of their appearance; the sweat almost glistens on their covers, like traces of the perspiration of their editors, racing to get the books on the shelves before the slow moment passes.)

Some kinds of slowness are, the Running Fathers think, truly called slow: If you just stopped working, stopped moving, stopped paying the rent or the mortgage, the children's tuition, then yes, you would be slow, off the track, standing still. But that kind of immobility is impossible, and the slowness that takes its place isn't really slow at all. If you set out to braise a leg of lamb, or to make a "classic" peasant pork stew, you are busy all day long. There are lardons to crisp and fat to skim and a hundred small slow decisions to make. Slow cooking offers no escape from the relentlessness of modern life; it just introduces a new and modish form of relentlessness.

Fast and slow, truth be told, will always catch up with each other. Anytime one attempts to insert speed into any system, slowness results. The traffic jam was the old, last-century proof of this truth. Airplane travel, so wonderfully speedy—imagine hinting to Ben Franklin that the day would come when you could get to Paris in seven hours!—becomes enbarnacled by an apparatus so slow (the freeway, the check-in, the security lines, the long drive through the congealing airport traffic on the other side) that the primary experience of air travel is its excruciating tedium.

But anytime you attempt to insert *slowness* into the system, life speeds up somewhere else. In aristocratic societies, it was possible at least to transfer the energy throughout a society: The leisure of Madame de Pompadour was supported by the desperate busyness of her servants. In modern bourgeois societies, though, where we are our own servants, any speed added produces slowness somewhere else *in your own life*—the equilibrium of slow and fast has become internalized in single bodies, a single consciousness. The balance that used to seek and spread across a civilization is now centered in a single soul; any slowness inserted to calm you down produces speed that wears you out. The economy of fast and slow, no matter how you try to adjust it, will always remain in perfect balance.

For here is the deep truth. There really is no fast. There is no slow. There is only time. Time is immovable; there is only so much of it, and it cannot be nudged or massaged or managed. *It* is the absolute thing, Time, and it is everywhere, like dust mites and smog.

The Running Fathers sit sipping lattes at the Starbucks on Columbus Avenue after the morning run, waiting with annoyance for two twentysomethings to pack up their computers so there will be free seats. But then what's the rush? When your work is done, they know, you are done. Each creature on earth has more or less exactly the same number of heartbeats, the same track to race around. The hummingbird uses his up in a week, the elephant in a century, but the consciousness, their experience of the time passed, is the same. We are calibrated to have as many heartbeats as we need. It is why retired athletes look dazed and drunken—they *are* dazed and drunken; they are finished. If you run, you use up your heartbeats. Running around the reservoir is a form of disguised middle-class suicide. It is no accident, a Running Father explains to another, that Mozart died at thirty-five, that Keats passed away at twenty-six: They had harvested themselves, used up their heartbeats. (Seemingly long-lived artists are always film directors or conductors or editors, who are inspired parasites leaching off others' heartbeats, others' music.)

The other Running Father nods. He recalls the moment that he got that, too. He was working out on the treadmill once, and pushing as hard as he could to derive the heartbeat-per-minute rate forward, and he ran faster, and then faster, but the heartbeat counter wouldn't move up! It just kept blinking, rising steadily from one to ten, and then falling back down to zero and then back up to ten, and then back down to zero—no matter how hard he pushed, or how much he strained, it would rise up and then fall back.

He thought that maybe he was having the beginnings of a heart attack until he realized that . . . he was looking at the wrong display! He wasn't looking at the heartbeat-per-minute rate. He was looking *at the seconds ticking by on the digital timer*—and they were so perfect, so smooth, so completely unchanging, so completely indifferent, that he was terrified. Nothing he did affected the polite, impassive digits, moving majestically onward.

"I just stopped running, and I was standing there sweating, just staring at them, and the heart rate went swooshing down to normal, but the second counter, the little digital clock, just went right on blinking, just imperturbable, like a child looking up at you, innocent and unaffected. And I realized what it was, and . . ." They nod together and sip: There is no fast. There is no slow. There is only time.

Why, then, do they run? They have learned from the trainer that running is futile; they have gathered from their wives that running is unnecessary; they have heard from their children that running is over; they know from their own knees and ankles that running is a pain. Given the realities of the body, the recalcitrance of the muscles, the illusion of aerobics, the fact that time is running out and heartbeats are being used up, why run at all? Why do we still see them, heads down, arms awkward, running around the reservoir every morning before work, every evening before dinner? Their knees ache and their lungs burn and they know that none of it helps anything. Knowing better, why do they persist? It is, perhaps, not exercise at all, not even a waste of heartbeats, that drives then forward, however clumsily. They are not racing to get anywhere, or rehearsing to overtake their competitors, or running to become faster runners tomorrow. They are not running in search of something, or toward someplace, or against someone. They are running away.

Fourth Thanksgiving: Propensities

Our children live in mazes / made of cards and screens and pages"—a description of the new reality in doggerel. The children *do* live in a maze of cards and screens and pages, and half our job as parents seems to be to guide them through it, particularly to keep them away from the screens, turn them toward the cards, and help them end up in the pages. The path from video addiction to book reading is a thorny one, a parental pilgrim's progress for our time.

This weekend, for instance, Luke and his friend Theo had a double sleepover: Friday night at Theo's family's loft in funky downtown, then Saturday night here, prissy uptown. Theo's dad, Peter Hoffman, and I decided, along with the boys, that it would be a no-screen weekend. Of course, when I say that we decided all together, I mean that the parents decided and the children, not yet having the weapons to contest it, accepted the decision and pretended they had helped to make it. Families remain autocracies, with the saving grace of all autocracies—not dictatorships where anything goes, but authoritarian centers that keep a jumpy and watchful eye on the mob, which will someday rule.

"No computer games? No video games?" The boys looked hurt as much as offended. No, nothing, we said. They spend too much time staring at screens; this would be the weekend to do something energetic and creative. "What are we going to do?" Luke asked—not indignant, just curious. What *were* they going to do? "Play music, do sports," we said. They looked dubious, and then they went downtown.

Once before, they had used a no-screen weekend imaginatively, to hold a fire sale of old Yu-Gi-Oh! cards. They both have outgrown the game in the past year and now view their beautiful old Rackhamish cards with disdain and the kind of disbelief about their enthusiasms of seven months ago that we have for pictures of ourselves in decades past—that haircut! those clothes! Childhood is just like life, only ten times faster. One of the reasons we still idolize the music of the sixties is that it moved at a genuinely childlike pace: Every six months the Beatles and Dylan had entered an entirely new moment, and what they had done a year ago in "Help!" or "The Times They Are A-Changin' " seemed as distant and incomprehensibly naive to them as Yu-Gi-Oh! now seems to Luke.

When the boys came back to our place after the first half of the sleepover, late on Saturday afternoon, their faces and eyes were alight.

"Hey, what did you guys do?" I asked semi-warily.

"We played pool!" they announced in unison, and then explained that Peter had taken them to a local pool hall—called, in deference to Wall Street faux-proletarian sensibilites, Soho Billiards but still, a pool hall—and taught them how to use a cue and rack 'em up. Then Peter had left them there among the slant-eyed sharks, and they had filled the afternoon learning the game.

"We got good," Luke said, eyes shining. "I think we could become, like, pool hustlers and all. I really do, Dad. You know, the kind of people who make you think they don't know how to play, and then they do?" (New York has made him into a "high" talker, ending every statement with the intonation of a question.)

I beamed with pleasure and relief. They had played pool! Pool hustlers! What could be better than learning how to adjust a cue to strike a ball into a pocket, as compared to another meaningless two-hour session in front of a screen doing mindless hand-eye–coordination games? They were not druggishly indulging in a cynically engineered entertainment. They were in touch with Americana, with history! With Jackie Gleason and Paul Newman in *The Hustler*, and with Seymour and Buddy Glass, for whom pool was a "Protestant reformation" in their New York lives. How wise we had been to make the screens off-limits, for it had led them to the billiard table and the pool hall! *This is going well,* I thought, and I told Martha about it.

She looked puzzled. "Wasn't pool sort of like the video game of nineteen-aught-three?" she asked. "I mean, isn't that what they get so exercised about in *The Music Man*? 'Trouble right here in River City, Trouble with a capital "T" and it rhymes with "P" and it stands for pool,' or however the hell it goes? It sounds like instead of letting them do mindless crap, you're getting them to do *dated* mindless crap."

"Yes," I conceded. "But that was . . . different." I couldn't say how, but I was convinced that it was.

That evening, staying at our house, the boys disappeared into Luke's room, where we keep the piano and the guitar. I heard banging and playing of various kinds. The next morning, when Peter came over to pick up Theo, they invited everyone to listen.

We all trooped in. "Listen to this, Dad," Theo said. They sat down: Luke on piano, Theo on guitar. Nods and mature headshakes, and then a solid, slightly out-of-order, but utterly rocking version of "Purple Haze" emerged from their fingers and their throats. They got it all: the stuttering bit at the beginning, the swoop in the middle, and the key slurrings of pronunciation, so that " 'Scuse me while I kiss the sky" became " 'Scuse me while I kiss this guy." Theo sang it right, too—stoned-sounding, but not too stoned.

Peter and I looked on, delighted, our heads bouncing to the remembered beat.

"You see what you guys can accomplish when you don't spend your whole day wrapped up in some screen?" I asked sapiently.

"Yeah, you were right," Luke said. "This was a lot better." He paused. "Hey, Dad," he added at last. "What's this song all about?"

"What do you mean?"

"Like, what's it about? I mean, 'purple haze all in my brain . . .' why? Why is there purple haze all in his brain?"

Still high with the pleasure of their weekend—Hendrix and pool, instead of GameCube and computer!—I said unguardedly, "Oh, it's a drug song. It's an acid song—Purple Haze was a way of referring to acid."

Peter corrected with a scholarly tilt of his head, "You know, actually, I think that it's a *psychedelic* song, but not really an *acid* song. It was a trippy kind of pot, I think. I think they started calling that stuff Purple Haze *after* the song was well known."

I nodded: good point. "Anyway," I said pedantically, "it's about an acid trip. It's an attempt to evoke the inner world of an acid trip."

The boys looked back at us.

"You mean it's a song about drugs?" Theo asked.

"Yeah, exactly," I said. "He was, you know, an addict."

"Is he dead?" Luke asked.

I nodded.

"Well, what did he die of?" asked Luke, always obsessed with questions of mortality.

"Oh, he died of a drug overdose. He's buried in Père-Lachaise," I added, with a pedantry growing lamer every moment, "you know, the cemetery in Paris." (He isn't, of course. I had the wrong dead rock star.)

"How old was he?" Luke asked.

"He was, I don't know, twenty-eight or twenty-nine."

"What kind of drugs did he die of?"

"I'm not sure. I think it was heroin, but a speedball or crystal meth, something like that. Hey, play it again," I said weakly. "You guys are great."

"What kind of drug?" Theo repeated, more maturely, evaluating it.

"Speed, I think," Peter said. EA Sports Madden NFL was looking more creative every moment. Reruns of *Gilligan's Island* were looking more creative.

"Why did he die of a drug overdose?" Luke asked, and, in line with my general principle of giving every one of his straight questions a straight answer, I explained what I could about musicians and their demons and their demands.

"See all the fun creative stuff you can do if you're not staring at a screen?" I added, lamely, as a coda. The boys went back to Hendrix.

. . .

I see, of course, the absurdity and comedy and even the hypocrisy of our parental struggle against the screens. The screen addiction is partly hateful because it is an addiction—an enslavement—and partly threatening, to be truthful, because it is not *our* addiction. Though many of our best memories are of staring at screens in our sometimes aimless and druggy adolescence, the thing we fear most for our kids is that they will end up druggy and mixed-up adolescents, staring at screens. Our screens, we tell ourselves virtuously (and the boys, when they will listen) were the screens of film societies and old television shows, which we now recycle to their bafflement; but the addiction was, in truth, the same, or very like.

Yet though I sense the absurdity, I still think there is an honest core, something worthwhile, at the heart of our struggle. We pull them away from the screens because, as always, we want them to be decentered, just a little. Our job as parents is still first to center our children constantly—to make them believe that they are uniquely valuable suns within a solar system of other people on whom they shine every day, that the light they cast is always welcome, daylight on another planet. But then our job is also continually to *de*center them—make them understand that theirs is not the first nor only nor most important consciousness in the world, and that half of life involves signaling to others that we recognize this fact, even if we don't quite believe it to be true. They may be suns, but they exist in nebulae and galaxies of billions of other suns. It is the problem of child flight, returning as it always does: We want them aloft, blessed by fairy dust, second star to the right and straight on to morning. And we want them flat-footed and realistic: You're lucky if you get to the corner in one piece, look both ways as you cross the street, do it twice. We want them aloft and alert, and at the same time.

The screens, video games, computer games, and online chat rooms center them very literally, by giving them the role of Gandalf, manager of the Yankees, God. It is perfectly true, as the contrarians insist, that video games teach a good deal, that they encourage the kids to improve their pattern recognition, hand-eye coordination, and whatever else. But that's exactly the problem: not that they don't learn anything from the screens but that they learn too much too easily. They earn a certain kind of limited mastery without interference from others. Really mastering something means learning it from someone else. You can't be a master without first having been an apprentice.

So the pleasure Peter and I felt as we watched the boys give up the new screens for the old vices was not, I think, entirely wrongheaded. The strongest decentering force in life is the past. When the children come into contact, however briefly or absurdly, with something that is outside themselves—the first notes of "Are You Experienced" or a pool cue and the hard stare of real pool players—it at least suggests that life is not a universe with the self at the center, but a river running through time, into which you are lucky to dip your hand and come up with minnows or diamonds or old Coke cans, tattered sheet music and cue chalk. A boy with a pool cue in his hand is doing himself some good just by standing in a long invisible line of other boys with pool cues, stretching out the pool hall door into the American past. I suspect that the people of *The Music Man*'s River City, exactly as appalled by their boys in a pool hall as we are by our boys staring at a video game, would have been relieved if their boys ran off to do the Tom Sawyerish things, play pirates in caves.

We don't really want them to practice the eternal virtues. Or rather, we do want them to practice the eternal virtues, but, short of that, we'll settle for the older vices. The older vices are our secret name for the eternal virtues. The older vices at least are old; you have to learn them from your fathers.

Olivia, at four, still plays with words, not screens, much less pool cues and broken chords. Her games are more purely verbal, games of discovery rather than acquisition. She likes to use long words to show her maturity, rather than short ones to show her cool. "Actually" and "obviously" have become her two favorites. "Actually" in a four-year-old's vocabulary means "surprisingly so," as, surprisingly, does "obviously." (Everything in a four-year-old's vocabulary means "surprisingly so," actually, not because everything is so surprising to her but because she wants you to know that she knows how surprising things can be, and therefore how unsurprised she is capable of being at them.)

"Actually, I like everyone in school," she says, adding, "I like everyone, actually, but I like my mother most of all." Or "Obviously, all the kids think that way." She needs some way to "mark" her recognition of a particular class of events—not strictly surprising but "more surprising than you might think." Much of human communication involves using the most extreme language to mean just "more than you might think" and "more often than you might imagine." We say "Geography makes destiny!" when we really mean "Geography matters far more than you might think." When Olivia says, "Actually, I like boys best," she means "I like them more than you might think I do."

Olivia and her friends have the normal vocabulary of four- and five-year-olds, with some peculiarities that I think may be purely local stuff. Their other marker word is "miscellaneous," which Olivia probably picked up from her super-sincere teacher. She uses it accurately enough—"There are some miscellaneous children in the class"—but uses it to mean "generally diffused throughout, unmarked by any distinctive feature." "Interact" is another word she likes. Having noticed me teasing the kids in her pre-K class (pretending to be unable to tell Sophie from Sylvia), one morning on the way to school, Olivia said to me quietly, "Dad, would you please not interact with the other children?" "The miscellaneous children, you mean?" I asked. She ignored me.

Actually, the four odd vocabulary "items" Olivia uses sum up all the marking you need for a New York life. What distinguishes life here is anonymity and intimacy, the dance of the two; marking out your decisive in-group from the vast indistinguishable and unknowable out-group. "Actually" marks the hard truth beneath appearances; "obviously" marks the consensus of in-group opinion, four-year-old opinion; "miscellaneous" is the great mass of common unmarked experience that surrounds you; and "interact" is what all of these obvious and miscellaneous forces actually do.

Late for school on a frozen day, we give up the usual bus route and grab a cab. (Hop in a taxi, as her friend Charlie Ravioli says.) The moment we get in, we're greeted by the deep thrumming sounds of chanting—not Gregorian but some other, more Asian kind. I check the driver's name: a long compound of vowels and "chg" consonants, Rumpole Chingoloalanana—something like that, though not that, obviously.

"Excuse me," I ask, "what is that beautiful music?"

He explains that it is the music of his home country, Nepal, or rather of the Sherpa peoples who inhabit the lower slopes of the Himalayas. "Sherpas like Sherpas?" I ask stupidly. "You mean the kind who guide Englishmen up Mount Everest?" Not Everest, he says, but—and he pronounces the long name of the mountain in his native language.

"What does that mean?" Olivia pipes up.

"The top of the world," he says proudly.

"Have you ever been to the top of the mountain?" Olivia asks, a New York child for once impressed.

"No," he admits. "I have been almost halfway up, to one of the bases. My family guides men up, but I have come here to make my living in this city, make more money here, and send it home."

The beautiful chanting continues. An odd feeling of peace descends on us both, I can tell. "What a journey!" I say sententiously to Olivia as we exit the cab. "Imagine this man climbing down from Mount Everest and coming all the way around the world to live in New York and drive a taxi!"

I tell Luke and Martha the story with great excitement, the chanting and the history, and turn to Olivia. "Wasn't it exciting?" I demand.

"Actually, it was obvious," she says calmly; extremely miscellaneous people are just part of life here.

While the children play with screens and cards, the grown-ups have their games, too. Martha and I have begun to play Mafia, a parlor game that has become popular among our friends. A "Mafia evening" is called, and a crowd—no fewer than fifteen, no more than twenty, writers and screenwriters and actors and publishers and lawyers—gathers at night in someone's living room or around someone's dining room table (in the rarer apartment where there is a dining room). Generally, two games are possible in a single evening, interrupted by Chinese takeout and excited discussion about the game just ended.

The rules of the game are so simple that to recite them is to make the game sound bafflingly dull. It's one of those games that plays much better than it sounds. The game begins when one player, with long experience of the game, takes on the role of God. He distributes, facedown, a playing card to each player. Three people get red cards and become, for this round, the Mafia; the rest, the ordinary black cards, become villagers; and the one who gets the joker becomes the Comandante, the policeman.

Night has fallen, "God" announces—and a small but real part of the pleasure of the game lies in having a "God" sufficiently persuasive and authoritative to make the game come alive, to make the night falling on the town feel serious, not playful. The Sicilian village (that is, the group of New Yorkers of the professional classes) falls asleep (that is, shuts their eyes tight).

"Mafia, make yourselves known to me," "God" says, and the three Mafia members "make themselves known": They open their eyes and look at one another, silently acknowledging the others in their sinister cenacle; then they look at "God" before going back to sleep. This is a thrillingly conspiratorial moment, particularly if the Mafia members are in some way ill sorted—a combo of newcomers and veterans. Then the "Comandante" makes himself known to the "God."

Then everyone opens his eyes, and the game begins. The villagers must try to identify the Mafia members among them, and then, at the end of each "day," a majority vote is enough to kill someone they believe to be a Mafia member. The Mafia, of course, try to mislead the villagers into killing the wrong—that is, non-Mafia—people without so obviously collaborating among themselves that their real identity is clear. Then, after the majority votes someone dead, "night" falls again (i.e., everybody shuts his eyes), and the Mafia members silently consult among themselves, instructing the "God" by pointing who it is they want to kill—usually someone whose conversation and questions and accusations suggested that he was on the track of the Mafia, but often enough a red herring. (I won't put quotes around all this from now on—"kill," "Mafia," etc.—because the quotes are the game. If you need quotes, you're not getting it.)

The Comandante then opens his eyes and silently points to any one of the sleeping players. God either nods, meaning that player is in the Mafia, or else shakes his head, meaning not. The Comandante must use this knowledge during the day without giving away the fact that he is the Comandante, which would result in his instant assassination that night, or "night." (I had to use quotes, just that once.) The game ends when the villagers have killed off all the Mafia, or the Mafia outnumber the surviving villagers. (Mafia wins are not unknown, but the village usually has the edge.)

Catching the Mafia begins with circumstantial evidence and pure guesswork—a rustle overhead in the night, a guilty smile on a naked face. For a villager, the best starting strategy seems to be a kind of "Blink" scan, simply and quickly to survey every face in the circle as soon as eyes are open, hoping to deduce from a thousand subtle, nonverbal clues just who looks guilty. This works better than you might think. As the game goes on, deductive reasoning comes, slightly, to the aid of intuitive guesswork. The wise villager tries to track the circles of accusation and assassination and figure out whose accuser is getting killed. It is perfectly possible—in fact, completely strategic—for the Mafia to accuse one another, so long as the accusation is deflected sufficiently never to result in a vote on the accused; and it is also possible for the Mafia to kill a perfectly innocent, nonaccusing villager one night, just to throw the others off the scent.

The game, which is said to have been invented by a sociologist in Russia, is meant to be a kind of devilish variation of Prisoner's Dilemma and other games in which cooperation and competition sit in uneasy equilibrium. The game demonstrates the many and pressing kinds of double-bind logic that fill a social group if its members suspect there are enemies within it. If you are in the Mafia, you have to kill all the people who correctly suspect that you are, but you can't be too obvious that the people being killed are the ones who suspect you, since that would confirm the truth of their suspicions. If you are a villager, you have to share information with the others in order to persuade them to vote the right way, but you can't share too much information, since some of the villagers with whom you're cooperating are certainly Mafia.

The ostensible pleasure of the game lies in testing your own skills as a dissembler and as a spotter of dissemblers—in lying and spotting liars. Both eager cooperation and absolute paranoia are essential to the strategic game. Yet the really fascinating thing about Mafia is seeing how much pure irrationality lingers in its play, how little real deduction and how much sheer panic govern its conduct. The game quickly breaks down, as social groups will, into small circles of belief, which become lynch mobs of mistrust on the next turn. As these small circles within the group form and break, the emotional authenticity of the alliances, the felt pleasure of trusting another, is startlingly, frighteningly real. "I think it's Larry—it must be Larry," George says to you, filling his eyes with sincere persuasiveness, leaning forward, confiding, conspiring. And you nod with conspiratorial glee: Yes, it must be Larry, look at him—and for that moment the bond between you and George is so intense as to overshadow your general and complete lack of interest in George as a person. You and George against the Mafia—but then the quick nightly shadow intrudes: What if George *is* the Mafia? Yet the proper suspicions, though they rise, rarely override these instant bonds. The impulse to trust and go on trusting a confidant is so strong that it often survives even overwhelming evidence that the confidant is a rat—just as, in the real Mafia, Big John Gotti went on trusting Sammy the Bull long after it should have been plain to him that Sammy the Bull was singing; the loss of Sammy—the loss of the idea of Big John and Sammy as a single mutually reinforcing unit—was so terrible to contemplate that Big John was prepared to put aside his own doubts rather than lose his friend, with, as we know, fatal results.

Trust, which we offer the children as a panacea, is dramatized in the game of Mafia, as it is in adult life, merely as a precondition to blindness. "Just trust me" in the grown-up game means "I'm probably lying," and the more trust you demand, the more likely it is to be a lie. "Just trust me" in the game means merely, "See me past the lie. Support me in the lie." "Just trust me" is the prelude to betrayal.

Some of the game's pleasure lies simply in its not being conversation: It is a relief not to have to make small talk with your neighbors at a dinner party. Instead of telling them elaborate social lies in an unformed context, you get to tell them elaborate social lies in a formal one. After all, the game offers a stylized version of the same game most of the players have been engaged in at offices and in meetings all day long, and would normally be playing that night, too, only less openly. Paranoid suspicion that your friends and fellow villagers are secretly trying to kill you is, after all, not very far from the beating heart of New York professional life. Beneath the surface of cooperation and villageness, of evening games and shared Chinese ribs and noodles, there lie murderous impulses; absolute paranoia about the motives of your friends—this is a game we know already. There is a smile of happy betrayal at the end of a successful Mafia game that is a smile of real triumph, uncomfortably intense, off-puttingly familiar. "We got you," the Mafia people cry, and they excitedly rehearse all the near-misses and shrewd killings. "I knew that Sally was about to suss us out, but we deflected it to Eileen, and then we got Sally that night." It comes to them a bit too easily.

Not that the evenings are not jolly, bright, and glowing, with the Chinese food and the absorbed, retrospective conversation ("I knew you were Mafia at the moment when . . ."). The game creates a kind of excited, genial ecstasy, an excessive feeling of happiness and release, not unlike that which we used to get from the more purple and hazy of drugs, come to think of it. The sense of happiness the game provides I take to be partly a token of its capacity to offer in symbolic form a chunk of real experience—to turn ordinary social betrayal into recreation—but I also take to be something more than merely social, something sexual and even erotic in its way.

For the truly exceptional thing about a Mafia evening is this: The game quickly degenerates, or advances, into a series of parallel duels between husband and wife (or lover and lover). The game is really played between couples as each one spots the other lying and tries to convince the rest of the room that he or she, uniquely, knows when this is so. A wife looks at her husband, a husband at his wife, a lover at a lover, squares eyes up, and says, "That's the way she *always* looks when she's lying."

And people are bursting to offer up to the group their familiarity with betrayal! As though the truth about our lovers that we cannot wait to tell the world, the thing we've been dying to say for years, is that they—our partners—are chronic but totally unskilled dissemblers. We can't wait to produce evidence about what a liar our loved one really is, and such a steady and poor liar that we can see right through him or her. We know each other perfectly, but it is only within the ritualized confines of a game, over sticky ribs on paper plates in someone's living room, that we can declare to the world: "She's a liar! Just look at that 'innocent' face." But she's *my* liar, and she can't fool me.

Yet here is the really odd thing: *No one credits the husband or the wife in suspicions about the spouse*—at least not any more than they credit all other suspicions and accusations in the game, including those that total strangers have or make about total strangers. Everyone believes himself to be especially good at spotting the prevarications of his sexual partner, but no one else believes this—because, I realize, they have decided that if we were really good at spotting what fakes our partners are, we never would have married them in the first place. The default assumption is that nothing one person in a relationship says about the other can have any probative value at all. "I know that smile. She had that smile on her face when she told me that she hadn't slept with her creative writing teacher," someone says, and everyone else thinks, *You needed the* smile *to tell you that?*

There is, after all, an irreducible element of impossibility about all other people's relationships, about everyone else's marriages. To each of us, in our hearts, the attraction of another person's mate must be a little unfathomable or self-deluding, illusory. We have no choice but to believe this; otherwise, they have made a better choice than we have. We have to convince ourselves over and over that our own choice was uniquely wise, and therefore that the spell everyone else casts on their mates is essentially spurious, phony, a threadbare thing of patches and obvious bits of makeup and neediness and self-delusion. He didn't see right through this person when he was deciding to buy a co-op and make love and have children with her, so why should we think that he is sharp enough to see through her now, in the middle of this game in someone else's living room on Lexington Avenue? *Now* she sees through him, suddenly, here? Why didn't she see through him the first time she heard that machine-gun laugh? He thinks she's lying now? But he still nods seriously when she makes the same fatuous remark about Bush being "you know, such a simple man," over and over again? Obviously, she *doesn't* know when he's faking, because he does it all the time, and she doesn't notice then. *Everyone* sees through her except him—so how can he claim to be seeing through her now?

You might expect an Updikean theater of adultery, of flirtation and seduction and sexual conquest and betrayal, to be going on at the same time within that same living room. The small subcircles of trust ought to become sexualized. But—and, twenty-five years married, I may well be missing something here, but I don't think I am—this doesn't seem to be going on. I am stirred by some of the women players—that excitement with which women play all games, once their tentativeness passes, without the tedious knowingness that men insist on introducing—and, who knows, there may be hidden threads, a pattern in the tablecloth visible only when you hold it to the light, that I am too dull to spot. But it seems to me that the eroticism of Mafia, like the apparent eroticism of the actual Mafia as we see it in the movies and read about it in the tabloids, lies in the renewal of sex among the already connected. The hit man's interest in his own wife is, they say, reawakened by the hit. *You're a liar, and I know it, but I'll sleep with you anyway* is, after all, the most intimate thing we can say to each other. It keeps the game—many games—going.

The screens have a hold on the children, but the cards hold them even closer. We live in New York, we tell other people timidly, for the cultural advantages, and for Luke, the major cultural advantage is Alex's MVP, a grungy sports memorabilia and card store on Eighty-ninth Street and Second Avenue. It sits in a basement crowded with old cards and comic books, and Luke's chief desire is to go there and buy more cards.

We found it first when we were bumming around one day. I was showing him the old neighborhood where Martha and I first lived, for three years, in our basement room on Eighty-seventh Street. It really was a neighborhood once, with a bad bakery, and German restaurants lining Eighty-sixth Street. On a memorable snowy night in the early eighties, I got my first job and we went out to celebrate at Kleine Konditorei, goose and duck with German sauces. All of that is gone now, wiped right off the map, not a sign anywhere of the kind of neighborhood it was just a quarter century ago.

Luke is indifferent to this, for obvious reasons—no child wants to hear his parents' mythology; his parents are already sufficiently mythological, evil emperor and good captive princess—and, trying to find something that he would like, I vaguely recalled a vintage comic-book store in the neighborhood. I said, "I think there's a cool card store around here somewhere."

"On Second Avenue and Eighty-ninth Street," a man going by announced helpfully. I stared at him in gratitude.

It was there, and Luke loved it. Small and grungy, with spiritualized sawdust on the floor. The smeared glass cases were crowded with dusty memorabilia at New York prices: a bat signed by Derek Jeter, a World Series program from 1932, a whole world of memories, some of them, a few of them, mine.

Luke wanted baseball cards. It is only a year now since I broke the news to him, finally and definitively, that the Rookie, the three-year-old fastballing pitcher of the bedtime story of his Paris years, was a fiction. He nodded cheerfully—a Santa moment—and then Martha made me abandon another fiction we had launched before, about the king of Central Park. At Alex's, he began instead to collect Major League Baseball Showdown packs, the new craze in the civilization of nine-year-olds. You collect baseball cards, new ones, showing players from across the decades, and then play a complicated dice-throwing game. (We actually had to send to Washington State for a peculiar twenty-sided die.) Each player pits his lineup against the others, and they follow the rules marked on the back of the cards, which span the decades: Whitey Ford can get out Johnny Damon; Barry Bonds can slug some off Walter Johnson. I love this game because it is, though part of their life now, still historical—it centers and decenters all at once, and for the price of a pack of baseball cards.

The other day we wandered over to Alex's—Olivia on her scooter; Luke has now "outgrown" his—and Luke bought a pack. He asked Olivia to kiss the pack for luck, and then he opened it.

He paused. "Dad, this is the kind of thing that only happens to me in my dreams," he said seriously, and he showed me what, or rather whom, he had in the pack: Willie McCovey, the great San Francisco Giants first baseman of the sixties. Apparently, McCovey, more than even better-known players, is hugely valuable within the game.

Luke had a good sense of McCovey's "icons," his particular status within the game, but only the most shadowy idea of who McCovey actually was, obviously, and I took delight in telling him the little I could remember, pretending that that little was more than it was. He listened seriously, with a real edge of respect for a past that reaches into the present: Who Willie McCovey was matters for who Willie McCovey is, for what he is worth in the game.

Then an odd thing happened. Every day Luke would come home from school with a kind of offer sheet for his McCovey card. "Dad, what if I traded McCovey for Bob Gibson?" he would ask over dinner, his face betraying only the slightest sign of deliberate taunting, of complicity in teasing Dad. "You'd be crazy," I would say flatly. The next night: "Dad—Daniel offered me Whitey Ford for him." I tried to distinguish between my own knowledge of the relative value of these ballplayers and their represented value on the face of the cards. I tried to be sage. But I didn't want him to trade the McCovey card. Every morning I would drop him off at school and cry out inwardly: *Don't trade the McCovey card!*

I don't know why it mattered to me. "You're going to be trading steak for hamburger!" I would warn him when he came home with a particularly lowball offer. But the truth was that, so far as I could see, some of the offers—Gibson for Willie, Ford for Willie—were pretty decent. I could sense that the card was burning a hole in his pocket—that possessing it was, perversely, urging him to surrender it, transform it, abandon it. It was, I suppose, a dream come true, and the only thing to do with a dream come true is give it up, so another dream can take its place. (Proust got a whole book out of this idea.)

Why did it matter to *me,* though? After all, one card or another . . . it's his game, I told myself relentlessly. It was, I came at last to understand, because the serendipity of the purchase of the card at Alex's was a marker in our own relationship, our own friendship, beginning to change, properly, with the passing years. We had bought it together, and I wanted it for us. If it became currency in his game of peer-group rivals—which is what it ought to be—then it was no longer a significant object in our history of father-son pleasures. This had occurred to him, too, or at least been sensed by him, driving him in just the opposite direction.

I came home from the office one day, and he was waiting for me by the door, a guilty smile on his face. "Dad, I traded the McCovey card today," he said, smiling but firm.

"What did you get for it?" I asked weakly, sadly.

He showed me: Whitey Ford, and Yogi Berra, and a throw-in member of the 1959 White Sox, Luis Aparicio. It was a pretty good haul of old ballplayers, I had to admit. Well, each man kills the thing he loves, and each nine-year-old has to trade his McCovey card. The cards are a way out into the adult world of exchange and judgment, of deceit and enterprise; they are there, above all, to be traded. Once the card is put in circulation, it is no longer his—but it is no longer mine, either. Parenting, however hard we discipline our hearts to make our children independent, involves an assertion of ownership; baseball cards, like money and desire, are a medium of exchange.

When we had another no-screen sleepover the other weekend, I walked into Luke's room and was annoyed to find the boys huddled over the computer. "It's okay, Dad," Luke said with winning innocence. "We're writing a screenplay."

They were, too—a story called "The New Finding," a sequel to *The Lord of the Rings.* They let me read a few pages. It was pretty clever, a transposition of Tolkien into Manhattan.

And what could we say? That they alone could not enter into the great gamble, the permanent game, of screenplay writing, into which all their parents would sooner or later plunge, as Mexican peasants plunge into the lottery, knowing the odds but dreaming of the jackpot? How could we forbid them that?

Considering the maze of screens and cards and pages, I ended up at last with a bitter, semi-Marxist conclusion: It is not that we want them free of screens, really. It is that we want them to be screen producers rather than screen consumers. We say that we don't want them enslaved to screens, but what we really want is for them to enslave other people to them. We want them to be Steve Jobs or Steven Spielberg—feudal screen lords rather than mere screen peasants, screen serfs. We do not mind if they play games, so long as they grow up to write the software. We will leave them alone for a weekend to write their screenplay, even if they have to huddle over a screen to do it.

The New York Mafia season passed with the coming of summer, when the players scattered, and then re-formed with the autumn. The game went on, but we noticed that the circle of players had altered slightly; there were certain couples whom we decided not to ask back to play with us—they were too loud, or too dull, or too unskilled—and then we noticed that certain other people, with whom we had played in the spring, were no longer playing—at least they must have given up the game, since we were not invited to their houses to play. Funny, that they lost interest . . .

And then it dawned on us: The game of Mafia we play at night is a ruse, a red herring, the game that conceals the real game. The real game of Mafia is the game of who asks whom back to play the game again. The apparent game of playacting and pretend death is just a subsystem, orbiting within the larger game not of pretend death but of brutally real social inclusion and exclusion. Over the Chinese takeout, murderous social judgments are being made: They're no fun, they're too giddy, they're too flat, they're too shrill. Silently, in the middle of the night in our Sicilian village—the real Sicilian village of New York, where the work of conspiracy is accomplished by cell-phone calls and e-mails—someone is being murdered and dropped right out of the game, the social circle, while others are being left to live. The real killers are an amorphous and self-appointed but fatal small inner circle within the larger innocent circle of players. A Mafia! One morning you wake up dead, though you don't know it until weeks go by and you realize that you have not been invited to the next game. You thought they were your friends, but they now turn out to be, well, Mafia. We are complicit in these murders, of course, as we, too, include and exclude, reinforcing our own circle. There is not one true Mafia, we realize, but several, Five Families, each whacking members of the other ones. The real "night" is the week's interval between games; the real murders the dropping off of friends; and the real God—well, there is no God, really.

On Thanksgiving, after the meal, with many friends we played Mafia because the children wanted us to; they are envious of our game-playing evenings out, the only thing we do without them. But the game feels rote in the absence of near-strangers with whom we can bond and break. That new game had decentered us as we want the old games to decenter the children; it left us reeling, just a little, with a usefully punctured ego. To have been killed, and by those people, too—to have been judged, so unfairly, as dull as all those others who deserved it! But then we have killed, we know, and just as cruelly, those friends on whom our social disdain has somehow landed, who could not have known that we would never ask them back. We were at the center, and now we are not. We have turned on our friends, and our friends have turned on us. We *are* a Mafia, after all, and more murderous than we pretend.

Death of a Fish

When our five-year-old daughter Olivia's goldfish, Bluie, died the other week, we were confronted by a crisis larger, or at least more intricate, than is entirely usual upon the death of a pet. Bluie's life and his passing came to involve so many larger elements—including the problem of consciousness and the plotline of Hitchcock's *Vertigo*—that it left us all bleary-eyed and a little shaken.

To begin with, Bluie, as his name suggests, was not actually a goldfish. He was a betta, a goldfish-size fish that the people in pet stores encourage you to buy in place of the tetchy and sickly true Asian goldfish. The betta is a handsome fish, with long, sweeping fins. It can be red or black or violet or blue, and it is, at least according to the pet-store people, the Vietcong of pet fish, evolved in rugged isolation in the rice-paddy puddles of Indochina and just about impossible to kill off. The only drawback is that male bettas fight with one another and have to be kept apart. It is not surprising these days to see a pair of them on a child's dresser in Manhattan, held in separate containers, in a kind of glass-bowl parody of the co-op apartment building that surrounds them, each fish furiously pacing its cubic foot of space and waiting for the other to turn up the stereo.

And then, in a deeper, damper sense, Bluie was not really a fish at all. He was, like so many New York fish and mice and turtles, a placeholder for other animals that the children would have preferred to have as pets, but which allergies and age and sheer self-preservation have kept their parents from buying. Olivia and her ten-year-old brother, Luke, desperately want a dog, and at Christmas Olivia brought the class hamster, Hamu, home from her preschool as an experiment in pet-keeping. Hamu stayed with us for a mostly happy, if sometimes jittery, holiday week, and we reluctantly agreed to add a hamster to the family.

We went to the second floor of PETCO, the mallish store on East Eighty-sixth Street, where all the rodents are kept together—rats and mice and guinea pigs and hamsters and gerbils. Looking at them, Martha had a foreboding sense of what Darwin must have felt, looking at the Galápagos finches: that these things were not nearly so distinct as they had been trying to make you believe. A hamster and a guinea pig and a gerbil are all rats, and the differences, tails and no tails, cute noses and not, are really bells and whistles, niche-marketing gimmicks. Having spent twenty-five years of her New York life struggling to keep rodents out, Martha couldn't see spending time and money to bring one in.

So we talked the children into goldfish, and then the weary fish salesman talked us into bettas instead. ("The goldfish will die," he said shortly. "Then what?") We bought them bowls and gravel and decorative architecture to swim around in, and took them home. Luke named his Django—a family joke, since he has often heard the story that this is what I had wanted to call him until his mother vetoed it, firmly—and Olivia gave hers the more descriptive name of Bluie. For a while, she seemed to accept his provisional, placeholding nature with equanimity.

For a pet condemned to live in so many brackets of meta-meaning, a fish passing as a hamster hoping to become a dog, Bluie had a pretty good life. In the constant struggle of parents of two children—one obviously large and one (especially to herself) irrefutably, infuriatingly small—to even life up, we got Bluie a castle, a bigger object for his tank than we got for Django. It sat on the gravel, and rose almost to the surface—a Disney-like princess's residence, with turrets and castellations and plastic pennants. There was even a route from the base of the castle to the top turret that Bluie could swim up. A third betta, won at a street fair, joined Bluie on Olivia's dresser, but this new guy, named Reddie, had only a bowl to swim in. Reddie, we thought, kept pressing to the edge of his bowl to stare at Bluie's real estate with a certain resentment, the way a guy who lives in a condo on Broadway and teaches at City College might regard a colleague who writes best sellers and lives in a penthouse on Central Park West.

One Sunday night around bedtime, my wife called me into Olivia's room. Bluie was stuck in one of the windows of his castle, wriggling and huffing, with just his head out, looking ahead and trying to swim away. He wasn't supposed to be able to swim up there into the windows—he was supposed to stay within the channel in the castle. But the castle obviously had a design flaw.

"Bluie's stuck in the window!" Olivia cried.

"Calm down, Olivia," Luke said. "He's just a fish."

"Bluie is my best friend," Olivia said. "I could tell him things I couldn't tell anyone else!" Until that moment, Bluie had seemed to be just a finny bit of decor, but at that moment, at least, he mattered to her crucially.

I watched Bluie wriggling in his window, staring out, stuck.

I felt for him, another victim of grandiose Manhattan real estate, undone by his own apartment. It was one of those moments, of which parenting is full, when you scream inside, *I don't know what to do about this!* while the parent you are impersonating says calmly, "I'll fix it."

I picked up Bluie's bowl and took him into the kitchen, leaving Martha to console Olivia. I slid the kitchen door shut and then reached into the water and tried gently to draw Bluie out of the window. I tugged lightly and then realized that he was really wedged in. I tugged again, just a touch harder. Nothing. I saw that if I pulled at all firmly I was likely to rip his fins right off. I tried pushing him on the nose, urging him back out the way he came. Still nothing. He was stuck.

I looked around the kitchen. The remains of a sea bass that we had eaten for dinner—and that had doubtless, when it was up and swimming, had a lot more personality than Bluie ever did—rested on the counter, filleted skeleton and staring, reproachful head, waiting to be tossed out.

"Why can't Bluie think, *I got into this mess by swimming forward, I'll go back the other way?*" Luke said. "It's like he doesn't have a rewind function in his brain."

He had slipped quietly into the kitchen beside me and was watching, an intern to my baffled surgeon. Like many ten-year-olds, he is obsessed by what philosophers call the problem of consciousness but he calls the thinking-and-feeling thing. "Does Bluie know he's Bluie?" he would ask when we watched the fish swimming in his bowl in Olivia's room. "I mean, I know he doesn't think, *Oh, I'm Bluie!* But what does he think—does he know he's him swimming around? Or is he just like a potato or something, only with fins, who swims but doesn't think anything?" What does it feel like, he wanted to know, to be a fish, a hamster, a monkey, a chimp? What does it feel like to be someone else?

When my sister, the developmental psychologist at Berkeley, came to visit, she sat Luke down and said, smoothly, that scientists once thought that life was a problem, but then they had not so much solved the problem as dissolved it, by understanding ever simpler forms of life. Luke's problem, why we know what it feels like to be alive, would probably dissolve into its parts, too. Luke had nodded politely, but I could see he still held that the problem of thinking and feeling certainly felt like a problem when you thought about it.

"Swim backward, Bluie," I implored. "Get out of there."

Bluie, of course, did nothing but wiggle some more, wedged in his window.

"Is he thinking, *I'm dying*?" Luke asked at last.

Finally, I settled on a cowardly postponement of what even then I knew to be inevitable. I walked back to Olivia's room. "Let's take Bluie to PETCO in the morning and see if the experts there can help him," I said to Olivia as we tucked her in. "They've probably got a whole team of guys who are specialists in castle extraction."

At five in the morning, I woke up to look in on Bluie. He was dead. I tried to think about what to do. I decided to take him out, still stuck in his castle window, and put him and the castle into a white plastic bag. Then I sat down to read at the kitchen table, in the gray light of the June Manhattan dawn, spring in Manhattan feeling so much more accelerated, so much quicker and time-lapsed and vivid than it does in any other city, a wave of pollen and warmth and renewal blowing in the window.

My sister had given me a kind of reading list to help me answer Luke's questions at a deeper level than I could on my own, and I had read many of the philosophers who have something to say about his problem. I read David Chalmers, who thinks that consciousness is the ghost in the machine, the secret irreducible presence in the mind that distinguishes us from computers and goldfish and other creatures who provide only a zombie-like imitation of our self-knowledge. I read those philosophers who think that what we call consciousness is just an illusion, and bears the same relation to the workings of our real minds that the White House press spokesman bears to the workings of the White House: It is there to find rationalizations and systematic reasons for feelings and decisions made by dim, hidden powers of whose pettish and irrational purposes it is aware only long after the fact.

Of all the theories that I came across, the most impressive was Daniel Dennett's. He argues that consciousness is a by-product, not a point—that it is just the sound that all those parallel processors inside our heads make as they run alongside one another, each doing its small robotic task. There is no "consciousness" apart from the working of all our mental states. Consciousness is not the ghost in the machine; it is the hum of the machinery. The louder the hum, the more conscious you feel. If Bluie had had a more interesting life, he would have known that he was having it. Bluie did not know that he was Bluie because there was not enough Bluie going on in his head to make being Bluie interesting even to Bluie.

Luke woke up and padded into the kitchen. He asked what had happened to Bluie, and I told him. We decided that we would bury Bluie before Olivia woke up, and then tell her that we had taken him to PETCO. That would buy some time, anyway. I emptied Bluie's bowl, hid it in the closet of my office, and Luke and I got dressed. We carried Bluie, in his castle, in his white bag, down the hall to the trash room. We held our caps over our hearts as he went down the chute. Then I took Luke to school. He was silent on the way, but at the school door, he turned to me.

"Dad, whatever you tell her, don't do a big Bluie's-in-the-fish-hospital thing," he counseled me. "That she'll never buy."

When I got home, I woke up Martha. "Bluie didn't make it," I whispered. "What are we going to do?"

"We're doing the full *Vertigo*," she announced, almost before her eyes were open. She had obviously been thinking about it since last night. "You're going to PETCO and buying a fish that looks just like Bluie, and then we're going to put him in the fishbowl and tell her that it's Bluie. If it worked with Kim Novak, it can work with a betta."

She was referring, of course, to the plot of the fifties Hitchcock classic, which we had seen as part of an impromptu Hitchcock festival about a week before. In *Vertigo*, James Stewart falls in love with a mysterious, cool blond beauty, played by Kim Novak, who he comes to believe is a mystical reincarnation of her long-dead great-grandmother, compelled to imitate her actions. When, like her great-grandmother, she launches herself to her death from a bell tower in a restored Mission town, Stewart is devastated. Haunted and desperate, he stumbles on a brunette shopgirl who looks eerily like Kim Novak, and forces her to dye her hair blond and dresses her in tailored gray suits, turning her into a precise replica of the Kim Novak character.

Actually, though, she *is* the Kim Novak character. She had been hired by the bad guy to play the part of the first Kim Novak character—another woman was thrown off that tower, as part of an insurance scam—and to make it even odder, the fact that this is so is given away by the second Kim Novak character (in a flashback) right in the middle of the movie, so that the viewer, unlike poor Jimmy Stewart, is never in doubt about the reason the new Kim Novak looks like the old Kim Novak. The meaning of Hitchcock's choice to give away the key plot point in the middle of the movie, against the advice of everyone around him, is, I have discovered, a subject as much argued about among the cineasts as the nature of consciousness is among the philosophers.

Martha went to wake Olivia and get her dressed for school.

"Bluie's in the fish hospital, darling," I heard her say. Boys and men don't believe in the fish hospital; mothers know that it is where all problems should be sent, while we wait to solve them.

She'll just walk in, like Jimmy Stewart, and will be strangely reminded of Bluie—then he'll become Bluie for her," Martha said a few hours later as we watched the new fish swim around in Olivia's tank, though I could tell that she was trying to reassure herself that this would work. I had gone to PETCO and bought a Bluie look-alike. It was easy—the bettas all looked like Bluie.

But I was beginning to doubt that this was such a good idea. I remembered that in the movie Jimmy Stewart goes nuts, and Kim Novak ends up throwing herself off that bell tower for real.

"Are we doing the wrong thing?" I asked. "I mean, won't she figure out at ten or so that Bluie died?"

All this while, Martha, as a New York mother in crisis, had her cell phone cradled under her jaw. Everybody had had a dead-pet problem. Goldfish had floated to the tops of bowls; hamsters had been found dead in their cages, their furry feet upward; and more gruesome pet-on-pet homicides had taken place, too. Each family had a different tack and a different theory. There were those who had gone the full *Vertigo* route and regretted it; those who had gone the tell-it-to-'em-straight route and regretted that. In fact, about all one could say, and not for the first time as a parent, is that whatever one did, one regretted it afterward.

I made only one call, and that was to my sister the developmental psychologist. She explained to me instantly that it was normal for children to develop intense attachments to pets, even "zombic" ones that did not reciprocate affection, and that a pair of Japanese psychologists, Hatano and Inagaki, had done studies of how children develop intuitive theories of biology by having pets.

"They claim that all kids, Western and Eastern, go from having primarily just psychology and physics to having a 'vitalist' biology right around age six," she told me. "That is, they start to think there is some vital spirit—you know, kind of like Chinese Chi—that keeps animals and humans alive, gets replenished by food, damaged by illness, and so on. And here's the cool thing. Hatano and Inagaki show, experimentally, that giving kids pet fish accelerates the development of this kind of vitalism. We give them fish as a learning device, though we don't know that when we do it. Olivia is probably in transition from a psychological conception of life to a biological one, which may be why she's so bewildered."

It seemed that the mere presence of a fish in a bowl, despite the barriers of glass and water and the fact of the fish's mindlessness, acted as a kind of empathy pump for five-year-olds, getting into the corners of their minds. Olivia was a vitalist, and Bluie was no longer vital. According to my sister, children's education proceeds in stages. At three, they're mostly psychologists, searching for a theory of mind; at six, they're biologists, searching for a theory of life. At ten, they're philosophers, searching to understand why our minds cannot make our lives go on forever.

"My sister doesn't think we're going to screw up Olivia's mind," I said to Martha a few moments later. "She does think that we're going to screw up her theories of biology." Martha was still watching the tank and trying to see if new Bluie would pass. "Olivia is going to think that dying things go away to PETCO and come back as good as new."

Luke was the first one home. He studied the new fish, too. "Does new Bluie know that he's not Bluie?" he asked. Reddie was looking at new Bluie, but we couldn't even guess what he was thinking.

In the end, when Olivia came home from school, we did neither the ingenious Hitchcockian thing nor the honest thing; New York liberals, we did the in-between, wishy-washy, split-the-difference thing. Martha told her that Bluie had been successfully extracted from his castle window by the fish specialists, but he had been so stressed by the experience that he was resting, and it might take a long time for him to recover. Meanwhile, they had given us Bluie's brother.

Olivia took one long, baleful look at the new Bluie.

"I hate this fish," she said. "I hate him. I want Bluie."

We tried to console her, but it was no use.

"But look, he's just like Bluie!" we protested weakly.

"He looks like Bluie," she admitted. "He looks like Bluie. But he's not Bluie. He's a stranger. He doesn't know me. He's not my friend, who I could talk to."

That evening we took turns staying up with her, sitting in the rocking chair in her room and rocking until she slept. The room, I realized, was full of Bluies: things that she had ascribed feelings and thoughts and intentions to, all the while knowing that they didn't really have them. There were Buzzes and Woodies, American Girl dolls, and stuffed animals from her infancy. Children, small children particularly, don't just have more consciousness than the rest of us. They believe in consciousness more than the rest of us; their default conviction is that everything might be able to think, feel, and talk. This conviction is one that entertainment companies both recognize and exploit, with talking toys and lovable sharks, though at some other level, the children are entertained by them because they know it's all made up—no child believes that her own toys in her own bedroom talk like Woody and Buzz in the movie. Ascribing feelings to things is a way of protecting your own right to have feelings. Expanding the circle of consciousness extends the rule of feelings.

Olivia loved Bluie because it is in a child's nature to ascribe intentions and emotions to things that don't have them, rather as Hitchcock did with actresses. She knows that she is Olivia because one of the things that she is capable of doing is imagining that Bluie is Bluie. Though you read about the condition "mind-blindness" in autistic children, the alternative, I saw, was not to be mind-sighted. The essential condition of youth is to be mind-visionary: to see everything as though it might have a mind. We begin as small children imagining that everything could have consciousness—fish, dolls, toy soldiers, even parents—and spend the rest of our lives paring the list down until we are left alone in bed, the only mind left.

And yet, though I had been instructed by my reading that we imagine minds as much as know them, I also realized, looking at the little girl who had cried herself to sleep, that the difference didn't quite matter. A pet is an act of empathy, a theory of love the child makes, but it is also a living thing, and when it dies, it moves briefly but decisively outside the realm of thought, where everything can be given the shape of our own mind, and into the cold climate of physical existence, where things are off or things are on. Science might be dissolving life and mind into smaller parts, but among the higher animals, at least, with eyes and skeletons and hungers, the line between life and non-life is pretty much fixed and hard; from the other side of that window, no traveler, or goldfish, has yet come home to his bowl.

The real proof of consciousness is the pain of loss. Reddie, swimming in his studio, did not know that Bluie had gone; Bluie himself may in some sense not have known that he had gone. But Olivia did. The pain we feel is not the same as the hum we know, and it is the pain, not the hum, that is the price of being conscious, and the point of being human. I looked at the sleeping child, hoping that she would be over her grief in the morning.

Mom," Luke said the next morning, "you shouldn't have done that big Bluie's-in-the-fish-hospital thing. It just stretched it out." The three of us were sitting at the kitchen table, waiting for Olivia to wake up.

"I didn't do a big Bluie's-in-the-fish-hospital thing," Martha objected querulously. She was pretty tired. "I did a big Bluie's-in-the-rehab-clinic-right-next-to-the-fish-hospital thing."

"Well, that makes it worse," Luke said.

"Let's try this," Martha said. "Let's tell her that, though Bluie did die, this Bluie is kind of Bluie reborn."

I thought she might have something, and in the next fifteen minutes, we did a quick, instinctive tour of the world's religions. We made up a risen-from-the-grave Christian story: the Passion of the Bluie. We considered a Buddhist story: Bluie goes round and round. We even played with a Jewish story: Bluie couldn't be kept alive by the doctors, but what a lovely bowl he left for his family!

Then we heard the door of Olivia's room open, and she came to the table, theatrically calm, and sat down. "I'm going to call the new fish

Lucky," she announced. "And can I please have the Honey Nut Cheerios?" She knew that the Honey Nut Cheerios were, strictly speaking, off limits, but that no one was going to call her on it this morning.

It was, I thought, an inventive stroke. Did the name refer to new Bluie's unearned good fortune in finding a home thanks to the death of the original Bluie? (He had, after all, fulfilled the oldest New York fantasy: He had found and moved into someone else's vacated and rent-controlled apartment.) Or did it refer to his good fortune in being alive at all to swim around in the world a little longer? Certainly luck seemed like a wiser thing to celebrate in a fish than reincarnation.

But then an odd thing happened. After a couple of days of everyone calling him Lucky, we noticed that Olivia, on her own, began to call the new fish Bluie. It was as if, having made a grand and instructive emotional tour, she had ended up right where she started. We begin with the problem of mind, pass through the experience of pain—and end up loving the same old fish.

I understood suddenly why Hitchcock had given away the secret in the middle of *Vertigo*. The surprise is revealed because Hitchcock could not see what was surprising. He didn't think that there was anything bizarre in the idea of someone constantly being remade in the image of someone else's schemes or desires or weird plot points, because he thought that this is what life and love consist of. Suspense, not surprise, was the element Hitchcock swam in—not *What next?* but *How will we get to the inevitable place again?* Hitchcock himself, after all, did not adapt to circumstances. He made circumstances adapt to him. When Grace Kelly married a prince, there was Kim Novak, and when Kim Novak rebelled, there was Tippi Hedren. Every five-year-old has one fish, as every great director has a single Blonde. What Hitchcock's films of the fifties have in common with all the world's religions is the faith that death can be overcome, or at least made tolerable, by repetitive obsession. First the mind, then the pain, and then the echo: That is the order of life. James Stewart learned this, and now Olivia had, too.

Luke had a much more sinister view about what had happened to Bluie—less *Vertigo* and more *Psycho*.

"What I think is," he said, "Reddie put Bluie up to swimming into that window and then laughed inside when he saw what happened. It was, like, the Revenge of Reddie. He hated Bluie all this time for having a bigger house than he did, and finally tricked him to his death. Reddie is the bad guy, with all these plots and schemes. Look at him! He's the villain."

And for a moment or two, watching poor Reddie swimming in his low-rent bowl, I did think I could see an evil gleam in his small fishy eye, a startling resemblance to Anthony Perkins in his drawn, nervous excitability and long-simmering rage. I watched him in slightly panicky wonder. He looked like a fish who knows his own mind.

Last of the Metrozoids

In the spring of 2003, the American art historian Kirk Varnedoe accepted the title of head coach of a football team called the Giant Metrozoids, which practiced then every week in Central Park. It was a busy time for him. He had just become a member of the Institute for Advanced Study, in Princeton, after thirteen years as the chief curator of painting and sculpture at the Museum of Modern Art in New York, and he was preparing the Mellon Lectures for the National Gallery of Art in Washington—a series of six lectures on abstract art that he was supposed to deliver that spring. He was also dying, with a metastasis in his lung of a colon cancer that had been discovered in 1996, and, at Memorial Sloan-Kettering Cancer Center in New York, he was running through all the possible varieties of chemotherapy, none of which did much good, at least not for very long.

The Giant Metrozoids were not, on the face of it, much of a challenge for him. They began with a group of eight-year-olds in my son Luke's second-grade class. Football had replaced Yu-Gi-Oh! cards and the sinister water yo-yo (poisonous) as a preoccupation and a craze. The boys had become wrapped up in the Tampa Bay Buccaneers' march to victory in the Super Bowl that winter, and they had made up their minds to be football players. They wanted a team—"a real team that practices and has T-shirts and knows plays and everything"—that could play flag football, against an as yet unknown opponent, and I set about trying to organize it. (The name was a compromise: Some of the boys had wanted to be called the Giants, while cool opinion had landed on the Freakazoids; Metrozoids was arrived at by some diplomatic back formation with "Metropolitan.")

Once I had the T-shirts, white and blue, we needed a coach, and Kirk, Luke's godfather, was the only choice; during one of his chemotherapy sessions, I suggested a little tentatively that he might try it. He had been a defensive-backfield coach at Williams College for a year after graduation, before he went to Stanford to do art history, and I knew that he had thought of taking up coaching as a full-time profession, only to decide, as he said once, "If you're going to spend your life coaching football, you have to be smart enough to do it well and dumb enough to think it matters." But he said yes eagerly. He gave me instructions on what he would need, and made a date with the boys.

On the first Friday afternoon, I took the red cones he had asked for and arranged them carefully on our chosen field, at the corner of Fifth Avenue and Seventy-ninth Street, just a couple of blocks from the Children's Gate. I looked over my shoulder at the pseudo-Renaissance mansion that houses NYU's Institute of Fine Arts, right across the street. We had met there, twenty-three years earlier, his first year at the Institute of Fine Arts, and mine, too. He had arrived from Stanford and Paris and Columbia, a young scholar, just thirty-four, who had made his reputation by cleaning up one of the messier stalls in the art-historical stable, the question of the authentic Rodin drawings. Then he had helped revive some unfairly forgotten reputations, particularly that of the misunderstood "academic" Impressionist Gustave Caillebotte.

But, as with Lawrence Taylor's first season with the Giants, though we knew he was supposed to be good, nobody was this good. He would come into the lecture room in turtleneck and sports jacket, professor-wear, and, staring at his shoes and without any preliminaries, wait for the lights to dim, demand, "First slide, please," and, pacing back and forth, look up at the image, no text in his hand but a list of slides. "Last time we left off looking at Cézanne in the eighties, when the conversation between his code, registered in the deliberately crippled, dot-dot-dash, telegraphic repetition of brushstrokes, and his construction, built up in the blocky, stage-set recessional spaces, set out like flats on a theater," he would begin, improvising, spitballing, seeing meaning in everything. A Judd box was as alive for him as a Rodin bronze, and his natural mode was to talk in terms of tension rather than harmony. What was weird about the pictures was exactly what there was to prize about them, and, his style implied, all the nettled and querulous critics who tried to homogenize the pictures into a single story undervalued them, because, in a sense, they undervalued life, which was never going to be harmonized, either.

It was football that made us friends. In that first fall, he had me typed as a clever guy, and his attitude was that in the professions of the mind, clever guys finish nowhere at all. That spring we organized a touch-football game at the institute, and although I am the most flat-footed, least-gifted touch-football player in the whole history of the world, I somehow managed to play in it. A bunch of us persuaded our young professor to come out and join in one Sunday. The game was meant to be a gentle co-ed touch game. But Kirk altered it by his presence. He was slamming so many bodies and dominating so much that a wary, alarmed circle of caution formed around him.

Finally, I insisted to John Wilson, the Texan Renaissance scholar in the huddle, that if he faked a short pass and everybody made a lot of noise—"I got it!," "There it is!," and so on—Kirk would react instantly and run toward the sound, and I could sneak behind him for the touchdown.

Well, the play worked, and, perhaps recognizing that it was an entirely verbal construction, Kirk spotted its author and came right over, narrow-eyed and almost angry. "Smart play," he said shortly, with the unspoken words "Smart-ass play" resonating in the leaves above our heads. But then he shook his fist happily, a sign meaning okay, nice one. He turned away. *He sees right through me,* I thought; *he knows exactly what I'm up to.* I began working harder, and we became friends.

A quarter century later, he was coming to the same field from the hospital. He was a handsome man, in a big-screen way, with the deep-set eyes and boyish smile and even the lumpy, interesting complexion of a Harrison Ford or a Robert Redford. The bull-like constitution that had kept him alive for seven years, as the doctors poured drugs into him like Drano into a clogged sink, might have explained why the chemo, which thinned and balded almost everyone else, had somehow made him gain weight and grow hair, so, though he was a little stocky now, and a little gray, his step was solid and his eyes were rimmed with oddly long Egyptian lashes.

The boys came running from school, excited to have been wearing their Metrozoid T-shirts all day, waiting for practice: Eric and Derek and Ken, good athletes, determined and knowing and nodding brief, been-there-before nods as they chucked the ball around; Jacob and Charlie and Garrett talking a little too quickly and uncertainly about how many downs you had and how many yards you had to go; Will and Luke and Matthew very verbal, evangelizing for a game, please, can't we, like, have a game with another team, right away, we're ready; and Gabriel just eager for a chance to get the ball and roll joyfully in the mud. I was curious to see what Kirk would do with them. He was, first and foremost, a teacher, and his lectures still resonated in the halls of the institute. But how would he teach these eight-year-olds to play football? Orate at them? Motivate them? Dazzle them with plays and schemes?

"Okay," he said very gently, as the boys gathered around him in an attentive, slightly wary circle. "Let's break it down. First thing is how you stand. Everybody get down in a three-point stance."

The boys dropped to their haunches confidently.

Kirk frowned. He walked up and down the line, shoving each one lightly on a shoulder or a knee and showing how a three-point stance could be a weak or strong tripod, a launching pad or a stopping place, one that let you push off strongly or one that held you back. At last he got everybody's stance correct. "Okay, let's run," he said. "Just run the length of the field, from these cones to those cones, and then turn back. Last guy does fifteen push-ups." Luke stumbled and was the last guy, and Kirk had him do fifteen push-ups. The point was made: no favorites.

Right around then a young park worker came up in one of those officious little green carts the park people ride around in. "I'm sorry," he said, "you can't play here. It's ruled off for games."

I was ready to get mad—I mean, hey, who was making these rules? We had been playing touch football here for years—when Kirk stepped in.

"We-ell," Kirk said, and the Southern accent he brought with him from his youth in Savannah was suddenly more intense, an airplane captain's accent. "Well, uh, we got ten young men here eager to play football. Where can we take them to play?"

To my surprise, the park worker was there for the enlisting. "Let me see—I'll come back," he said. We went on with the drills, and ten minutes later, the guy scooted up again in his cart.

"I think I've found just the place," he said. "If you go off there, right over the road, and take the left fork, you'll find this field that's hidden there behind the parking lot." He added almost confidentially, "It's just opposite the toilets near the Ramble, but it's flat and large, and I think it's perfect."

"Much obliged," Kirk said, and he gestured to the boys, a big arm-sweeping gesture, and led them off in search of the promised field. They followed him like Israelites. We walked across the road, took the left, went down a hill, and there it was—a little glade that I had never seen before, flat and fringed by tall trees, offering shade to the waiting moms and dads. It had a slightly derelict look—I could imagine that in a livelier era, this field might have been a Francis Bacon mural, men struggling in the grass—but today it was perfect.

"Gentlemen," Kirk said clearly to the boys as they straggled on, looking around a little dubiously at the tufts of grass and the facing bathrooms. "Welcome to Metrozoid Field. This is the place we have been looking for." He set out the red cones again around the fringes.

"Okay, let's scrimmage," he ordered. He divided the guys in half with a firm, cutting gesture, and they began an intense, slightly nervous touch-football game. Kirk watched them, smiling and silent.

"Shouldn't we teach them a play?" I suggested.

"No," he said. "They're off to a good start. Running and standing is a good start."

The scrimmage ended, and the winning team began to hurrah and high-five.

"Hey," he said, stepping forward, and for the first time I heard his classroom voice, his full-out voice, a combination of Southern drawl and acquired New England sharpness.

"No celebrations," he said, arriving at the middle of the field. "This is a scrimmage. It's just the first step. We're all one team. We are the Giant Metrozoids." He said the ridiculous name as though it were Fighting Irish, or Rambling Wrecks, an old and hallowed name in the American pigskin tradition. The kids stopped, subdued and puzzled. "Hands together," he said, and stretched his out, and solemnly, the boys laid their hands on his, one after another. "One, two, three, together!" and all the hands sprang up. He had replaced a ritual of celebration with one of solidarity, and the boys sensed that solidarity was somehow at once more solemn and more fun than any passing victory could be.

He had, I realized on the way home, accomplished a lot of things. He had taught them how to stand and how to kneel—not just how to do these things but that there was a right way to do these things. He had taught them that playing was a form of learning—that a scrimmage was a step somewhere on the way toward a goal. And he had taught them that they were the Giant Metrozoids. It was actually a lot for one hour.

When I say that I began working harder, I can barely begin to explain what his idea of working hard meant: It was Bear Bryant's idea of hard work circa 1955, it was General Patton's idea of being driven, only more military. It was coupled with a complete openness and equality, a vulnerability to his students' criticisms so great that it was almost alarming. Kirk was working that hard, and was as eager to have you spot his weights as he was to spot yours. In what now seems like the halcyon days of 1984, a Saturday morning in winter would begin with a phone call and a voice booming, breaking right through the diaphanous protection of the answering machine, "Hey, folks, it's

Kirk. I got up early to walk the pooch, and I think I got some progress made on this here problem. What say we meet at eleven and trade papers?" I would curse, get out of bed, get to work, and be ready three hours later with a new draft of whatever the hell I was supposed to be working on. We would meet at the little island that separates Soho, where we lived, and Tribeca, where he and his wife, the artist Elyn Zimmerman, had their loft, and, standing there, he would turn the pages, and I would turn the pages, and he would show me all the ways in which I had missed the boat. Above all, he would insist, break it down: Who were the artists? What were the pictures? Give me the dates. Compile lists, make them inclusive, walk through it. You break it down in order to build it back up. What does it mean, why does it matter, for this artist, for art history, for the development of human consciousness? I would go back to work, and the phone would ring again at three. "Hey, folks, it's Kirk. What do you say we meet and go over this new draft I've done and then maybe get some dinner?" And we would meet, and all four—or six or eight or ten—people would come together around him, and have dinner, and drink a good bottle of white wine and a good bottle of red wine and finally, exhausted, I would get to bed.

And then the phone would ring again. "Hey, folks, it's Kirk. I got to walk the pooch one last time, and I was just thinking that I may finally have sorted out the locomotive from the caboose in this thing. What do you say . . ." And I would put a coat on over my pajamas and go out one last time, in the whipping cold of midnight, and he would open the envelope right there and start reading, signaling to me to do the same, while his black Chow raced around, and we would try one more time to clarify exactly why Picasso looked at African art or why Gauguin went to Tahiti, while a generation walked by us in Astor Place haircuts and long vintage coats on their way to the Odeon.

He gave football all the credit. He had discovered himself playing football, first at his prep school, St. Andrew's in Delaware, as an overweight and, by all reports, unimpressive adolescent, and then at Williams, where, improbably, he became a starting defensive end. The appeal of football wasn't that it "built character"—he knew just how cruddy a character a football player could have. It was that it allowed you to make a self. You were one kind of person with one kind of body and one set of possibilities, and then you worked at it and you were another. This model was so simple and so powerful that you could apply it to anything. It was ordinary magic: You worked harder than the next guy, and you were better than the next guy. It put your fate in your own hands.

I had always loved football, too, and we watched it together on Saturday afternoons and Monday nights for years. We saw a lot of good games, but we missed the big one. In 1984 we went up to New England to celebrate Thanksgiving, and we were supposed to watch what promised to be the greatest college football game of all time, Boston College–Miami, Doug Flutie versus Bernie Kosar. But our wives wanted to do something else—go look at things at a Shaker fair, I think—and we came home to find that we'd skipped the greatest college football game of all time, which Flutie had won by a Hail Mary, a long desperation heave on the last play of the game. We stared at each other in disbelief—we missed that?—and for the next twenty years, "Boston College–Miami" was code between us for something you really, really wanted to do but couldn't, because your wife wanted to do something else. "You want to try and grab a burger at six?" "Uh—Boston College–Miami." It was code between us also for the ironies of life, our great, overlooked game, the one that got away.

I think I'm going to make the motivational speech," I said to Luke as we walked over to Metrozoid Field the next Friday. I had been working on the motivational speech for several days. I didn't see a role for myself on the Metrozoids as a leader, and I thought I might make a contribution as the Tommy Lasorda type, raising everyone's spirits and bleeding Metrozoid blue.

"Okay," he said, relenting for the moment. "Tell it to me again."

"We're here to separate the men from the boys," I said, stopping at the Miners' Gate entrance to the park, at Seventy-ninth Street, and trying to growl like Gary Busey as the Bear, "and then we're going to separate the warriors from the men." I paused to let this sink in. "And then we're going to separate the heroes from the warriors—and then we're going to separate the legends from the heroes. And then, at last, we're going to separate the gods from the legends. So, if you're not ready to be a football god, you don't want to be a Metrozoid." Long pause. "Now, won't that make the guys motivated?"

He reflected. "I don't know if they'll be *motivated*. They'll certainly be *nauseated*. Nobody wants to be motivated to play football, Dad. They want to play football."

Kirk ran another minimalist practice on this second week, and he missed the next because he was too sick from the chemo. I ran the session, and I thought ambitiously that it would be good to try a play at last, so I set about teaching them a simple stop-and-go. I got them to line up and run short, stop, and then go long. They ran it one by one, but none of them could get the timing quite right, and the boy who was supposed to be quarterbacking the thing couldn't get the right zip on the ball. Everyone was more annoyed than motivated, so I stopped after ten minutes and sent them back to scrimmaging. They were restless for their coach.

It wasn't any surprise that he missed a practice; the surprise was that he made as many as he did. The chemo he was getting was so caustic that it had to be infused gradually, over sessions lasting three or four hours. Years of chemotherapy had left the veins in his arms so collapsed that sometimes it took half an hour for a nurse just to find an entry. He would grimace while being poked at with the needle, and then go on talking. He had the chemotherapy at one of the midtown extensions of the hospital, where the walls were earnestly decorated with Impressionist posters, Manet and Monet and Renoir—the art that he had taught a generation to relish for its spring-coiled internal contradictions and tensions there as something soothing for dying patients to look at.

He would talk for hours. Sometimes he talked about the Metrozoids, and sometimes about Dylan or Elvis, but mostly, he tried to talk through the Mellon Lectures he was to give in Washington. He was, he said, going to speak without a text, just with a slide list. This was partly a bravura performer's desire to do one last bravura performance. It was also because he had come to believe that in art history, description was all the theory you needed; if you could describe what was there and what it meant (to the painter, to his time, to you), you didn't need a deeper supporting theory. Art wasn't meaningful because, after you looked at it, someone explained it; art explained itself by being there to look at.

He thought that modern art was a part of modern life: not a reaction against it, or a subversion of it, but set within its values and contradictions, as surely as Renaissance art was set in its time. His book on the origins of modernism, *A Fine Disregard,* used an analogy from the history of rugby to illuminate the moment of artistic innovation: During a soccer game at the Rugby School, in England, an unknown young man named William Webb Ellis picked up the ball and ran with it, and a new game came into being. A lot of people thought that Kirk was celebrating a Romantic view of invention. But his was a liberal, not a Romantic, view of art. It began with an individual and extended to a community. What fascinated him was the circumstances that let someone act creatively and other people applaud instead of blowing the whistle.

That was what he loved to talk about when he talked about Elvis. He revered the moment when, in 1954, Elvis walked into a studio and played with Scotty and Bill and Sam, and everything suddenly came together. Had any of the elements been absent, as they easily might have been, as they usually are—had the guitarist Scotty Moore been less adaptable, the producer Sam Phillips less patient—then Elvis would have crooned his songs, no one would have cared, and nothing would have happened. The readiness was all. These moments were Kirk's faith, his stations: Picasso and Braque in their studios cutting the headlines right out of the newspapers and pasting them on the pictures to make collage; Richard Serra (first among Kirk's contemporary heroes) throwing hot lead in a studio corner and finding art in its rococo patterns.

Toward the end of one chemotherapy session, as he worried his way through his themes, a young man wearing the usual wool cap on his head came around the usually inviolable barrier of drapery that separated one "suite" from the next.

"You are professor?" he asked shyly, with a Russian accent, and Kirk shook his head.

"No, you are professor. I know. We have treatment at same time, every week. Same three hours," and he gestured toward his cap with a short we're-in-this-together smile. "I used to bring book, but now I just listen to you."

That Sunday of the first Mellon lecture, Kirk walked to the lectern after an introduction. The room was sold out, and the overflow had been sent to another lecture room. "Can I have the lights down, please," he said, and I saw that he had kept his word: He had no text, no notes, just a list of slides. He began to show and describe objects from sixties American minimalism—plywood boxes and laid-out bricks and striped paintings. He didn't offer a "theory" or a historical point. He tried instead to explain that a landscape that looked simple—there had been Abstract Expressionist splashes, and then there were all these boxes—was actually extraordinarily complex: There was a big difference between the boxes of Donald Judd, elegizing New York Canal Street culture, and the gleaming body-shop boxes of the West Coast minimalists, glorifying California car culture.

"The less there is to look at," he said, pacing, as he always did, "the more important it is that we look at it closely and carefully. Small differences make all the difference. So, for example, the next time somebody tries to sell you on the mechanical exactitude of Frank Stella's stripes, think again about the beautiful, delicate breathing space in these stripes, the incredible feathered edge of the touch of the picture, which has everything to do with its kind of espresso-grounds, Beat Generation blackness that gives the picture its particular relationship to its epoch and time."

So he walked people through it. There were the bright Matissean stripes of Ellsworth Kelly, made from the traced shapes of Parisian shadows, and those dark espresso-bar simplicities of Stella. There was the tradition of the Bauhaus diaspora, all those German refugee artists who had been forced to go to South America and who had proselytized for a kind of utopian, geometric abstraction—which had then appeared in New York just as New York artists were using geometric forms to indicate a cool-guy stoical distaste for utopian aspirations, creating a comedy of misunderstanding and crossbreeding. An art that had seemed like a group of quadratic equations set by a joyless teacher had been revealed as a sequence of inventions thought up by people. Where there seemed to be things, there were stories. The audience, at the end of the hour, was riveted. Someone was breaking it down and then was going to build it back up. You didn't want to miss it.

Okay, we're going to learn a play," he said the next Friday at Metrozoid practice. The boys were standing on Metrozoid Field in their Metrozoid shirts in a semicircle around him. He showed them the play he had in mind, tracing it in the dirt with a stick: The quarterback takes the ball from the center and laterals to the halfback, who looks for one of three downfield receivers, who go in overlapping paths down the right sideline—one long, one medium, one short. The boys clapped hands and ran to the center of the field, terrier-quick and terrier-eager.

"No, no. Don't run. Just walk through it the first few times."

The boys then ostentatiously walked through the play, clowning around a bit, as though in slow motion. He laughed at that. But he had them do it anyway, five or six times, at a walk.

"Now let's just amble through it, same thing." The play took on a courtly quality, like a seventeenth-century dance. The boys did it at that pace, again and again: Hike and pitch and look and throw.

"Now let's just run easy." The boys trotted through their pattern, and Garrett, the chosen quarterback, kept overthrowing the ball. Gently but firmly, Kirk changed the running back with the quarterback—Ken for Garrett, so that Garrett had the honor of being official quarterback but wouldn't have to throw—and then had them trot through it again. Ken threw hard, and the ball was caught.

After twenty minutes, Kirk clapped his hands. "Full speed. Everybody run." The boys got in their stances, and took off—really zoomed. The ball came nervously back, the quarterback tossed it to the halfback, he turned and threw it to the short receiver.

"Great!" At top eight-year-old speed, the ball had been thrown for a completion. The Metrozoids had mastered a play.

"Now let's do it again," Kirk said. I heard him whisper to Matthew, the short receiver, as he lined up, "Fall down!" They started the play, Garrett to Ken. Matthew fell down. Ken's eyes showed a moment of panic, but then he looked up and saw the next boy, the middle receiver, Luke, waiting right in line, and he threw there. Complete.

"Nice read," Kirk said, clapping his hands. "Nice read, nice throw, nice catch. Well-executed play."

The boys beamed at one another.

"You break it down, and then you build it back up," Kirk said as they met at the center of the field to do the pile of hands. "The hardest play you learn is just steps put together."

By the fourth and fifth weeks of the Mellons, the scene at the National Gallery was almost absurd. People were lining up at nine in the morning for the two o'clock lecture; I met a woman who had driven down from Maine to be there. The overflow room had to be supplied with its own overflow room, and the museum finally printed a slightly short-tempered handout. ("But what if I need to use the restroom while standing in line?" "If you need to use the restroom while in line, ask your neighbor to save your place.")

The fifth lecture would, Kirk thought, be the toughest to put over. He found it easy to make an audience feel the variety, the humanity, of abstract art, even an art as refined and obstinate as the art of Judd or the young Frank Stella. But it was harder to make people accept and relish that art's perversity, and harder still to make them see that its perversity was exactly the humanism it offered. In the lecture hall, he explained that, as E. H. Gombrich had shown half a century ago in his Mellon Lectures, representational artists were always making forms and then matching them—taking inherited stereotypes and "correcting" them in the light of new things seen. Leonardo, for instance, had inherited the heraldic image of a horse, and he had bent it and reshaped it until it looked like an actual animal. Abstract artists were always making forms and then trying to *un*match them, to make sure that their art didn't look like things in the world. Sooner or later, though, they always did, and this meant that, alongside abstraction, there was a kind of sardonic running commentary, which jumped on it anytime that it did look like some banal familiar thing.

Pop art was the most obvious source and form of this mockery: Roy Lichtenstein made fun of the abstract Op artist Victor Vasarely for making pictures that looked like the bottom of a sneaker, and Andy Warhol thumbed his nose at Barnett Newman for making pictures that looked like matchbook covers, and so on. But this countertradition wasn't mere jeering. It was generative, too: It forced and inspired new art. It kept abstraction from wallowing complacently in a vague mystical humanism. In the parody and satire of abstraction, its apparent negation, lay its renewal.

This process, Kirk explained, easily visible in the dialogue of minimalism and Pop, was just as vital, if less obvious, in the relationship between Jackson Pollock and Cy Twombly, two of his heroes. Twombly's squiggles and scribbles were not dutifully inspired by but actually parodied Pollock's method: "Everything that Twombly achieves, he achieves by the ironic distancing of himself from Pollock. Everything that is liquid is turned dry. Everything that is light is turned dark. Everything that is simple and spontaneous and athletic is turned obsessive, repetitive, self-conscious in Twombly. By this kind of negation, he re-realizes, on a completely different scale and completely different terms, the exact immediacy of energy conveyed to canvas that Pollock has." Negation and parody were forms of influence as powerful as any solemn "transmission" of received icons. Doubt led to argument; argument made art.

That Friday, out on Metrozoid Field, Kirk divided the boys into two teams. "A team runs the play, and B team defends," he said.

"But they'll know what we're gonna do," someone on the A team complained.

"That's okay. Most of the time the other team knows what you're gonna do. That's called your tendency. The key is to do it anyway."

"But if they know—"

"Just run the play. Most of the time the other team knows. The hard part is doing it right even when you know exactly what's coming."

The offense boys ran their one play, the flea flicker, and the defense boys ran around trying to stop it. Standing on the sidelines, I was amazed to see how hard it was to stop the play even if you *did* know it was coming. The boys on defense ran around, nettled, converging on the wrong receiver and waving their hands blindly at the ball. The boys on offense looked a little smug.

Kirk called them together. "You know what they're going to do. Why can't you stop it?"

The boys on the B team, slightly out of breath, shrugged.

"You can't stop it because they know what they're going to do, but you don't know what you're going to do against it. One team has a plan, and the other team doesn't. One team knows what it's doing, and the other team knows what they're doing, but it doesn't know what it's doing. Now let's figure out what you're going to do."

He went to work. Who's the fastest kid they have? Okay, let's put the fastest kid we have on him. Or, better, what if each guy takes a part of the field and just stays there and knocks the ball down if it comes near him? Don't move now; just stay there and knock it down. They tried both ways—man-to-man and zone—and found that both ways worked. The play lost its luster. The boys on the B team now seemed smug, and the boys on the A team lost.

"Maybe you need another wrinkle," Kirk said to the A team. "Let's work on it."

Watching him on Metrozoid Field, you could see what made him a great teacher on bigger questions for bigger kids. Football was a set of steps, art a set of actions. The mysterious, baffling things—modern art, the zone defense—weren't so mysterious or baffling if you broke them down. By the end of the spring practice, the eight-year-olds were instinctively rotating out of man-to-man into a zone and the offense audibling out of a spread formation into a halfback option, just as the grown-ups in Washington were suddenly seeing the differences and similarities between Pollock's drips and Twombly's scrawls.

One particularly bright kid, Jacob, was scared of the ball, the onrushing object and the thousand intricate adjustments you had to make to catch it. He would throw out his arms and look away instead of bringing his hands together. Kirk worked with him. He stood nearby and threw Jacob the ball, underhanded, and then got him to do one thing right. When he caught it, Kirk wasn't too encouraging; when he dropped one, he wasn't too hard. He did not make him think it was easy. He did not make him think that he had done it when he hadn't. He made him think that he could do it if he chose.

It is said sometimes that the great teachers and mentors, the wise men and gurus, achieve their ends by inducting the disciple into a kind of secret circle of knowledge and belief, make of their charisma a kind of gift. The more I think about it, though, the more I suspect that the best teachers—and, for that matter, the truly long-term winning coaches, the Walshes and Woodens and Weavers—do something else. They don't mystify the work and offer themselves as a model of oracular authority, a practice that nearly always lapses into a history of acolytes and excommunications. The real teachers and coaches may offer a charismatic model—they probably have to—but then they insist that all the magic they have to offer is a commitment to repetition and perseverance. The great oracles may enthrall, but the really great teachers demystify. They make particle physics into a series of diagrams that anyone can follow, football into a series of steps that anyone can master, and art into a series of slides that anyone can see. A guru gives us himself and then his system; a teacher gives us his subject, and then ourselves.

If this story was the made-for-television movie that every story about early death threatens to become, we would have arranged one fiery game between the Giant Metrozoids and another team, a bigger, faster, slightly evil team, and the Metrozoids would win it for their coach. It didn't happen like that. Not that the Metrozoids didn't want a game. As their self-confidence increased, they kept urging us to find some other team of eight-year-olds that they could test themselves against. I was all for it, but Kirk, I sensed, was not. Whenever the boys raised the possibility, he would say diffidently, "Let's wait till the fall," knowing, of course, that the fall, his fall, would never come.

I understood the hold he had on the Metrozoids. But when I thought about his hesitation, I started to understand the hold that the

Metrozoids had on him. I had once said something fatuous to him about enjoying tonight's sunset, whatever tomorrow would bring, and he had replied that when you know you are dying, you cannot simply "live in the moment." You loved a fine sunset because it slipped so easily into a history, yours and the world's; part of the pleasure lay in knowing that it was one in a stream of sunsets you had loved, each good, some better, one or two perfect, moving forward in an open series. Once you knew that this one could be the last, it filled you with a sense of dread; what was the point of collecting paintings in a museum you knew was doomed to burn down?

But there were pleasures in life that were meaningful in themselves, that did not depend on their place in an ongoing story, now interrupted. These pleasures were not "aesthetic" thrills—not the hang gliding you had never done or the trip to Maui you had never taken—but things that existed outside the passage of time, things that were beyond comparison or, rather, beside comparison, off to one side of it. He loved the Metrozoid practices, I came to see, because for him they weren't really practicing. The game would never come, and the game didn't matter. What mattered was doing it.

At the last practice of the school year, the boys ran their plays and scrimmaged, and the familiar forms of football, of protection and pass routes and coverages, were all there, almost magically emerging from the chaos of eight-year-olds in motion. At the end, the boys came running up to him, and he stood in place and low-fived each one of them. "See you in September," the kids cried, and Kirk let the small hands slap his broad one and smiled. "We'll work again in the fall," he said, and I knew he meant that someone would.

That Sunday he did something that surprised me. It was the last lecture of the Mellons, and he talked about death. Until then I had never heard him mention it in public. He had dealt with it by refusing to describe it—from Kirk, the ultimate insult. Now, in this last lecture, he turned on the audience and quoted a line from a favorite movie, *Blade Runner,* in which the android leader says, "Time to die," and at the very end Kirk showed them one of his favorite works, a Richard Serra *Torqued Ellipse,* and he showed them how the work itself, in the physical experiences it offered—inside and outside, safe and precarious, cold and warm—made all the case that needed to be made for the complexity, the emotional urgency, of abstract art. Then he began to talk about his faith. "But what kind of faith?" he asked. "Not a faith in absolutes. Not a religious kind of faith. A faith only in possibility, a faith not that we will know something, finally, but a faith in not knowing, a faith in our ignorance, a faith in our being confounded and dumbfounded, as something fertile with possible meaning and growth. . . . Because it can be done, it will be done. And now I am done." The applause, when it came, was stadium applause, and it went on a long time.

By July, the doctors had passed him right out of even the compassionate trials and were into the world of guesses and radiation. "It's a Hail Mary," he said of a new radiation therapy that they were proposing. "But, who knows, maybe I'll get the Doug Flutie of radiologists." Then a slight ache in his back that he thought was a disk he'd hurt water-skiing turned out to be a large tumor in his spine, and the end came quickly.

His wife, Elyn, had to be out of the city, and I spent the last Saturday afternoon of his life with him. In the old way, I went into his office to work on something I was writing. Kirk went to see what was on television. He had, I noticed, a team photograph of the Metrozoids at their last practice propped up on the coffee table. By then he could hardly walk, and his breath came hard.

But he called out, "Yo. You got to come here."

"What?"

"You won't believe this. Boston College–Miami."

Damned if it wasn't. ESPN Classics had a "Hail Mary" Saturday, all the great games decided on the last play, and now, twenty years late, they were showing the game from beginning to end: the whole game, with the old graphics and the announcer's promos, exactly as it had first been shown.

So we finally got to watch the game. And it was 1984 again, and the game was still thrilling, even though you knew what the outcome would be and how it would happen. Kirk's brother, Sam, came around, and he watched, too, the three of us just enjoying a good game, until at last here we were at that famous, miraculous, final Hail Mary, Doug Flutie dropping back and rolling out to heave the ball desperately downfield.

"Look at that!" Kirk cried, and the ball was still in midair out of view, up above the television screen.

"What?" I asked, as the ball made its arc and fell into the hands of Gerard Phelan and the announcers went wild.

"That's no Hail Mary. Watch it again and you'll see. That's a coverage breakdown." The old defensive-backfield coach spoke evenly, as, twenty years before, the crowd jumped and screamed. "Safety steps up too soon because he doesn't think Flutie can make that throw on the run. What he doesn't see is that Flutie has time to square around and get his feet set on the rollout, which adds fifteen yards to his range. Safety steps up too soon, Phelan runs a standard post route, and that's it. That safety sees Flutie get his feet set, makes the right read, and there's no completion." Turning to us, he said, "That is no Hail Mary, friends. That's no miracle. That is just the play you make. That is one gentleman making the right read and running the right pattern and the other gentleman making the wrong read." And for one moment he looked as happy as I had ever known him: one more piece of the world's mysteries demystified without being debunked, a thing legendary and hallowed broken down into the real pattern of human initiative and human weakness and human action that had made it happen. We had been waiting twenty years to see a miracle, and what we saw—what he saw, once again, and showed us—was one more work of art, a pattern made by people out of the possibilities the moment offered to a ready mind. It was no Hail Mary, friends; it was a play you made.

He turned to me and Sam, and, still elated by the revelation of what had really happened all those years ago, we began to talk about Ralph Emerson and Richard Serra. And then Kirk said heavily, "There is nothing in the world I would rather be doing than taking part in this conversation. But I have to lie down." He died four days afterward, late at night, having spent the day talking about Hitchcock films and eighteenth-century hospital architecture.

Luke and Elyn and I went up to the football field at Williams last fall and, with some other friends, spread his ashes in the end zone, under the goalposts. At his memorial, at the Metropolitan Museum of Art, Renée Fleming sang and the violinist Arnold Steinhardt played and the art world of New York turned out and listened and recalled him. I think a lot of them must have been puzzled, in the slide show that Elyn had prepared to begin the evening, and which recapitulated his career, from Savannah to Princeton, to see toward the end a separate section gravely entitled "The Giant Metrozoids," with the big figure surrounded by small boys. But I'm sure he would have been glad to see them there. The Metrozoids are getting back in business again, with an inadequate coach. I've thought about finally making the motivational speech, but I don't think I need to. The Metrozoids don't need to learn how to separate the men from the heroes. They know.

Last Thanksgiving: Immensities

The Gates went up in Central Park, and we took the children through them. We entered the park at the Children's Gate, Seventy-sixth and Fifth, but now the pathways and walks, usually so open and Narnian, their old-fashioned streetlamps glowing at twilight, have been hung with countless orange shower curtains, more of them than you had thought possible.

And yet it works; the effect makes its effect. I had been, for what little it's worth, opposed to the idea, on the grounds that Central Park, a perfect and miraculous work of art, hardly needed to be italicized or commented on by an inferior work of art. I opposed it on the grounds of the park not being mere grounds. And yet the scale of Christo and Jeanne-Claude's invention, the expanse, the perspective—orange veils not here and there but everywhere, a vast infestation, yet orderly, obviously human-tailored, premeditated—all of it was, if not artful, then at least impressive, a form of the organized sublime.

They revealed and emphasized the park's expanse. I watched a small boy enter the park at the south end, where the pond and skating rink are, and saw him muttering. Drawing closer, I could hear him: "Sixty-four, sixty-five, sixty-six . . ." he counted. He intended to check the reported number for himself. (Actually, there were around 7,500.) They showed, also, how small the park is, how man-made: 7,500 is, after all, a number far from nature's millions, an amount a boy can hope to count. Density was transformed into immensity; the close-packed park, usually limited by what is going on right in front of you, by the local proscenium of incident, is transformed by the tick-tock metronomic regularity of the curtains, marching away in every direction, into something ordered, regimented, overwhelming, and vast. The park, experientially quite segmented, becomes by the repetition of a single measuring unit perceptually quite large. We can no longer see the park in separate chunks. Someone has taken an orange ruler to it: My, how big you've grown!

And grant these gates their good effect on the city. So many people came to walk through them, even in the cold—pushing strollers and reaching up to touch, the children racing beneath and the old folks watching from the benches, as though expecting them to speak, to say something that mattered. The thing worked, no doubt about it. It seemed, in fact, like a regular annual festival that we had somehow forgotten to practice for a while—a festival dreamed up by the king of Central Park, which we had abandoned as we waited for him to come home.

But a festival celebrating what, exactly? A secular ritual for what faith? I could easily imagine generations of betrothed West Siders who had been expected to parade beneath the orange; or that, for a century, no fourteen-year-old East Sider could confidently begin high school without a ramble through the curtains, but of course, none of this was so. The Gates were there as a secular ritual of ritualized secularism, an invented festival of the power of festive inventions, a celebration of themselves.

Perhaps all liberal-secular celebrations are like that. Even this season, our great American Thanksgiving, we know now, does not come to us direct from the Pilgrims but is as invented as the Gates, dreamed up by an aesthetic entrepreneur, a magazine editor, as a festival of festivity. The liberal city constantly invents and forgets itself with its festivals—the marathon, the parades, the Gates—whose primary purpose is entirely frivolous, to break the dull round of the commercial year into the appearance of seasons and to give an occasion for another style of shopping. Sacred ritual is like stories in stained glass: We gaze and hope someday to understand. Secular ritual is a form of mistletoe; we hang it up and wait for something hot to happen underneath.

. . .

The children are gliding this year. Mobility and escape are not metaphors for kids; they are kids' whole purpose in life, and the beautiful thing is that they believe escape exists. They are in training. They glide and scoot and bike and skate, and though they always come home, for now, they believe, effortlessly, that, like POWs in a World War II movie, they are getting ready for the big one, the Great Escape, when they will flee their comfortable quarters for the world beyond, taking with them (we hope) a fond memory of kindly jailors.

The children pretended to fly over London a few years ago; now the hope of levitation has become a more practical daily activity, one of smooth movement in the opposite direction, away from home. We grown-ups, looking at them, see only the illusions of mobility and the possibility of harm: They will fall, break limbs, bruise knees, skin ankles. And so, New York parents, we wrap them up in swaddling of a kind: helmets that perch absurdly oversize on their heads, wrist pads and knee pads. Martha gasps as the children whiz by. But, though they accept the regalia with more or less good grace, they keep on in motion, getting ready for the day when the signal comes from resistance headquarters and they go for the fences.

The current rage in the civilization of childhood in New York is still for those Heelys—sneakers with small wheels embedded in their soles. They enable a walking child suddenly to become a whizzing, gliding child, floating down the sidewalk, free. Luke found his pair at Modell's in September and began practicing on the sidewalk outside our building; it is harder to do than it looks, and it took him a while to get it right: the stutter-start beginning, the almost imperceptible push and one-footed glide that follow, the long whoosh home with the second foot dragging behind. The Heely has erased the Razor scooter, the child mover of five years ago (which can now be had, I've noticed, for thirty dollars, on sale at Modell's).

The more specific appeal, I think, lies in the secretive nature of the wheels; a normal kid becomes a super-kid, rolling down Eighty-ninth Street like a motorcyclist. It is the revelation, as much as the glide, that stirs them. Luke went to visit the M's, where Emily was sitting shiva for her mother, and solemnly, beautifully glided down their long Riverside Drive hall to take her hand in sorrow.

Olivia tags along, desperate to catch up with her brother and his mates and their fads, the latest thing. She is too small, so far, for Heelys, which do not come in her size. On the evening we had a bunch of boys over for chili and a World Series game, *all* the boys had their Heelys on, and they went outside to go for a roll (having been forbidden by a scuff- and neighbor-conscious mother to do it inside). Olivia disappeared into Luke's room while the boys were away. We looked in later. She had, we saw, tried to Scotch-tape, and then to glue, two AA batteries to the soles of her sneakers, to create a makeshift homemade wheel. Heartbreaking ingenuity of the smaller nation!

We found Heelys in her size at last—but now Luke, of course, has moved on, indifferently, to the Next Cool Thing, which for the moment is not scooting, or flying, or gliding, but making things. He and the rest of the ten-year-old boys have discovered a new game. It is called Warhammer, and it involves neither screens nor even cards but actual miniature figures, some taken from *The Lord of the Rings,* which you painstakingly assemble and then even more painstakingly prime and paint, in order—eventually—to stage a battle. ("Warhammer" actually refers to an earlier game made by the same company, but is used as a generic term for the activity.)

The game itself, which, like all such games, never actually seems to happen—any more than Yu-Gi-Oh! games happened, or any more than Major League Baseball Showdown led to major-league showdowns—is another of those bafflingly complicated sword-and-sorcery book games. You present a particular situation from Tolkien—the confrontation at the Mines of Moria, the Uruk-hai outside Helm's Deep—with enough variation (this troll here, that Rider of Rohan moved there) to create a different outcome from the one in the books. You find out what the new outcome ought to be by consulting the telephone-book-thick manuals that go with the game, which give the precise appropriate result for each confrontation: Two trolls confronting six Riders of Rohan, armed with swords, in the presence of a Wizard, produces one lost troll and three wounded riders, and so on. As with his other games, the narrative can be transformed into an infinite number of possibilities. This time the Tower may not fall. . . .

Of all the games he has obsessively played—or prepared to play—

it is the most baffling. The preparation is endless: Constructing the miniatures takes forever and must be done in a ventilated room, which means, in a New York apartment, the kitchen with the window wide open to the November wind. The priming takes another day, and then the painting is meticulously detailed and painstaking, including—according to the honor code of ten-year-old boys—intensely realized modeling and shading, down to splashes of bright red blood around the troll's horrible mouth. Luke has decided to specialize in Evil Armies, on the reasonable grounds that goodness is already popular among his friends; an army of Orcs and trolls and Ringwraiths will give him an edge. "I'm interested in good," he said seriously to the equally serious vendor at the hobby store, which promotes the games as relentlessly as Bloomingdale's promotes perfumes, "but I thought I'd sort of concentrate on evil first."

The game combines, so far as I can see, the joys of being a Malaysian child laborer in a small-goods sweatshop with the excitement of double-entry bookkeeping. But it is their addiction, and they spend hours and hours on it. Our fears that they would be swallowed up by the screens are passing. Fashion, replacing last year's enthusiasm with this year's passion, neutralizes the seduction of the screens by promoting a new and opposed seduction, a much more effective force than parental disapproval. Hemlines go up because hemlines were down before, and the children escape the screens not because they have been liberated by their parents but because they have become fatigued with their enslavement.

Luke and his friends now sit together in the kitchen soberly and silently making tiny figures out of glue and plastic and pain. The GameCube is, like, so over. At least the new game is a way into the pages. Motivated more by the game than even the movies, the boys are reading Tolkien—not just reading but scrutinizing, trying to find the mythological logic behind their mythologizing game. The screens have been defeated by the combined force of airplane glue and literature.

. . .

It is amazing to contemplate the number of games Luke has embraced obsessively and discarded definitively in four short years. Each one, I see now, was a kind of cocoon against all that has been unfairly harsh and perplexing in his experience: chess tournaments and the Yankees right after 9/11, Yu-Gi-Oh! and football to get him through his godfather's illness and death. The wise men tell us that all the games we play—social games, language games, and sexual games—are a way of straight-arming harsh and perplexing experience, a way of building fences against the dreadful things that lie just outside the circle. We grown-ups play games in the face of fear and pain and death. Children do that, too, but with an added charge, an extra fillip, of abstraction, of doing the thing for the thing's sake. They play games in the face of grown-ups. Each poem we write may be a concrete way of organizing difficult experience, controlling it by giving it form; but each game children play is an abstract way of organizing experience for its own sake—see, you can control *something.*

But then the force of fashion among small boys in New York has by now become much keener than it is among grown women, who will remain loyal to a favorite dress, an old look, or a trusted pair of shoes for longer than you might suppose. Women have, in their overstressed, overbusy world, a kind of permanent truce to admire one another's Narcissos when they wear them, and the rest of the time to forgive one another their tracksuits and sneakers. Everyone knows which moment is which, and though the old jokes about cattiness and competitiveness are not entirely false, they no longer apply consistently. The mothers are like warriors; they are in the arena, or they are not.

Luke and his friends, on the other hand, are as fashion- and trend-conscious as the people in *The Way of the World*, miniature Millamants and Mirabells. They wear only T-shirts and request new haircuts ("I want to have a sort of heavy-head look," one boy in the crowd explained to his mother). They are, like all fashion-conscious people, at once intently conformist—the Charvet shirts and corduroy pants Martha brought back from Paris would be unthinkable for Luke now, even if they still fit—and at the same time insanely conscious of small details: this T-shirt, with this cryptic insignia of broken words and pattern, is cool; this one, with the Knicks insignia writ large upon it, is not.

The reason they are the fashionable group is clear enough: They are the leisure class. They are occupied, of course, with school and homework, too much of both. But where their mothers have conceded polish to exhaustion—one sees beautiful women standing bleary-eyed outside Artists & Anglers in baseball caps and jogging pants—the boys still share modishness with one another. Students are always at once a leisure and a laboring class, and, like the boys at Oxford in *Brideshead*, our boys make up for their implicit subservience with dandyism. Kenneth Clark, in his beautiful account of his Edwardian childhood, writes of sitting soberly in his sailor suit while the childless ladies of fashion paraded themselves for his judgment. Now it is the children who are the masters of fashion, and the beautiful young matrons, their mothers, watch from nearby, in uniform, as they parade.

They are leaving us, they are going away, they have a date across the water, like the Elves in Tolkien, whom Luke so carefully constructs, on the rare days when he invests in the Good. The children *are* Tolkien's Elves, a superior race of poets living among us mere mortals, on their way to the sea—from which they will return, of course, as more mere mortals. They are becoming artists, writers, themselves makers of stories and shapers of experience, no longer merely their parents' subjects. Luke is writing his memoirs for school, and they are, I find to my delight, largely about the funny, mixed-up things his father has done: the time I thought I was ordering strawberries in Italy and got string beans instead, the time I forgot the word for the cheese I wanted and, finally recalling it, shouted out "Pecorino!" on the beach, as though it were a hunting cry. He has the soul of a writer, getting even in the guise of geniality.

It will be a long time before our children are really gone, but we feel them getting ready, picking out disguises for the break, eyeing the laundry trucks. Our friends the M's, with one boy in college and another in tenth grade, are, miraculously, a couple again, going to movies and restaurants, dating. We hear the distant bells of possibility, too, and we try to make love in the afternoon. From our bed, we see the window washers suddenly rise up on their scaffolding with the timing of a Buster Keaton comedy, and Martha dives beneath the covers, and love is over. I watch the window washers, who try to look studiedly indifferent, high-mindedly virtuous. The scaffold takes them up to the higher, dirtier windows, and at last they are just boots.

Maybe there is no city left, and these familar comedies of density—the window washers rising on their scaffolding to stare in the windows, the children whooshing down the sidewalks on their Heelys as the matrons shriek—are busy parts of a soon-to-be consigned past; we are in a Brueghel painting and not wise enough to know it yet. New York, which was lost, and then found, and then lost again, only to be found again, at least for now, may be as doomed as the dodo no matter what we do or whom we vote for.

This is the thesis of several new books that I have been reading about the crisis of New York: For good or ill, the city—not just this one but all of them—as we have known it is a relic, and it will disintegrate as we watch. The Venetian metaphor is no metaphor. It's no accident that New York, as Paris did twenty years ago, is becoming a tourist spot (a tourist trap). People come to see the streets where bohemians once roamed. The city is dead, killed by the growth of the edge cities where suburban sprawl meets the semi-urban mall; by the final triumph of the car; by the need for schools and lawns and cheap shopping. Terrorism has done its part, too, making concentrations of people too dangerous. Flight from the city, which seemed, in the past twenty years, to have been stemmed by the property tycoon's childbearing revolution, the late-arriving baby, is really (the argument goes) a force as inevitable as continental drift or evolution itself. All of life will soon be an exchange of pixels from seated positions in secure rooms.

So cities are dying, though their death will not be, as we long thought, slow and violent. They are just being strangled. Cities will die sighing, not screaming, but they will die. They will be inherited not by feral gangs and rampaging hordes but by aging yuppies, professionals, like ourselves, who will linger to remember the Last Bohemia, Soho and the Village, after their children have fled to the edge or to the Sunbelt, as they age and their apartments drip value, like coffee filters, year after year. If the city remains intact at all, it will be as a relic, just as Venice is now, which people will visit for "culture" (rather than for the life of art) and for recreation (meaning sex in a hotel room, for people who can afford it). London is already nearly Londonland, Paris already a city of the rich and retired, and there is no more Venice at all, really, just a kind of simulacra of it, drained of inhabitants, if not of floodwater, and all in the past twenty-five years. Ten years ago New York seemed as much a city as Dickensian London was a city—a great grim lamp shining with greed and need, drawing people, like insects, to a doom they didn't quite mind. Now New York is sinking beneath our feet.

I have an interest in this, as someone whose entire wealth, or, rather, whose entire weight of optimistic debt, is sunk into the city, and as one who has learned that he will never be able to drive (or sail or swim or do anything save walk), and so I do not want it to be true. But when I walk the streets, I don't feel something coming to an end, as one did in the early seventies, when the previous New York of immigrant manufacture was dying and no new thing was yet clearly being born. What I feel instead is a thing coming into being through common need, which is all a city is. The immigrant stories of this generation will be epic when the immigrant children come to write them: Already the children's babysitters have included a Korean girl, now at law school, whose family's rise from twenty-four-hour groceries will be every bit as astounding as my own family's rise from Ellis Island, which passed by way of groceries, too.

A sense of still-here pervades even the bits that are long-standing. To stand in Fairway on a Saturday afternoon, where the olive-oil tasting goes on alongside the search for monster boxes of All, or to walk through the meatpacking district, now decarcassed, where the twentysomethings with their BlackBerrys send each other—what, exactly, I don't know—billets-doux of the newer kind, is to see a world of engagement, of brief exchanges, of bumping into, something that certainly feels necessary and urgent, not indulgent and nostalgic. Every time I take a taxi home from La Guardia, I don't feel anything like nostalgia (as I must admit I do when the cab from the airport turns toward Paris) but rather wonder, relief—relief that it's still there, that I will be there soon, delivered from the netherworld of other places, my flat feet solidly on the flat ground.

We no longer take homeland security alerts as seriously as we once did, as perhaps we still should. The mayor went on television to say, "They're coming," and New Yorkers said, "So what if they do?" We have not outgrown fear but been worn out by it. What we practice is not resignation, really, but a kind of self-deluding guessing at the averages—what baseball managers call playing the percentages. If it happens, it is, given the size of the city, unlikely to happen to me, to us. On the way to work, I took the weird, newly renamed W train, thinking in some desperate deal-making-with-the-demons part of my superstitious soul that Osama bin Laden has certainly never heard of the W and that, out-of-towner that he is, he will think only of the 6, and the Broadway local, like Sauron looking past the Shire.

It is not exactly an inspiring sight, this subway car on the W train—our usual car filled with a look so full of exhaustion that you might think we had been riding on this car forever. But one senses that if you look hard enough, you can see the things that draw people to cities, that drew my grandfather here seventy years ago and drew me here, too: possibility, and plurality, keep us riding still. I suppose that possibility is just as possible in the suburbs of Dallas or Phoenix, in some edge city near Atlanta, some floating island of residence levitating between two malls, but I don't quite believe it. Possibility still, in some significant part, depends on density; hope is the thing in a sweatshirt, riding the W train and reading the *Daily News*, a bird of another feather.

In five years, we have been through the hyper-excitements of the millennial arrival, through the darkest slough of despond there has been, then through a long nervous night, to emerge at last, not in the sunny uplands—there are no sunny uplands—but on the rational plateau, back to the park, where liberal pleasures were long ago planned from resistant materials. The amazing thing is not that we have gotten the children through it—they are made to be adaptable—but that they have gotten us through it, and made us glad. From the overstressed, ironic exasperation we felt when we first came home, to fear, to a tender appreciation of the city's rituals and joys underlined by its new vulnerability to—well, I suppose I ought to say to a deeper, more mature understanding, but really, it's just the old ironic exasperation, now revealed to be a kind of love. Every time the exasperation and the expense and even the plain worry rises, which it does regularly—why are we doing this? what for?—something holds us back. There's a lovely Dave Frishberg song about a man who leaves Manhattan, "Do You Still Miss New York?" He does. We would. We do already, when we think about it. The rush of emotion that rises as the car pulls down the Hudson Parkway, as the cab comes across the Triborough Bridge from La Guardia, the sense of a scale too big to be credited and of a potential too large to be quite real—all that remains available, which is the most you can say of any emotion. The other emotions—the daily frustrations, the long-term fears—remain available, too. The city we are in, the home we have made, and the other city we long for all remain in existence, and we travel with the children back and forth between, just the way I did when I was a child.

Perhaps the virtual world is the true immensity. (That's something I read, too.) The computers encircle the city, like the Orcs around Minas Tirith, and their grip on us is palpable. (The switch hotel was the first tent of the new occupation, and we as New Yorkers have become mere parakeets, interesting oddballs.)

To a frightening degree, our life is already like that of a minor, failed wizard in Tolkien: staring all day into a palantir, a seeing stone—for what else is an Internet connection? Denethor, the last Steward of Gondor in *The Return of the King,* goes mad because he stares into his seeing stone and sees not what is actually there, the real Middle Earth muddle, but only what Mordor wants him to see: the massed Orcs, the hopeless mortals, the gathering armies of the night.

We, in the same way, see only our own Mordor, the wasteland where metaphor and extended argument have all been blasted away, and all that remains are the massed Orcs of attitude and opinion.

This is Denethor's fallacy, Denethor's folly. In truth, just as there was more resistance left in the West than he was allowed to see, there are more variety and resilience and common sense and eccentric appetite and just plain individual taste in America than the partial view can provide. Every day when we look up from the screens and smell the coffee—in this case, the triple-grande cappuccinos that have overtaken the continent—hope begins again. The screens give a good sense of the American unconscious, but a very poor, or partial, sense of American life.

The Internet is a picture not of our life but of our dream world, where each of us is a little emperor of appetite and opinion and everyone has to listen. Our real life is the usual muddle of bounded desires and disappointments that we have trained ourselves to believe are actually wishes fulfilled in another way. To get back out into that common life, to force ourselves into the world—that is hard, and each of us must do it in some different way. The truly hard work is not to connect—we connect too damned easily—but to disconnect, to separate the noise and rage of the virtual world from the decent muddle of the real world. To decenter the children and unplug ourselves. If only we could!

In the end, the immensities of communication lead right back to the densities of people talking and touching. Luke has become, like all his friends, an IM fiend. The instant message is as much his form as the eight-line epistle was Horace Walpole's. This is true of all the ten-year-olds. They sit doing their homework, and despite a chorus of parental nos—your brain will shrink to the size of a walnut!—they are conducting three or four, sometimes six or seven, IM conversations at the same time.

Instant messaging demonstrates a profound truth: that manners do not follow the new comforts of technology, but that whatever technology offers next becomes the new form of manners. Fashion once again is our improbable savior, our real God. How laborious instant messaging is, and how scant and impoverished in information: not the warm instantaneous presence of a voice, with all its inflections of feeling, but laboriously keyboarded-in information, placed in code from sheer fatigue: "LOL" and "Whazzup?" and "GTG." They are, it seems, moving relentlessly backward toward Morse code.

Had the instant message come first, and the telephone conversation second, what a triumphant technological breakthrough the phone call would now seem! How proudly the papers would unveil it, how breathlessly the business pages and *Wired* magazine would celebrate the innovation. Real-time conversation! Actual voices! Effortless dial-up-and-speak communication! No need to wear your fingers out just to say hello, how are you! At last the realm of the real voice; hear your sweetheart's breathing! Listen when your best friends cough. Enjoy! You are there, really there, at last. Steve Jobs would hold a press conference, holding the phone up high, with amazement. And the next day the back page of the business pages would have one of those defiant, declarative full-page ads: "Real speech! Real Time! The Real You." It would be on the cover of all the newsmagazines the following week. (And there would be contrarian op-ed pieces in the *Times:* "Why I Will Never Make a 'Phone' Call"; "The 'Phone Call'—Is It Killing the Keyboard?")

Yet the children, who are free to pick up the phone and talk to one another just as we did, exchanging gossip and long-division tips, actually prefer the cryptic and limited vocabulary of the instant message. Partly, they prefer it for the same reason that they now prefer the *Lord of the Ring* miniatures to EA sports. Fashion always overwhelms logic. But I think, as I watch Luke doing his homework—the radio on Disney, playing the new kind of pop, keening, minor-key power ballads of loss rather than our peppy old ballads of fun or sweet ballads of love, love and loss now pounded together in a single chord sequence and drum pattern—that they also like it because of the control it offers. Talking is a form of the adult world's social ordering, and the IM is a powerful tool of children's independence. The keyboard is power; you give away just as much, just as often, as you want to.

Luke checks IMs idly as he works—just, let truth be told, as I check my e-mail steadily—and I realize that both are popular because that is what we really want: not to connect, not to disconnect, but to *sorta* connect, to turn even our strongest ties into weaker ties, where we can control them, reward them with little prepackaged bursts of geniality or warmth without being drawn into an open-ended exchange where anything might happen. (How well I recall the aimless hours on the telephone from my own youth, when we would meander far and wide and end up with hurt feelings or frustration, girls being adept at winding down a conversation you were trying to key up. The split screen in the movies was invented, of necessity, to represent these exchanges, this war.) IMing saves face; if you send it out and get no reply, there are a million rationalizations at hand. Make a phone call and you put yourself at risk. The great advantage of e-mail, as it is of the Internet generally, is the isolation it provides even as it offers the appearance of interaction. What we want is not an exchange of ideas but a mutual tolerance of soliloquies.

It was the instant message, in fact, that for a while seemed to keep the day of reckoning, the day of flight, away. Every parent knows that there is going to come a time when your child will become, or begin to become, an adolescent, and you will become remote, distant, even despised. Yet knowing this and accepting it, we don't quite believe it. It is the mortality of parenting: You know for certain that it will happen, just as you know for certain that you are going to die, and that this is right and necessary, part of What Must Happen. But in some secret part of the soul we don't actually think it's going to happen to *us*. Just as we don't really believe we'll die, no matter how many deaths we've known, we don't believe that our children will be thirteen, no matter how many times we have seen thirteen, despite having *been* thirteen.

New York being New York, everything a gear faster, thirteen now begins around eleven. Every day now, Luke comes home from school at three-fifteen and I greet him at the door. I ask him how school has been, and where he used to answer, sometimes fully, now he just shrugs the high-shouldered shrug of the exasperated, and silently stalks into his room. This is the universal tragedy of three-fifteen p.m., as sure in its foreordained certainty as any Greek myth. The bell rings, the eleven-year-old enters—and the parent, knowing as surely as

Oedipus knew never to doubt the Sphinx, knowing that he should never ask "How was school?" goes ahead and asks it anyway. Every parent is doomed to ask it, even as the Chorus of Parents Past chants at him not to.

And every parent is rewarded with the inevitable shrug and head-down glare, and then the boy walking into his room and shutting the door—not slamming it, certainly, but shutting it. And yet every day you do it again.

Then silence. You know that, can be pretty sure that, among other things, he's on his computer, IMing exasperatedly to his equally exasperated friends. Once again, you might feel safer with the old vices: You sort of wish you could smell the wholesome whiff of marijuana, the sounds of adolescent groping, the keening endless tedium of a phone call. Instead there is the silence of the multivoice instant message, passing from eleven-year-old to eleven-year-old, seven or eight running side by side on his screen at a time.

For a long time, I was shut out from instant messaging. It had seemed so remote. A curtain falls around the age of forty, and whatever the medium of electronic communication that was in place then remains the medium you use. If you were forty when the fax machine was in flower, you still send faxes, for all their snaky, mid-eighties kind of flimsiness. My parents still SPEAK UP on long-distance telephone calls, as they did in their early middle-age—while the children take a friend ringing in from Paris or Tokyo on the cell phone as just what happens, no more surprising than Sally dropping in at seven from upstairs. My grandfather still wanted to send telegrams to his grandchildren on their birthdays, was furious that he couldn't. Though I lived on e-mail and caffeine—just got onto *that* subway as the doors were closing—I had never sent or received an instant message.

Luke, though, who is always urging software onto me—Pandora! Skype! Limewire!—urged me to download the IM software from AOL and I did, that little man running nowhere in particular. And then that week, after the ritual observance of the three-fifteen tragedy, I saw the little IM icon on the bottom of the screen pinging and bouncing, urgently, happily. It was Luke! An IM from my son!

"Hey, Dad! Whazzup?" he wrote. "Nothing much. Whazzup with

you?" I wrote back. "Not much." "How was school?" "OK. I guess." And then at three seventeen—minutes after having already established that nothing had happened all day at school, we had the conversation that he had denied at the door: what he'd done that day, what he wanted to do that evening, homework to finish, movies to watch. . . . Everything we hadn't talked about face to face we exchanged in the IMs from fifteen feet apart. The three-thirty IM exchange became the best part of the day. It was practically Japanese in its formality: The doorbell would ring, I'd open the door, we'd bow at each other, he'd go silently into his room, I'd go into mine, and within moments the ping would happen and we'd write to each other about the events of the day, as though we were miles apart, days away.

I understood what he was doing. To submit to the parental three-fifteen is to surrender autonomy; to send complete messages from your own computer is to seize control of the means of communication, allowing you to declare both your autonomy and your essential goodwill. He was doing what children have to do: He was making me, his strongest tie, into a weaker tie, and then strengthening the tie again, but on his own terms. He is getting ready to go. He is putting his first shirt in the bottom of his eventual suitcase.

Still, here for a while, he taught me the language of instant message, all the simple abbreviations that make it work. He explained them to me when I was puzzled as they appeared on my computer screen: GTG means Got To Go. BRB: Be Right Back. U2: You, too. And above all, LOL—well, *that* one he didn't have to explain to me. It was obvious, as Olivia would say. It meant "Lots of Love." I could tell because it occurred at the end of so many of his instant messages. So I sent it right back to him: LOL, Dad. LOL, Luke. I felt delighted. Whatever inevitable conflicts we might have, at the end of every one of these exchanges, we could still tell each other that we loved each other, and lots. He used it in response to the e-mails I sent him, even in the sententious, just-do-the-things-you-have-to-do ones. Despite the coming of adolescence, beckoning like a sad Thanksgiving, we could still send each other love.

And I adored this about IMing in general, the way that in three capital letters you could send lots of love to anyone you liked. My sister was getting divorced, and I sent her a message "I'm with you, and beside you. LOL, your brother." A friend got terrible and unfair reviews for a book; I sent him LOL. Everyone for six months—editors, friends, I was riding the ecstacy of love messages that I was sending out, instantly.

Finally, after about six months of this, I was sitting in an airport lounge at eleven on a Friday night, off on one more trip—online, writing a goodbye IM to Luke. Explaining how much I hated being away from him for another weekend, how I had to do it to pay for his school, for our life. Heartfelt, heart-full, I signed it "LOL, Dad." Then a pause. And I see appearing on my screen these words.

"Dad: what exactly do you think LOL means?"

"Lots of Love, obviously," I replied.

A longer pause, and then a flurry of caps appeared on my screen, as though an urgent message was incoming from NORAD:

"NO, DAD! LOL MEANS 'LAUGHING OUT LOUD'!!!!!"

"NO it doesn't!" I wrote back.

Then the icon of a big embarrassed face, an incredulous face:

"YES IT DOES DAD!!"

And of course it does. I realized that for the past six months I had been jeering at him sardonically when I thought I was sending him all my love. And he had been mocking my sententiousness when I thought he was responding to my wisdoms. I had been jeering sardonically at *everyone*, without knowing it, and now I was going to have to go back to all the people I'd been sending an instant message to and apologize for ridiculing them in the midst of their pain. I would have to repeal six months' worth of LOLs. I decided to give up instant messaging. I am too old for it. It is for the young in one another's screens, with nimbler fingers and quicker minds than mine.

All afternoon as I write, I listen to Mike and the Mad Dog, the Kramden and Norton of New York sports radio, dissecting the Yankees, the Mets, the Rangers. I love Mike's tired knowingness, contrasted with the Dog's eager, obsequious fatuity: "Dog, you know—this is just—

just the most asinine phone call we've ever received . . ." "Yeah, Mike, you're right, you're right!" I can make Luke laugh by impersonating the two of them, Mr. Know-It-All and the Village Idiot, as Phil Mushnick calls them in the *New York Post*.

Yet I listen, storing up Yankees news. Luke remains a Yankees fan. I have, amazingly, become one myself, in the wary, ironic way that one can be a Yankees fan now, a pigeon watching the antics of the hawks from a safe distance. We are all Yankees fans now, having lived through Aaron Boone's walk-off home run and, with an odd kind of masochistic glee, the Red Sox's great comeback the following year, three games down and winning four in a row. No, not masochistic glee, more a kind of detached affection—we are Yankees fans, certainly, we go out to the stadium and dodge the obscenities and sit up in the nosebleed seats where we can buy tickets. I wear their simple NY on my cap when I take the kids to school, we watch and listen to Mike and Mad Dog debate the off-season signings and read Phil Mushnick's doubts on them. But we also recognize that baseball is a mess of drugs and greed and a certain amount of ugliness—we're there, but we don't go all the way. What is lost in purity is gained in wisdom. (As they play a video game at a friend's house, I hear one of the boys say about a virtual player, "Is this before or after he's on steroids?") We have accepted the Yankees, more than we have embraced them. They are another New York accommodation that we have made.

When a new phone-caller comes on to give the expected greeting to Mike and the Dog, my heart lifts. "Longtime, first time," the caller always says as he begins to make his well-intended contribution, only to get jumped on by Mike ("What are you saying? Whoa, whoa—you puttin' A-Rod on the couch here?"). Longtime listener, first-time caller: This is the endless mantra of Mike and the Mad Dog. I have long been part of your audience, and now, suddenly, by an act of grace and good fortune, I am up there with you. The eventfulness of this idea—a listener, one of the anonymous mass, suddenly becomes a participant, pitting his wits against the wits of Mike Francesca—there is something absurd and beautiful about it, something bar mitzvah and first communion: I was a listener, and today I become a caller. Longtime, first time. Half the time in New York, I think that I am a longtime observer, first-time participant. Longtime shopper, first-time lover. First-time observer, longtime resident. Longtime first time, all the time.

Olivia is watching *The Lion King* in the bedroom. She turns to Martha and asks, out of the blue, "Will you and Daddy ever get divorced?"

"No. We love each other."

"Will you ever leave me? Even when you die?"

Martha doesn't know what to say.

"When you die, you'll go to heaven," Olivia answers before Martha can say anything. "And then when I die, I'll go to heaven, too, and we'll be a family again." She smiles and returns to *The Lion King*. She is the only believer in the house.

At six, she still belongs to Narnia, not middle Earth. She believes not in the unending contest, but in the undiscovered country, the World Around the Corner, where small girls are queens and animals talk. I wrote a "comprehensive" take on Lewis's penchant for the fatuous allegory and then took the kids to see the Narnia movie. Luke liked it well enough but Olivia loved it: The cobbler's children have no shoes, and the critic's children have no crabby opinions, or at least not the crabby opinions of the critic. A six-year-old girl who discovers another world! Whom everyone condescends to as if she were a baby, but who then is proven absolutely right! And becomes a queen. Good stories are simple stories, and speak to our condition. We went to see it again, and she glided away from me.

"You don't know anything, Dad," she says suddenly. I am hurt, offended, and I say, "Olivia, how can you say that?"

She catches herself. "I mean, you don't *know* anything, Dad. You're always just guessing."

I am, too. Trust me though she does, she sees the limits of my knowledge.

. . .

Verticality, possibility, plurality. The towers over there and the small apartment over here, the Blue Room and the Big Store, just as it was when we were young and had just arrived. The dialogue between the dense and the isolated, the lady down the hall who lives alone and plays Christmas carols on Christmas Eve after we started to play them, too. Hyper-intimacy and absolute isolation, less dancing partners than planets in uncomfortable relation, pulled toward each other as their orbits change, threatening to collide and then spinning off again. The downstairs neighbors waiting to be infuriated, listening for a sound, and the upstairs neighbors making their sounds while we listen. There is a whole world, a dense network of connections in a city that can't be reproduced on the Web and can't be mirrored by a nation in cars, a constant daily dialogue between big and small, vast and tiny, the individual experience and common fate. In a big town, you can't avoid the dialogue completely. So why not stay here, in the biggest?

I'll believe this forever, even after Martha bundles me at last off to Connecticut and I'm having people who drive over for six o'clock cocktails after riding the happy mower on the happy lawn, happily.

Out of the blue, a letter arrives from the granddaughter of Molly Hughes: I've been asked to write a new preface to *A London Child of the 1870's*. I'm stunned. It has been years since I thought of Molly. When Martha and I first came to New York, we lived for three distant, disquieting, and now very long-ago-seeming years in that tiny basement room, nine feet by eleven feet, whose only conventional attraction was that its high-up window looked past a playground onto the back of the stained-glass windows of the Church of the Holy Trinity on Eighty-eighth Street. In that room, only blocks away from this room where I write now, Molly Hughes's book had become our favorite, our only, reading. It tells the story of an ordinary family in London from the 1870s to World War I, as related by the one daughter—Molly—in the 1930s. I read it out loud to Martha every night in those first couple of New York years.

It's *David Copperfield* from the point of view of the Micawber children. "We were just an ordinary, suburban, Victorian family, undistinguished ourselves and unacquainted with distinguished people," Molly says at the beginning. She writes simply and vivaciously of the life she shared with her four brothers, Barnholt, Vivian, Tom, and Charles; of going to the Criterion Theatre in Piccadilly Circus, and supper at the grill in the theater afterward; of walking a mazelike route of side streets from Canonbury to St. Paul's on Christmas Day; of going on excursions up the Thames to Kew—a whole world of small comforts now lost but still living.

It's a beautiful book, but *A London Child* ends tragically. Molly's father is run over and killed in a railway accident. "During the years that followed my mother used to sit in the dusk, in a chair facing the gate. . . . I think she almost hoped that the past was only a nightmare, and that she would surely see my father coming up the garden path with his springy step, and would hear his familiar knock," Molly wrote.

Afterward, Molly was courted by a very good, very poor young lawyer—a clerk, really—named Arthur Hughes. After an agonizingly long engagement, they married and had an incandescent little girl named Bronwen. But Bronwen dies, too, suddenly and cruelly, just after her first birthday. Finally, in an unspeakable irony, Arthur is killed in the same kind of accident that claimed Molly's father.

Yet Molly resolutely shook off despair. She wrote two more books after *A London Child*—*A London Girl* and *A London Home*. As Martha and I neared the end of the trilogy, we realized that Molly had written all three books as an old lady, living alone in the 1930s in a cottage in the country, though she had kept to the end all the clarity and mischief of a happy child. I suppose there is something sentimental in Molly's writing, but sentimentality in such circumstances seems a way of organizing harsh and perplexing experience, as worthy and admirable as classical stoicism or medieval chivalry or modern irony.

In our first New York years, Molly's world seemed to us less an imaginative alternative to our world than an extension and equivalent of it. Molly's experience of London was utterly true to our own experience of New York. We began to feel that there was some real connection between our world and Molly's, as though, beneath Second Avenue, we had stumbled on a great abandoned tunnel (coffer-roofed, gas-lit, something from a Doré engraving) that had long ago connected Canonbury Road and East Eighty-seventh Street.

This turned out to be true, in a small and serendipitous way: The stained-glass windows that faced us on Eighty-seventh Street were designed by Henry Holiday, the illustrator of "The Hunting of the Snark," Molly's favorite poem; and the path we used to take home from Parsons, across Astor Place and up lower Broadway, when I would collect Martha, who in those days was studying fashion design, was exactly the view Molly had sketched from her hotel window on her single visit to New York as a traveling teacher in the 1890s. I made our love for her book, and our discovery of those serendipitous and occult overlays of experience between two utterly unlike times and lives, into the subject of my first long story published in *The New Yorker.* "The Blue Room," it was called, and its publication was the event of my writing life, the proof that our basement years in New York had not been wasted. I walk with the children past the window now and then, on our way to and from Alex's MVP, the memorabilia shop. They listen to the stories of our first New York years with exactly the same polite inattention that I gave my grandfather's endlessly repeated stories of his life in the old country (Cossacks, cellars) before he arrived at Ellis Island.

With the letter in front of me and the commission in mind, I sat down to read the book again. I was much changed by the quarter century, and so my reading of Molly Hughes had changed, too. I think as well of her memoirs as I ever did, better, if anything. Yet I realize now how much she had to make up and cover up in order to write a life at all. I have come to suspect her more as a witness, admire her more as a writer.

Much of what she wrote in those lovely, high-spirited, beguiling pages, I learned from the letter, covers up pain and grief deeper than she could admit. Her beloved father, whose death in the book forces the family's expulsion from the perfect nursery-garden of Canonbury Road, actually took his own life in 1878, apparently in despair at having been caught in the kind of financial scandal we know so well from Trollope and Thackeray. This archetypically Victorian disaster casts an almost unbearably poignant light on her father's remark to her mother, which superintends this book as a motto of married love: "Oh, well, nothing matters, because you and I are in the same boat." The "nothing" that mattered was more than we knew.

There were, I learned from the letter, still darker truths: Molly's father may have carried on an affair with one of his son's women friends. Yet that Molly would remake her father's death in the pattern of her husband's (which she reports truthfully) seemed, after my twenty-five years of adult life, less cover-up than constellation searching, the consequence of a diligent will to meaning and pattern, the kind we all force retrospectively onto life. The cradle rocks above an abyss, Nabokov tells us, and the middle-class nursery is perched above a chasm of debt and dread. There could not have been, I know now, a single easy moment in all this history for Molly, or for her parents, or for her husband, Arthur. Her mother's courage in the face of her father's suicide and the shame that must have attached to it are staggering. People who call Molly's work narrowly nostalgic or who imagine that she provides a somehow "comfortable" view miss the desperation of her subjects and their real grace in the face of it. There is much that is comforting in Molly Hughes's writing, but nothing that is comfortable.

Having realized this, I now recognize, too, as I could not when I first read Molly Hughes, the true subject of the urban middle-class existence of family homes and haunts, the kind she describes so beautifully and so fully. What runs beneath the surface of her books is money. The need for it, the lack of it—that is the hidden ostinato of these charming memoirs. A family life like the Thomases'—entirely respectable and fixed, resting on a foundation completely precarious and unsure—is familiar to that same class today.

The problem, then and now, lies in the difficulty of what we long for. For Molly's middle-class, literary-minded, high-Victorian London family lived, as we still do, according to a pattern of pleasures established by older, richer, more leisured classes. Theaters and novels, Shakespeare and classical music, the theater and the ball: These are inherited, the pastimes of Jane Austen's young ladies and gentlemen pursued by Dickens's characters. (I see now that Dickens understood this himself. It is what gives *his* precarious people their poignancy and their dignity.) Molly's people must fight for each pleasure, each matinee or amateur theatrical, in adverse circumstances that they gallantly refuse to see. They have all the bourgeois pleasures and ailments save boredom.

No society has set itself so much to pursuing pleasure as the commercial urban society whose first high period of joy Molly celebrates, and to which we still belong—and no society has been so essentially a magnificent swindle. The Thomas family love of shops and cities, stage doors and Saturday matinees, is not reciprocated by its objects, which look as warm as gaslight but feel as cold as ice. The joys that fill this book nearly all rise from what the Marxists call commodity fetishism, and they exist to make money for the people who propose them. It is a web of social relation from which the Thomases and everybody else is sure to be shut out cold the moment they stop making enough. Even the organ-grinder and his monkey in Canonbury Park are not there to be picturesque; they are there to raise a profit, and all their charm lies in the plaintive improbability of their doing it well, or at all.

So my youthful surprise at the similarity of Molly's Victorian city and our own Reagan-era town now seems to me, well, jejune. Our cities felt alike because they *were* alike, because the urban commercial world of cities and shops is still governed by the iron logic of the menu and the bill, the music hall and the countinghouse. Molly's recital of pleasures and affinities, of altruisms and worthy educational institutions, takes place before a backdrop of calculation and graspingness and want, as much as any medieval memoir takes place against a background of cruelty and hunger.

And yet, as Molly grasped and illuminated, these small shared pleasures were, and remain, not less moving or beautiful or real for being so precarious. They remind us of the precariousness of all things that exist in time. A life whose meaning is found not in a faith in the past, or in the afterlife, but in family, in children, is fragile as no other can be.

Molly died, I was startled to discover from her granddaughter's letter, in the year that I was born; and though I make exactly as little of this as it deserves, still and all, it suggests something for me that I cannot avoid mentioning. Not a fact of metempsychosis, certainly, but the dawning of a duty, a burden passed on. At least my own ambitions, since those early years, have narrowed enough to make me, in an irony I could not have imagined during those world-devouring days, hope to be a faithful chronicler of another middle-class world and family life in another great and precarious city, where the threat of disaster looms every day, and the reality of daily happiness is all that there is to make it ache a little less. I read Molly now not merely as a metaphysical occult "Other," but as an end to be achieved, a writer to be imitated, a pattern to apply, the obvious example at hand. To press a few pleasures within the book of time, as country people press their flowers, seems to me nearly all that city writers can do—not because there is no higher subject than family pleasure, but because every family pleasure carries within it the knowledge of the larger fact, of family heartbreak and family pain. We see light only because the shadows set it off.

Liberal civilization creates the conditions in which Molly can live an enviable life, but it could not create the conditions in which such a life would seem, as it should, noble, even heroic. It is, I suppose, possible to see something unreal in Molly's avoidance of all and every truth. But no realism can encompass all that is real. Death and loss are enough pain to season any sunny memoir. If there is something evasive about her celebration, there is also, in its minute detailing of a life gone already by the time she wrote it, something beautiful and permanent—happiness not merely recorded but actually wrought, from a time and circumstances more iron and resistant than she is prepared to allow. Realism, like Parnassus, has many mansions, and a mantelpiece is as real as a marriage bed. The heroism of children, seeking happiness in the midst of their parents' anxieties—this is a kind of heroism, too. Molly's book seems to me more painful now than it did when I first read it, but even finer as writing. The pain I didn't understand is part of the fineness that was, in those days, beyond my grasp.

After I reread Molly Hughes, I went for the first time since we came home, though it lies mere blocks away, to look closely, not just in passing, at our old apartment and the church windows it looked toward.

The apartment was still there, its basement window grilled as before. But the church windows were gone, or invisible. The asphalt playground that lay open before them and let us look at the church had been sold, and the lot's new owners had built a "splinter" tower, a high, thin building crowded jeeringly with apartments, each with its tiny terrace, completely eradicating the view. Like almost everything else that had been part of our first New York—twenty-five years ago, it's true, but still, only twenty-five years, a blink in Paris or London time—the view was gone, just as the German restaurants were gone, and the deli on the corner and even our Gristede's. (It had become another Duane Reed drugstore.) Now you had to walk all the way around to Eighty-eighth Street to get into the church, and you could see the windows only from inside, from their front-facing side. I went in and looked at the windows and, getting no sense of a usable past, went home. I did say a prayer, though.

I am not connected to Molly by the strange serendipity of things. I am not connected to her because our lives are alike. I am connected to her because there are no ordinary lives.

Last night we took the children to see *The Nutcracker*, as we do every year, and I enjoyed it greatly, as I always do. But I was struck uneasily, as I have been for the last few years at the performance, by how much tragic foreboding there is implicit in it. The two civilizations that came together to produce it, after all—the German Romantic civilization that E. T. A. Hoffmann came from, and the Russian one that Tchaikovsky celebrated—would both in the next century know catastrophes that would be unique in human history, if the other one wasn't arguably worse.

And one sees, in the first act of *The Nutcracker*, offered as play, the original source of the disasters: the small boys in a late-nineteenth-century Russian house all march as make-believe soldiers in mock drill, and everyone is delighted to watch them. It puts one inescapably in mind of John Keegan's point that it was the mass militarization of civilian culture in the late nineteenth century—the cultural change that had monarchs out of their court robes and into military uniforms, complete with medals—that was the entirely new thing of the time, leading directly to the catastrophe of World War I. The boys in the Nutcracker house are in training for a war whose extent and destructive force they don't yet conceive. Watching the children play at war beneath the Christmas tree, I can't help but recall how easily liberal civilizations have been driven to suicide in the recent past by an infatuation with war and a fear of national humiliation. What awaits our own Nutcracker house is unknown, but the suicidal impulses are there every morning on the front page.

No matter how well I know the children, no matter how many books I read to them, and no matter how many meals I cook for them, I will never know them as well as their mother does, because she knows them better than they know themselves. She was away on a rare trip to see *her* mother, and we lost the remote control for the television. We three searched the bedroom, high and low, and couldn't find it, and were reduced to changing the channels manually, as though it were 1964. Since Luke's sports are around Channel 9 and Olivia's shows on the Disney Channel, up around 56, it was wearing on the dad's fingers. I sighed and explained it to Martha when she called.

"What kind of movie were you watching when you lost it?" Martha asked.

"I don't know—one of the *Star Wars* things, I think. Why does it matter?"

"Oh. Then it's behind the bed, on the floor behind the bed, on your side."

"We looked there, *obviously.*"

"Well, look again."

And of course it was. "How did you know that?" I asked when she came home.

She sighed. "When Luke is watching a mildly scary movie he always plays nervously with the remote, and Olivia scoots over to be near you. He let it slip down back there while he wasn't paying attention and then Olivia would have been the one to look behind the bed, since she was closest. Her arms are too short to find anything that's slipped all the way down, though—but she absolutely wouldn't admit that, so when you asked her if she'd searched there, she'd say she had. It was obvious."

It is three in the morning. I wake up and go into the darkened living room, looking out on the quiet avenue, and flick on my computer's AirPort, looking for ether. In the five years since we came home at the height of that enraptured millennial moment, we have been intending to join our century, get plugged in to a decent broadband line and have a Wi-Fi connection in the apartment. But something—the complexities of changing cable companies, Martha's distaste for cables snaking through the apartment—has kept us from it. So at night I become a thief, the only larceny I have ever practiced, stealing from my neighbor's Wi-Fi hot spots. I don't want to do it, and I apologize for doing it—I intend to get us wired, though I am baffled by how exactly to accomplish this—but I do it anyway.

Forgive me, neighbors. I promise that when (next week or next month, in the unknowable but surely approaching future) we claim our little bit of air, you will all be welcome. *All welcome, do you hear.* But for the moment I am awed by your presence, I see you on the AirPort menu of my Mac and I know you are there, clutching *your* laptop at your window, somewhere in this enormous building, tapping out, here in the middle of the night above the avenue, your blog or your schedule or your money or your life. ("Your money or your life!" the man said to Jack Benny, and he said, "I'm thinking it over." Luke and I laughed when I told him that one, a great Jewish joke.)

I'm thinking it over, like we think of fleeing, and I flip open our laptop again and position my hands above the keyboard. This intermingling of essence, this sharing of ether, surely makes us more than neighbors. We are connected in a city of anonymity, where I must pass you at the Food Emporium as we buy dubious-looking fresh-chopped pineapple. Which are you, my ethereal neighbor? How can I pick you out, secret sharer, from among all the anonymous neighbors, the extra-weak ties? Are you the one who reads *Food & Wine* in the check-out line as we wait, moving your lips to remember the recipe without buying the commodity? The grumpy man who buys brisket at the butcher's, or the beautiful woman in the wineshop? Is that you, Bob; is that your gaze I avoid in line, Marilyn? Let it be so. We are united in this strange act of staring at a screen and making marks on it that aren't even really marks, just electric registers, like the lightning in Ben Franklin's bottle so long ago.

But the air around us, the atmosphere that just sits here, is filled with us. Intimacy and anonymity, the two New York poles between which our lives endlessly oscillate, continue to produce their own kind of field. We live in it. We can't ride the light. There isn't really any light to ride. But we can share the air.

My fingers hover above the keyboard. I ought to go to sleep, but insomnia has me in its hold, as it does most nights. My eyes spring open at three, and I wander around the apartment, look for something to do. The dangerous thing is to go online, into that seductive world of foreign headlines, where it is already midmorning in Paris or London and the world's day has already begun to be organized. Or, worse, to go into the bloggy netherworld of angry opinion and attitude.

I try instead to write a few of the lines I might lose tomorrow, and then I wander through the apartment, "checking" on the children, as I promise them I will every night before they go to bed. "Check on me, Dad?" Luke asks, and of course I say yes, though I know—and he knows—that a sleeper cannot check that he is being checked on. I tell him I will, and he sets no test to be sure that I have done it. Olivia now asks for the same thing every night.

Check for what? I think secretly. That they are breathing, as Martha does? That they are safe? But what could that mean? Though I tell them they are safe, none of us really knows what safety is, or means, or looks like when it is asleep. So I check on the children, and then on their fish, for whom the sign of safety is simply swimming, movement, obvious signs of fishy life. New Bluie and Reddie seem okay; Django is vital.

I realize, in the middle of the night, that the love I feel for the children is not at every moment remote enough from the need I feel for them; all the discipline I attempt to prepare to let them go into their own world, where they make up their own minds and fly away on their own wings, gets lost when I look at them. I want them here, safe, I want them this age forever, I want this situation—two small children puzzled and, on the whole, happy at home, in a big city, not to change, even though I know that the parent's task is building up and letting go, Kirk's formula for the Metrozoids raised to a moral principle: break it down and build it back up, help them to break down life enough to make their own plays, their own Hail Marys. Life *does* have many worthwhile aspects, but the trouble is that the really worthwhile ones are worth too much and last only awhile. That the dear doctor forgot to say.

Just before I went to sleep, I had had a last IM exchange with Luke, five feet away from me in his bedroom. He sent me LOL, and I sent it right back to him. We do it a lot now, again. In the end, after all my embarrassment about LOL, we didn't reject the ambiguity, give up after the misunderstanding. No, now we live within the ambiguity—we sustain the misunderstanding, have kept the miscommunication going back and forth across the net.

My sister had confided in me that she, too, had made the same mistake, keyed off by mine—using LOL for love when it was really meant for laughter—and that her children had eventually mocked her, as Luke had me. And for a while I had thought that this was the essential exchange of parent and child: We give them lots of love, they laugh out loud, and we don't even know that they've done it.

But now I think that the really significant thing was that, through all those months of my not knowing what LOL really meant, Luke had never protested—he had never thought it weird or strange or odd that I had been laughing at him, or thought it odd that I had never complained when he was laughing out loud at me. The truth is that between parents and children, there are very few circumstances where saying, "I love you a lot," and saying, "I am laughing out loud in your presence," don't effectively mean the same thing. Though love and laughter are not entirely interchangeable—if they were, we would not grieve when those we love die—they are near relations, brothers and sisters. There are, in fact, very few letters we can write where the final words "lots of love" and "laugh out loud" are that different in meaning—where the vast apparent difference in private languages do not add up to nearly the same thing, a near-miss, a close enough application. In the great majority of messages we send, electronically or face-to-face, what we mean by "LOL"—lots of love—and what some other language game players, the children in this case, mean by "LOL"—laugh out loud—turn out to be strangely synchronous, oddly the same, acceptably close. Luke was puzzled by my strange and private use of the abbreviation, but he never was puzzled enough to object. It *just* worked—just, but it worked. Saying, "I am laughing out loud in your presence," and saying, "I love you," are close enough to count.

They are close, too, because in the end neither is really that complex. We can't entirely screw up loving our children, as we can't entirely screw up laughing at old Jewish jokes, as we can't entirely screw up games or Christmas music. They work, in some odd way. Laughter and love are close enough for a creative misreading to be a decent half-truth.

So now the very last thing we write to each other every night is LOL. LOL, Dad, LOL, Luke, and it doesn't really matter what it means. It means what it means at that moment, to us. We turn its meanings off and on like a light.

So I shall send out LOL to whoever happens to catch it, and whatever it may mean to the one who does. There are other lights on in other windows, across the way, just a few—but a few in this city means, when you count them, a great many. Density is fate, and density also makes firefly-like light, flickering at nearby windows even in the middle of the night. The light is on in the supermarket across the way, and a manager in a white apron goes in, just as my grandfather, who bore the name of the island, did into his grocery store at five every morning. The newspapers still blow on the pavement, and the little man who walks on the stoplight still bends forward, and then the ominous staying orange hand appears next on the stoplight, like the hand of Saruman on the shield of a Warhammer Orc.

Down Eighty-eighth Street, looking east, I can see . . . my goodness! a solitary light, hyper-bright, shining low in the sky, just above the buildings: a planet, surely, the morning star! Whatever the hell that is—Venus? I think so. What do I know from stars? I am a New Yorker and know only from stoplights. (Old Henny Youngman joke: Two men pursued by a monster. "What kind of animal do you think that is?" "What do I look like, a furrier?" Tell it to Luke when he wakes up.)

All of us still awake at this moment would form, if seen from above, a kind of cartoon drawing, in black and white, a thousand solitary insomniacs at our windows with our keyboards, looking for the light of another writer across the way. LOL to you all, companions of the night, friends along the way, LOL! Though not too loudly, please, your family is sleeping, as mine is, but still, LOL, whatever it may mean in the private language you write and that we, sometimes anyway, share, all of us at home at night in the city sitting in our windows, making sentences and serving time, LOL to everybody waiting for the light of a New York morning to fight its way past buildings, come in the window, and start the common day again.

Released into sleep, I doze on the window seat and wake to find Olivia, early morning, already dressed in overalls and the Jason Giambi Yankees jersey that we bought for her the last time we went to the stadium. She sees my computer lying open and asks me what I am writing, and I tell her, a book about her and Luke growing up in New York. I tell her that I am thinking of calling it *Through the Children's Gate.*

She frowns. "I think it should be called *Through the Silver Gate,* not *Through the Children's Gate,*" she says. "Because it's very high, and it's good for grown-ups, it's a funny book for grown-ups, maybe, but it isn't a good thing for children—it just doesn't sound right for children. If I wasn't your daughter, I wouldn't get that title. I would pick *Through the Silver Gate,* because it's more beautiful, because kids like it more, because it's silvery, it's more beautiful, than children walking through a gate. Another good title would be *Through the Door.* It's just a simple name. Or *The Open Door* or something . . ." She pauses.

I sit up. She has the equable, short patience of every editor I have ever lunched with, every publisher in whose office I have ever so uneasily sat. She'll give you the benefit of her views, which are sure and true, but she won't give them to you for too long. You're worth talking to but not worth really persuading. Neither of my children can any longer be my subjects. Her brother is a poet, but she is something far more potent and unstoppable; she is thinking like a publisher.

It's not for children, exactly, I explain, it's about children partly, about her and Luke. "But how about us? Did you write about Luke's lost tooth? Well, you should write about that. Did you write about my school play? You should have. Did you write about Ravioli? That's, like, so over for me. All my friends are teenagers now."

"Do you *like* being a child?" I ask her. I never have before.

She nods. "Being a child is the most awesomest thing."

"Why?"

She shrugs. "Because your brains are, like, fresher and less filled up with memory. You have more free brains."

And then she returns to her subject, just as an editor should. "Well, maybe, now that I know what it's about, I think . . . but . . . No. No. Not *Through the Gate* because, like, *every* book is named that. It's just going to be, like, when you grow up"—and here she looks at my doubtless wearied face and gently edits her words—"I mean not when you grow up but, like, when you're old, really, *really* old, you're going to ask yourself again and again, why did I name my book *Through the Children's Gate*? I know I'm right. Just trust me."

Permissions Acknowledgments

Grateful acknowledgment is made
to the following for permission to reprint
previously published material:

Random House, Inc.: Excerpt from "September 1, 1939," from *Collected Poems* by W. H. Auden. Copyright © 1940 and renewed 1968 by W. H. Auden. Reprinted by permission of Random House, Inc.

A Note About the Author

Adam Gopnik has been writing for *The New Yorker* since 1986. He is a three-time winner of the National Magazine Award for Essays and for Criticism and the George Polk Award for Magazine Reporting. From 1995 to 2000, he lived in Paris; he now lives in New York City with his wife and their two children.